D1522702

NIETZSCHE'S GENEALOGY

NIETZSCHE'S GENEALOGY

NIHILISM AND THE WILL TO KNOWLEDGE

R ANDALL H AVAS

CORNELL UNIVERSITY PRESS

ITHACA AND LONDON

First published 1995 by Cornell University Press.

Printed in the United States of America

⊗ The paper in this book meets the minimum requirements
of the American National Standard for Information Sciences—
Permanence of Paper for Printed Library Materials, ANSI Z39.48-1984.

Library of Congress Cataloging-in-Publication Data

Havas, Randall, 1957–
    Nietzsche's genealogy : nihilism and the will to knowledge /
Randall Havas.
        p.   cm.
    Includes bibliographical references and index.
    ISBN 0-8014-2962-5 (cloth : alk. paper)
    1. Nietzsche, Friedrich Wilhelm, 1844–1900.   2. Truth.   I. Title.
B3318.T78H38   1995
193—dc20   94-40871

For my father

CONTENTS

ABBREVIATIONS

The following works are cited in the text by abbreviation and by section and page number:

AC   *The Antichrist*, trans. R. J. Hollingdale (New York: Penguin, 1968)

BGE   *Beyond Good and Evil*, trans. Walter Kaufmann (New York: Vintage, 1969)

BT   *The Birth of Tragedy*, trans. Walter Kaufmann (New York: Vintage, 1967)

D   *Daybreak*, trans. R. J. Hollingdale (Cambridge: Cambridge University Press, 1982)

EH   *Ecce Homo*, trans. Walter Kaufmann (New York: Vintage, 1967)

GM   *On the Genealogy of Morals*, trans. Walter Kaufmann (New York: Vintage, 1967)

GS   *The Gay Science*, trans. Walter Kaufmann (New York: Vintage, 1974)

HAH   *Human, All Too Human*, trans. R. J. Hollingdale (Cambridge: Cambridge University Press, 1986)

TI   *Twilight of the Idols*, trans. R. J. Hollingdale (New York: Penguin, 1968)

WP   *The Will to Power*, trans. Walter Kaufmann and R. J. Hollingdale (New York: Vintage Books, 1967)

All that exists that can be denied deserves to be denied; and being truthful means: to believe in an existence that can in no way be denied and which is itself true and without falsehood. That is why the truthful man feels that the meaning of his activity is metaphysical, explicable through the laws of another and higher life, and in the profoundest sense affirmative: however much all that he does may appear to be destructive of the laws of this life and a crime against them. So it is that all his acts must become an uninterrupted suffering; but he knows what Meister Eckhart also knows: "The beast that bears you fastest to perfection is suffering".

—*Schopenhauer as Educator*

PREFACE

> The greatest recent event—that "God is dead," that the belief
> in the Christian god has become unbelievable—is already begin-
> ning to cast its first shadows over Europe.
>
> *The Gay Science,* sec. 343

Talking about the death of God appears to be Nietzsche's way of talking
about what he thinks it makes sense to believe. It is not altogether clear,
however, that one can in fact talk about what it makes sense to believe.
For it is not obvious what standpoint one would have to adopt in order
to do so. Either one can say something that it makes sense to believe,
or one can try to say something that it makes no sense to believe. But
to try to stand, as we might wish to say, outside the realm of what it
makes sense to believe—and proclaim from there that it makes or fails
to make sense to believe this or that—leaves one in the philosophically
awkward position of trying to account for the status of claims it is not
clear it makes sense to believe. It is not just that one will be asked the
troubling question how one knows what it does and does not make
sense to believe. Rather, the difficulty is that it is not clear that such a
specification of what it does and does not make sense to believe is
possible at all.

These more or less familiar difficulties surrounding questions of
sense and nonsense are not at all foreign to that aspect of Nietzsche's
thinking about the state of our lives in the present age with which we
will be concerned in this book. In the special sense of the term at stake
here, what is amiss with our lives as they stand can be understood,
according to Nietzsche, as a problem of culture. But, as we will see, he
does not fall prey to the temptation to try to talk about modern culture
from without. Nor, however, does he merely offer local criticism from

within. Rather, he insists that, as I will put the point, we in the present age fail to count as a culture at all.[1] My aim in *Nietzsche's Genealogy* is to understand and to assess this claim.

Nietzsche was deeply concerned with the special character of modernity—with the nature and significance of human life in the present age.[2] He wanted, in particular, to understand the special character of what he took to be the specifically modern commitment to truthfulness, what he called the 'will to knowledge' or the 'will to truth'.[3] For he says that we live in the wake of the death of God—that given our commitment to truthfulness, we can no longer allow ourselves the 'lie involved in the belief in God'. But he complains that this fact does not make the right sort of difference to us.

To say that God is dead is to say, roughly, that we must take a certain sort of responsibility for what we say about the world, rather than try to deny the fact of such responsibility by means of a fantasy of access to the world's nature that would be wholly independent of our 'human, all too human' interests and aims. To treat the death of God as an event[4] is to say, in effect, that we have to take responsibility for having to take responsibility for what we say, to acknowledge its necessity as a fact about ourselves. Nietzsche is convinced that, by and large, we fail on both counts, a claim he expresses in *On the Genealogy of Morals* (hereafter, the *Genealogy*) by saying that, as we stand, we lack the right to make promises. The interpretative problem in either case, however, is that it is not at all clear how we should think of the relevant notion of

---

[1] I will be using the word 'culture' here in the sense I understand Nietzsche to give it in the *Untimely Meditations:* culture not, in other words, in the sense of artistic or intellectual cultivation or tradition, but rather in the sense of a grasp of the demands that life's intelligibility places upon each of us. I explain this sense of the term in Chapter 1 in the context of my analysis of Nietzsche's attack on Socratism.

[2] For a recent discussion of Nietzsche's work from this perspective, see Robert Pippin, *Modernism as a Philosophical Problem* (Cambridge: Blackwell, 1991).

[3] I use the expression 'commitment to truthfulness' to render Nietzsche's 'will to knowledge' or 'will to truth' in order to underscore my contention in this book that though Nietzsche is uninterested in putative problems about the *nature* of truth, he is nevertheless deeply concerned with what he understands to be the distinctively modern devotion *to* it. In this connection, it seems to me that the term 'truthfulness' is much less likely to mislead contemporary readers than is the term 'truth'. For Nietzsche, I will argue, truth is just truth, and there is no room for philosophical theorizing about what sort of 'property' it is. But truthfulness is what is supposed to distinguish modern individuals from their more pious predecessors, and there is a good deal of room for psychological theorizing about the differences between the two.

[4] See the preceding passage from *The Gay Science,* where the death of God is called the greatest event, as well as *The Gay Science,* sec. 125, where Nietzsche calls it a "tremendous event." The German word in both cases is *Ereigniss.*

responsibility.[5] For, as we will see, there seems to be nothing obviously unreasonable about claiming perfect indifference toward either development.

From Nietzsche's point of view, however, such indifference amounts to a form of nihilism. It is an indifference that characterizes the lives of those he calls 'the herd', and one that he believes threatens the very possibility of individuality in the present age. We need, therefore, to make clear the relationship between this form of nihilism and Nietzsche's conception of the individual, and to appreciate the intimacy of the connection he sees between the notions of nihilism, truthfulness, and individuality. Though it is common enough to suppose that the life of the authentically Nietzschean individual would be governed by some value other than truthfulness, I think Nietzsche is better read as insisting that the would-be individual recognize that value as her own, rather than that she should throw it over in favor of something else.

Nietzschean nihilism is usually thought of as a transitional stage between two different ways of evaluating human life, between two different 'tables of values'. According to a common reading, while we once measured our lives by a divine standard, and found them wanting,[6] we have, in the present age, come to distrust this standard—to find it unbelievable. As long as we have nothing with which to replace that standard, we will continue, as we do presently, to find our lives worthless.[7] In the future, however, some of us may come to love our lives even in the absence of an external standard by which to measure their value. Those of us who fail to do so will have to learn to live with the thought that not only does human life lack the value that we once hoped it had, but it lacks any other value as well.[8]

[5] I hope my appeal to the idea of having to take responsibility for what one says does not, at the outset, strike the reader as wholly foreign to Nietzsche's concerns. As we will see, he is quite explicitly concerned with this question in the second essay of On the Genealogy of Morals. I mean to show, however, that the question of responsibility underwrites his entire conception of life in the present age. And the latter conception is, I contend, central to his project as a philosopher.

[6] Of course, as we will see, a principal problem with putting Nietzsche's point in this way is his insistence that it is only because we find life wanting in the first place that we construct philosophical, religious, and moral visions of something better. One way to think of Nietzsche's interest in philosophy, therefore, is to see him as trying to understand how—in the absence of such a standard—we could get so far as to think one up. This is another way of asking what he thinks 'life-denial' is.

[7] Such a reading relies on passages like the following: "Nihilism represents a pathological transition state (what is pathological is the tremendous generalization, the inference that there is no meaning at all): whether the productive forces are not yet strong enough or whether decadence still hesitates and has not yet invented its remedies" (WP, sec. 13, p. 14).

[8] For an eloquent expression of this view, see Tracy Strong, Friedrich Nietzsche and the Politics of Transfiguration (Berkeley: University of California Press, 1975). Strong

The form of nihilism I wish to discuss here, however, should be understood as the state one may be said to be in when nothing truly matters to one. Overcoming nihilism, on this reading, is not so much a matter of replacing old values with new ones, as it is coming to value something where previously one, in effect, valued nothing. This understanding of the notion of nihilism, that is, seeks to distinguish two forms of life: one in which meaning can be found, and one in which it cannot. The more genetic picture of nihilism sketched in the preceding paragraph can be useful for bringing out the intended contrast, but it tends misleadingly to suggest that Nietzsche sought somehow to supply new values in the sense of offering a concrete specification of some new set of institutions and practices that might provide content to modern life.[9] As Nietzsche sees it, however, the problem with the way we live our lives in the present age is, very roughly, not that we care about the wrong things, but rather that we care—in the relevant sense—about nothing at all. Our cares are sham cares, our promises hollow ones. We can, as readers of Nietzsche's work, use the expression 'new values', but we must not lose sight of this fundamental distinction.

Nietzsche knows full well, however, that the nihilist will want to dismiss his talk of a crisis in our highest values as hyperbole and will treat Nietzschean aspirations for new values as an expression of nostalgia.[10] As I read him, Nietzsche's concern with this sort of response is absolutely central to his conception of the present age and, therefore, central to his work as a philosopher. Nietzsche and the nihilist *agree* that God is dead, and they appear, moreover, to *mean* the same thing by this expression. But the nihilist pretends not to care about it—a reaction Nietzsche considers unintelligible.

I am therefore less concerned in this book with Nietzsche's arguments—such as they are—for what *The Will to Power* calls 'the advent of nihilism' than with how he conceives of what he believes has taken place. On the reading I present here, the present age is, for Nietzsche, a period of transition between two different ways of responding to the

---

writes, "Nietzsche . . . is saying that, in the past, men based their lives on (for example) God, that this foundation is, for particular historical and logical reasons, no longer available, *and that there is nothing else*" (p. 12). He goes on, "The problem confronting modern times, then, is for Nietzsche that the presuppositions, which made, for example, morality possible, no longer exist" (pp. 12–13).

[9] It is, of course, common to complain that Nietzsche in fact failed to make any such specification. But the point is that, on the reading in question, it appears reasonable at least to expect one. It is this expectation that I think Nietzsche means to call into question.

[10] This, I take it, is Richard Rorty's response to similar considerations. For the phrase, "highest values," see *WP*, sec. 2, p. 9.

announcement of the death of God. This period, I will argue, is the gap that separates the individual from the herd.

In a way, then, this book returns to what should be familiar ground. I want to understand what is, in effect, a principal unifying theme in Nietzsche's writing: his conception of life in the present age. The many threads that make up the fabric of Nietzsche's thinking often appear to run in competing directions. But while the theme I discuss in this book is only one among many, it is quite central to his thought as a whole. Thus, although I do not mean to deny—indeed, quite the contrary—that Nietzsche sometimes spoke of replacing our old values with new ones, such talk often reflects a temptation to which he knew himself to be prone, not his considered view of the matter.

For the reasons I have suggested, my concern to understand Nietzsche's conception of modern life dictates that I will be talking about nihilism and the problem of individuality. And for reasons that will become clear in the Introduction, I will have a good deal to say about Nietzsche's understanding of the will to knowledge. Nihilism, on my view, stems from an unwillingness to question our modern commitment to truthfulness, but Nietzsche, as I have suggested, does not wish to replace that commitment with anything else.

Such a reading might seem to place me in the camp of those who believe Nietzsche's work is purely negative in character.[11] But I mean to

---

[11] Both Jacques Derrida and Paul de Man are often accused of holding a view of Nietzsche as a purely critical thinker, one not concerned—or perhaps not able—to offer positive alternatives to the views he rejects. (See a recent example, Michael C. Milam, "The Misuse of Nietzsche in Literary Theory," *Philosophy and Literature* 16 [October 1992]: 320–32.) I think I understand what gives rise to this charge, but it seems to me nevertheless to miss the point of these commentators' best writing. Derrida, in particular, is responding to Heidegger's reading of Nietzsche. Heidegger claims that Nietzsche's thought 'completes metaphysics' since Plato, but he maintains that it fails to 'overcome' that metaphysics. The claim that Nietzsche's thought remained tied to 'metaphysics' seems naturally to invite attempts to deny that it did, and Derrida, for example, appears to do just that. If I follow him, however, Derrida, is trying to understand just what Heidegger could *mean* by talking about 'the end of philosophy' and wisely refuses to take his ostensibly critical claims about Nietzsche at face value. His aim is not—or anyway should not be—to show that Nietzsche said what Heidegger pretends to have been the first to have uncovered. De Man's suggestion that, for what he considers rhetorical reasons, Nietzsche's writing cannot extricate itself from metaphysics has, I think, a similar goal. Richard Rorty, on the other hand, seems to believe that, though both Nietzsche and Heidegger (and Derrida and de Man, for that matter) remain to some degree tied to 'metaphysics', it should not be terribly difficult—or, if difficult, then not interestingly so—to bracket those portions of their works for later disposal. See Rorty's *Consequences of Pragmatism* (Minneapolis: University of Minnesota Press, 1982) and *Contingency, Irony, and Solidarity* (Cambridge: Cambridge University Press, 1989).

question the alleged distinction between the 'positive' and 'negative' or critical aspects of Nietzsche's thinking about the present age. The distinction he draws between two different responses to the death of God is not best understood as differentiating two competing understandings of our current situation. From Nietzsche's point of view, the nihilist fails to understand the obvious, and attempts to deny the undeniable. The distinction Nietzsche has in mind, then, is that between understanding and failing to understand the death of God.

This is a book about a specific and central aspect of Nietzsche's conception of life in the present age: namely, the nature of what he takes to be the decisively modern commitment to truthfulness. Nietzsche believed that the commitment remains essentially intact even if we abstain, as he thinks we now must, from specifically philosophical conceptions of the *nature* of truth. And I argue that, appearances notwithstanding, Nietzsche meant to strengthen, not to weaken it.[12]

In my focus on the question of Nietzsche's understanding of modernity, as well as in my understanding of the nature of what he takes to be our commitment to truthfulness, my interpretation of Nietzsche owes an obvious debt to the work of Martin Heidegger. It is appropriate to comment briefly on that debt here.

Heidegger understood Nietzsche to be *the* philosopher of modernity, and his reading is in large measure a sustained attempt to elaborate this very claim.[13] More specifically, he was convinced that only in Nietzsche's philosophy can a proper understanding of the 'technological' character of modern life be found. In particular, the Nietzschean doctrines of will to power and of the 'overman' illuminate, in Heidegger's view, the nature of modern technology, on the one hand, and what he took to be the thoughtlessness of our response to it, on the other. Though the details of this arguably idiosyncratic reading of Nietzsche do not concern me here, I do think that Heidegger was right to focus on

---

[12] Maudemarie Clark makes an ostensibly similar point in her *Nietzsche on Truth and Philosophy* (Cambridge: Cambridge University Press, 1990). As I understand her, however, she thinks Nietzsche does have a positive conception of the nature of truth, albeit a very thin one, and that though he retains the value of truth, he does so by assigning to it a different purpose than he thinks it has had hitherto, by making it serve a 'new ideal'. On the reading I present, on the other hand, Nietzsche has *no* conception of the nature of truth, and does not seek *any* independent justification for our continued commitment to it.

[13] I offer an interpretative framework for Heidegger's reading of Nietzsche in "Who Is Heidegger's Nietzsche?" in *Heidegger: A Critical Reader*, ed. Hubert L. Dreyfus and Harrison Hall (Cambridge: Blackwell, 1992), pp. 231–46. For an interesting discussion and criticism of Heidegger's idea of a 'metaphysics of the age', see Vincent Descombes, *The Barometer of Modern Reason* (New York: Oxford University Press, 1993).

Nietzsche's conception of life in the present age, and I have adopted a similar orientation in this book. It seems to me undeniable that a concern with the character of modern life—both with what is wrong with it and with its promise for the future—is as central to Nietzsche's thinking as is the idea of the death of God.

Besides this shared focus, I use—especially in Chapters 2 and 3—a quasi-Heideggerian vocabulary of 'responsiveness' to characterize what seems to me the particular conception of *commitment* that is at work in Nietzsche's notion of the modern 'will to truth'. Some readers will doubtless find this choice of terminology jarring, but I do not believe that it represents an unwarranted interpretative imposition of Nietzsche's text. Let me explain.

One is sometimes tempted to read Nietzsche as though he sought to encourage his readers to take responsibility for their view of the world in the special philosophical sense of acknowledging that it is 'merely' their view, and thus to open themselves up to the possibility of different views. In my view, however, this is a temptation worth resisting. My thesis, once again, is that Nietzsche meant to strengthen, not to weaken, our commitment to truthfulness. Accordingly, the Nietzschean notion of responsibility should, if I am right, be understood in terms of the notion of commitment. As I read him, specifically philosophical talk of 'taking responsibility' for a commitment represents for Nietzsche one more attempt to distance ourselves from that commitment. What Nietzsche demands instead, I think, is something much more like Heideggerian 'responsiveness', a kind of openness to what matters to us. And, according to Nietzsche, what matters to *us* (at least to those of us he considers his rightful readers) is the truth.

I do not suppose that a vocabulary of responsiveness is the only appropriate one for articulating Nietzsche's thought about these matters. Indeed, if we had an unproblematic grasp of the notion of commitment, talk of 'commitment to truthfulness' might do just as well for getting at the notion of the will in Nietzsche's will to truth. But I think that talk of responsiveness, as well as helping us avoid a tempting misunderstanding of Nietzsche, is suggestive in this context in large part because we simply do *not* have a good grasp of the notion of commitment. It is also, as we shall see, a natural way to understand the upshot of Nietzsche's attack on Socratism.

Like Nietzsche, Heidegger—both early and late—may be read as trying to undermine certain forms of both philosophical and nonphilosophical 'detachment' from what conditions us. To put it crudely, both thinkers endeavor to bring home the futility of our attempts to transcend what neither of them would happily call 'the human condition'.

Heidegger, in particular, is concerned to make plain the emptiness both of our attempts to view ourselves and our place in the world from a perspective radically external to our ordinary practices of judgment and of the recommendation that we learn to accept the so-called limits of human cognition. As he sees it, both those attempts and the recommendation to renounce them partake of the same sorts of prephilosophical confusion. Accordingly, Heidegger sought to reestablish a kind of intimacy with the world that can be maintained only by foregoing both traditional philosophical speculation *and* an antiphilosophical rejection of such speculation. As I suggested, such intimacy is to be achieved, if at all, not by accepting that there is something that we cannot do, some limit to the scope of human reason, but rather by seeing that there is simply nothing of the sort that we might initially have been inclined to say that we wanted to do.

As I read his talk about the life-denying character of the ascetic ideal generally, Nietzsche also sought to display the emptiness of the expression we give to what he considered our human, all too human wish to be more than human. It is important to put this point in this fashion, because it is easy to mistake Nietzsche's condemnation of what he calls 'life-denial' as advocating that, in effect, we simply stop trying to measure the value of this life in terms of a better one. His view, however, is not that we find our lives wanting when compared to some external standard, for he finds the very idea of such a standard incomprehensible. His point is rather that we first find our lives wanting and only *then* (subsequently, that is) concoct the fantasy of a standard against which to measure their value. In his insistence that we not accept a philosophical description of the problems facing us (he more often calls it a 'moral' description), Nietzsche's thinking bears this strong connection to Heidegger's—a connection that I emphasize in this book.

Nietzsche describes the wish to deny life in many ways. Most broadly, however, he characterizes it as our 'ill will against time'. On his view, we endeavor in a variety of ways to deny the fact of having a history.[14] This theme is, as should be clear, as central to Nietzsche's thinking as is the idea of eternal recurrence. (Indeed, it is plausible to take the latter doctrine to be a reflection on the very nature of human history.) A hatred of history, according to Nietzsche, gives rise to the various attitudes of detachment from life that he condemns as life-denying. In a

[14] One relatively clear statement of this view can be found in *Twilight of the Idols,* "'Reason' in Philosophy," sec. 1: "You ask me about the idiosyncrasies of philosophers? . . . There is their lack of historical sense, their hatred of even the idea of becoming, their Egyptianism. They think they are doing a thing *honour* when they dehistoricize it, *sub specie aeterni*—when they make a mummy of it" (p. 35).

more blatantly philosophical context, Platonism represents the most obvious version of such an attitude. The Platonist seeks to tie the meaning of what we say to something lying wholly outside the actual empirical and temporal conditions of human speech. The particular form of such detachment at stake in this book, however, consists in the attempt to deny the historical character of our commitment to truthfulness. Nietzsche wants us to accept the historical character of that commitment, but urges that we do so in such a way as thereby to acknowledge its authority or necessity for us.

How the ideas of history and necessity come together for Nietzsche in this context is the subject of Chapter 4. Rather than offer an interpretation of Nietzsche's conception of history, however, I have tried to understand this central aspect of his conception of modernity in the light of his criticism of Socratism. The reasons for this approach are twofold. On the one hand, because, in Nietzsche's view, Socratism is at the root of the modern commitment to truthfulness, it is worthwhile to understand both how Nietzsche thinks that commitment began with a certain conception of the nature of truth and how he thinks it survives the collapse of that conception. There is, on the other hand, it seems to me, a great deal of good philosophy in Nietzsche's attack on Socratism. That attack allows us in particular to understand his conception of the nature and possibility of the general philosophical enterprise. And that conception has, as I have suggested, important ramifications for uncritical assumptions and presuppositions that tend to guide our reading of a writer so deeply concerned with the apparent impossibility of a certain kind of thinking.

However much the reading of Nietzsche I propose here goes against the grain of what seem to me the usual expectations—and though that reading is clearly no one's responsibility but my own—it did not develop in a vacuum. Indeed, people who have helped me in a variety of ways should be acknowledged here. Rüdiger Bittner, David Cerbone, Hubert Dreyfus, Harry Frankfurt, Raymond Geuss, Michel Haar, and Irad Kimhi have very generously commented on drafts of various parts of the book. I am grateful for their time and attention. I have also benefited from conversation with Christopher Dustin, Jonathan Lear, Richard Moran, Alexander Nehamas, and Jamie Tappenden. I am particularly grateful to Richard Moran for pressing me on more than one occasion to be more circumspect in my use of the term 'philosophy' than has at times been my wont. As is often the case with academic books, this one began as a lecture course, and I acknowledge here the help of my teaching assistant Ron Katwan during the time that I tried to teach the material. I also thank Yale University for providing me with a Morse Fellowship for the academic year 1990–91, during which time I began work on this book in earnest. Finally, thanks are due to the anonymous readers for Cornell University Press who took the trouble to make clear to me ways in which to improve the book as a whole.

Over the years, I have, in different ways, learned much about Heidegger from both Hubert Dreyfus and Stanley Cavell, and, to the extent that my reading of Nietzsche is, in the way I indicated above, broadly Heideggerian in inspiration, it bears the marks of my attempt to come to terms with their often conflicting appraisals of the significance of Heidegger's attack on epistemology.

I also owe much to Douglas Winblad. We have discussed the ideas in this book—both in the form in which they appear here and in other forms—since graduate school. I consider myself fortunate to have had the benefit of his intelligence and integrity as well as his friendship for so many years.

My understanding of the relationship between obedience and responsibility is heavily indebted to the work of Vicki Hearne, especially to *Adam's Task: Calling Animals by Name.* Our conversations last year about the dangers, both intellectual and otherwise, of pity have been for me a source of genuine insight, and I thank her here for taking the time to talk about these matters.

I am grateful most of all to Edward Minar and Melissa Weissberg for their friendship and guidance over the past several years. My ongoing conversations with Ed about meaning and responsibility and Melissa's tireless efforts to teach me the importance and burdens of writing clearly are the intellectual conscience of this book.

Finally, I thank my editor, Roger Haydon, for his confidence in this project and for his patience with me while I finished it.

RANDALL HAVAS

New Haven, Connecticut

NIETZSCHE'S GENEALOGY

NIHILISM AND THE
WILL TO KNOWLEDGE

> And here I again touch on my problem, on our problem, my *unknown* friends (for as yet I *know* of no friend): what meaning would our whole being possess if it were not this, that in us the will to truth becomes conscious of itself as a *problem?*
>
> As the will to truth thus gains in self-consciousness—there can be no doubt of that—morality will gradually *perish* now.
>
> *On the Genealogy of Morals* III, sec. 27, p. 161

My aim in this book is to understand Nietzsche's conception of modernity—his conception of life in the present age. It is his most fundamental conviction that, while a commitment to truthfulness is in some way definitive of modern life, we nevertheless seek to avoid taking responsibility for that commitment. That is to say, we fail to understand the significance of the death of God.[1] Such a failure leads to the specific form of nihilism with which I will be concerned here: what we might think of as a nihilism of indifference with respect to what we have become in the present age.[2] This is the form of nihilism Nietzsche diagnoses in his readers. The principal claim for which I will be arguing is that such nihilism is overcome to the degree that we acknowledge the

[1] Nietzsche's most famous depiction of this failure can be found in sec. 125 of *The Gay Science*, "The Madman." As I noted in the Preface, to say that God is dead is simply to say that one is committed to truthfulness—that one finds *these* beliefs to be false and therefore unbelievable.

[2] As I noted in the Preface, this is not the only form of nihilism with which Nietzsche is concerned, but it is such indifference that he thinks threatens to wreck our modern commitment to the truth. And it is this form of nihilism that is most relevant for understanding Nietzsche's conception of life in the present age.

1

authority that the value of knowledge has for us. Nietzsche, as I said, seeks to strengthen our commitment to truthfulness, not to weaken it.

As I will try to show, we can best understand what Nietzsche takes to be our failure properly to comprehend the death of God in terms of the distinction he draws between the individual and the herd. Though this distinction can appear to mark the difference between two opposing classes of action, it should be understood, in the present age, to designate two different ways of responding to the special kind of responsibility Nietzsche believes we bear for our commitment to truthfulness. I suggest, roughly, that the herd seeks to turn away from such responsibility (and pressures the individual to do so as well), whereas the individual takes that responsibility upon himself (and must struggle against the herd's attempts to prevent him from doing so). The content of the relevant notion of responsibility, however, can be difficult to grasp at first. In order to make sense of the ideas of herd and individual we need to understand why Nietzsche's conception of responsibility is not at odds with the idea of commitment.

This interpretation of Nietzsche's conception of our modern commitment to truthfulness, and of his notions of the herd and the individual, can seem unorthodox. But we will see that we lack any truly compelling reason to attribute to Nietzsche the view that the will to truth is something that we ought to envision one day foregoing. I will argue, moreover, that, contrary to a natural but misleading interpretation of his notion of individuality, Nietzsche in fact rejects as unintelligible the idea that the would-be individual must stand outside his or her historical or cultural community and view the world from a radically different standpoint. But if the perhaps romantic ideal of the individual as someone who in this way turns her back on the community is indeed incoherent, then we must reexamine the idea of the *antagonism* between individual and community. One of Nietzsche's principal goals as a philosopher is to provide such a reexamination, and in this book I try to make clear what that reexamination entails.

While the centrality of the concepts of individual and community to Nietzsche's criticism of morality is clear, the importance of those concepts for understanding the value he attaches to *truthfulness* has gone largely unremarked. It can be tempting, as I have said, to think that Nietzsche meant somehow to emphasize what one might understand as the contingency of our commitment to the truth. As I see it, however, Nietzsche *rejects* the idea that we should in any way seek to distance ourselves from that commitment. He is hostile in particular to the idea that we might look forward to a time when something else might take its place.[3] The first four chapters of this book are therefore concerned specifically with Nietzsche's conception of the character of that commitment, and hence with the fate of Socratism.

My claim, then, is that Nietzsche's interest in the will to knowledge can be adequately assessed only in the light of his conception of life in the present age. It was his contention that the modern will to knowledge had come to provide the most coherent focus to human life at the end of the nineteenth century. From his point of view, to be an individual in the modern age meant to be a member of the community of knowers. He feared, however, that as long as the character of the modern commitment to truthfulness remained unexamined, no such community would be possible. This absence of community, in fact, is the kind of nihilism with which we will be concerned here.[4] In such circumstances, individuality should be understood as a matter of standing apart from those who refuse to question their commitment to truthfulness. But to call that commitment into question, as the *Genealogy* suggests we must, is fully to adopt it as one's own, rather than, as one might suppose, to discard it in favor of another. Only in this way can nihilism be avoided.

Thus, though I explore at length certain of Nietzsche's views about knowledge, I do not pretend here to articulate an interpretation of his epistemology.[5] For, as I have claimed, the views I discuss can be adequately assessed only in the context of his conception of the individual

[3] Thus, when, at the end of the *Genealogy*, he says that morality perishes as the will to truth gains in self-consciousness, he is not suggesting that calling the value of truth into question loosens that value's hold on us, but rather that, in questioning it, he aims to reinforce its hold by clarifying the nature of our commitment to it. My goal in Chapters 3 and 4 is to make clear what questioning and self-consciousness mean in this context.

[4] If we understand nihilism as something like a modern crisis of meaninglessness, then Nietzsche's worries about nihilism should be understood in broadly Emersonian, not existentialist, terms. The existentialist claims to have recognized the meaninglessness of life in general, and proposes a distinction between those who can face up to this fact and those who cannot. Nietzsche, in contrast, claims to have recognized the meaninglessness of our lives *as we now live them,* but he also insists on the possibility of rectifying the situation. Making sense of this possibility is the aim of this book. I therefore use the term 'nihilism' in the sense in which Nietzsche uses it in the preface to the *Genealogy:* "I understood the ever spreading morality of pity that had seized even on philosophers and made them ill, as the most sinister symptom of a European culture that had itself become sinister, perhaps as its by-pass to a new Buddhism? to a Buddhism for Europeans? to—*nihilism?*" (*GM,* preface, sec. 5, p. 19). It is the burden of Chapter 5 to make clear the relationship between this form of nihilism and the so-called morality of pity.

[5] Indeed, I argue that Nietzsche means to undermine the intelligibility of the standpoint from which epistemological questions are most commonly raised, thereby questioning the need for an epistemology altogether.

and the community. This means, in turn, that his ethical concerns with
how we live our lives and conceive of our relationships to one another
cannot be divorced from his interest in the will to knowledge. Making
this last connection clear is my goal in the fifth and last chapter of
this book.[6]

Much recent commentary in English has been devoted to understanding Nietzsche's ostensibly epistemological views in their own right.
Maudemarie Clark, Alexander Nehamas, Richard Schacht, and John
Wilcox, for example, each develop detailed interpretations of Nietzsche's
views about truth.[7] But little has been said about the place of those
views within the overall context of Nietzsche's conception of life in the
present age. Only in that context, however, can we appreciate the point
of many of Nietzsche's remarks about rationality, knowledge, and truth.
That context suggests that Nietzsche's aim is hardly to articulate for its
own sake a philosophically defensible view of the nature of knowledge
or truth.[8]

Like Kierkegaard and Heidegger, Nietzsche believes that an especially high estimation of the value of knowledge is in some way defini-

[6] I mean to suggest, in other words, that it is wrong to separate Nietzsche's ostensibly 'ethical' concerns from his 'epistemological' ones, for they are of a piece, and
should not be compartmentalized.

[7] See, for example, Maudemarie Clark, *Nietzsche on Truth and Philosophy* (Cam-
bridge: Cambridge University Press, 1990), Alexander Nehamas, *Nietzsche: Life as
Literature* (Cambridge: Harvard University Press, 1985), Richard Schacht, *Nietzsche*
(London: Routledge and Kegan Paul, 1983), John Wilcox, *Truth and Value in Nietzsche*
(Ann Arbor: University of Michigan Press, 1974), and Brian Leiter, "Perspectivism in
Nietzsche's *Genealogy of Morals*," in *Nietzsche, Genealogy, Morality: Essays on Nietzsche's
Genealogy of Morals*, ed. Richard Schacht (Berkeley: University of California Press,
1994), pp. 334–57. See also Rüdiger Bittner, "Nietzsche's Begriff der Wahrheit,"
Nietzsche-Studien 16 (1987): 70–90. Bittner's article also contains a useful bibliography
of recent writing in German on Nietzsche's purported conception of truth. In group-
ing these commentators together in this fashion, I by no means wish to suggest
that they all agree with one another. (Nehamas, in particular, questions whether
Nietzsche really has views on the nature of truth at all. Clark, on the other hand,
has done the most to tease a coherent—if extremely thin—conception of truth from
Nietzsche's writings.) But none of these commentators adequately acknowledges the
connection between Nietzsche's interest in something we might call 'the problem of
knowledge' and his conception of life in the present age, and it is this latter connection that is of interest to me here.

[8] By insisting on the historically situated character of Nietzsche's interest in the
problem of knowledge, I am following Heidegger, who claims that, as the philosopher
of the present age, Nietzsche has something important to say about the significance
of contemporary human life. Heidegger's emphasis on what he calls 'the will to
power as knowledge' is meant, among other things, to underscore the idea that, for
Nietzsche, to be modern means to have a particular commitment to knowledge.
According to Heidegger's Nietzsche, we cannot make sense of our contemporary
situation except in terms of that commitment.

tive of modern life. But, as I have suggested, unlike those thinkers and contrary to a very common reading of his work, Nietzsche does not wish to replace our commitment to truthfulness with something else, but rather to understand and to undermine certain forms of resistance to it.[9] He insists that we tend to misrepresent to ourselves the authority of truthfulness, either by treating that commitment as the inevitable progress of reason or by representing it merely as one way among others of approaching the world. Nietzsche is convinced that these ways of talking about the value we attach to knowledge blind us to ourselves: "We are," as he says at the beginning of the *Genealogy*, "unknown to ourselves, we men of knowledge . . . we are necessarily strangers to ourselves, we do not comprehend ourselves, we have to misunderstand ourselves" (*GM*, preface, sec. 1, p. 15). As I suggested above, he diagnoses—and seeks to overcome—precisely this lack of self-understanding in his readers. The men of knowledge misunderstand themselves insofar as they are not yet self-conscious about their will to truth. Though to say that they have to misunderstand themselves suggests that such self-consciousness would change them as they are, there is an important sense in which they remain the same.

On the reading I develop here, to understand the significance of modern life is, for Nietzsche, to understand what it means to be committed to the truth in such a way that, in his words, belief in God becomes unbelievable. Those who are capable of understanding the death of God, and who nevertheless fail to do so, Nietzsche calls 'men of knowledge', and it is to them that he dedicates those portions of his work with which we will be concerned. It is they who, in Nietzsche's view, have not yet adequately questioned their will to truth.[10]

[9] In another context, it would be appropriate to challenge the suggestion that Heidegger meant to supplant his version of the will to knowledge with something else. The situation with respect to Kierkegaard's views is, I think, more complicated.

[10] The expression 'men of knowledge' translates the German *Erkennenden*. There may be room to speculate about possible differences between what might be called a 'masculine' and a 'feminine' commitment to knowledge, as well as about the different sorts of self-blindness such a commitment might engender in each case, but these are not the questions that will occupy me here. Nevertheless, despite what might conceivably be considered to be the sexist overtones of Kaufmann's translations of *Erkennenden* and *Erkennender*, I retain those translations. Additionally, I almost always refer to the philosopher as 'he'. I doubt that I am being unfair to Nietzsche in doing so. Here again, however, there may be room to wonder whether in criticizing philosophy Nietzsche is criticizing what might be called a masculine outlook. In particular, Nietzsche thinks of philosophy as operating in service of a fantasy of activity turned against the necessity of a certain sort of passivity. I have, however, nothing helpful to say about the question of whether such activity might in any significant sense be said to be masculine or about whether the passivity with which I find Nietzsche to be occupied could be meaningfully said to be feminine.

As the actual number of such individuals is only as great as that of persons unconditionally committed to the value of truthfulness, it is not always clear just what segment of the book-buying population Nietzsche counts as his own.[11] At times, of course, he considers their number vanishingly small: in *The Antichrist*, for example, he says that he writes for "the very few." "Perhaps none of them is even living yet" (*AC*, p. 114).[12] Thus, when I speak in this context of the significance of modern life, I do not mean to suggest that in my view Nietzsche's concern with the value we place on knowledge exhausts his interest in the present age. Clearly, he has much to say about the cultural situation of his day which is not directly related to what he takes to be the distinctively modern estimation of the value of knowledge. As we will see, however, only a commitment to truthfulness can provide us with what Nietzsche considers a true culture in the special sense of the term that interests me here.

By now, of course, the metaphor of God's death is quite worn. But Nietzsche's basic point is that good sense can no longer be made of the idea that the ways in which we view the world are justified by something standing above, beyond, or behind the world itself.[13] Or rather to say that God is dead is to say that the only good sense that a man of knowledge can make of the idea of justifying this world in terms of some other is that it answers to nothing more than historically and psychologically conditioned human needs. Christianity, Nietzsche says, is 'Platonism for the people'.[14] And it is precisely such Platonism that the death of God renders unbelievable. Nietzsche maintains that the unbelievability of Platonism is forced upon anyone committed 'at any price', as he says, to the value of knowledge.[15] He believes, in other

[11] It should be obvious that the truth of Nietzsche's claim is not to be settled by statistical means. The men of knowledge are those who, with respect to their religious, philosophical, and moral beliefs, should by now, as we might like to put the point, know better. And, from Nietzsche's point of view, that could, I take it, be anyone, even though by and large it might well be no one.

[12] *Thus Spoke Zarathustra*, by apparent contrast, is 'a book for all and for none'.

[13] This is how sec. 125 of *The Gay Science*, for example, explains that phrase. As I argue, however, to claim that God is dead is simply to claim that one is committed to the truth—indeed, precisely to those truths that render belief in God incredible. In other words, when Nietzsche suggests that we do not understand the death of God, then, he is suggesting that we do not understand the nature of our commitment to truth.

[14] See *Beyond Good and Evil*, preface, p. 3.

[15] See, for example, *On the Genealogy of Morals* III, sec. 27 (Nietzsche is quoting *The Gay Science*, sec. 357): "Christian morality itself, the concept of truthfulness taken more and more strictly, the confessional subtlety of the Christian conscience translated and sublimated into the scientific conscience, into intellectual cleanliness *at any price*" (p. 161, my emphasis). See also *The Gay Science*, sec. 344: "'At any price': how

words, that whoever can afford to tell the truth about himself will come to find unintelligible the idea that the sense he makes of the world is either inherent in the world or imposed upon it from the outside. Consequently, he concludes, we ourselves must be in some way responsible for it. Nietzsche maintains, however, that men of knowledge fail properly to comprehend the unbelievability of Platonism because they do not understand the needs to which it responded. From his point of view, they wrongly dismiss those needs as needs for rational foundations and thus emptily suggest that honesty demands that we now learn to live without such foundations.

According to Nietzsche, it is a particular form of *morality*—an understanding of ourselves and of our relationships to one another expressed in what he calls 'the morality of pity'—that hampers the self-understanding of those committed to truthfulness. At its most general level, Nietzsche's criticism of morality takes aim at our self-blindness.[16] More particularly, however, the goal of what the *Genealogy* calls a 'critique of the morality of pity' is to understand the obstacles morality presents to self-knowledge in the present age. More particularly still, the goal is to understand the way in which morality blinds the man of knowledge to his own nature. This aspect of Nietzsche's attack on morality, however, takes a surprising turn. For as I argue in Chapter 5, the morality of pity is, in Nietzsche's view, an obstacle to self-knowledge precisely insofar as it prevents men of knowledge from reading his own works in the right way.[17] It prevents them from understanding the special status of, for example, the *Genealogy*'s reflections on life in the present age. More specifically, the morality of pity lies at the root of the common misunderstanding that leads one to ask whether Nietzsche directs his criticism of modern life from *within* or from *outside* modern culture. Insofar as his insistence that we 'modern Europeans' fail to count as a culture cannot be understood in these terms, a proper understanding of his criticism of morality cannot be divorced from an ade-

---

well we understand these words once we have offered and slaughtered one faith after another on this altar [of unconditional truthfulness]" (p. 281).

[16] It is important to remember that Nietzsche understands the notion of morality *very* broadly indeed. As Chapter 1 makes clear, in this context, 'morality' can be understood as whatever gives voice to the philosophical demand for reasons. The intelligibility of this demand turns, as I shall argue, on an important misunderstanding of the nature of judgment. But this misunderstanding does not express the sort of self-blindness to which Nietzsche feels the modern man of knowledge is especially prey.

[17] The morality of pity, in other words, is an obstacle to reading writing that, in particular, helps to make explicit the consequences of our commitment to truthfulness.

quate understanding of his conception of *reading*.[18] It is not at all clear what kind of authority Nietzsche can claim for his charge that we fail to count as a culture. But, as we will see, though he does not exactly have an argument for this view, it is not clear that argument here is what is called for anyway.

On the reading I develop in this book, we in the present age are constituted as a culture, in Nietzsche's sense of the term, to the degree that our commitment to truthfulness becomes, as Nietzsche says, 'self-conscious'.[19] Such self-consciousness, however, turns on an appropriate understanding of the past,[20] an understanding he believes can be afforded by a genealogy of morals. Such self-consciousness is the form of self-knowledge that, in Nietzsche's view, our current ways of life deny us.

As I indicated above, however, when Nietzsche says that we in the present age are unknown to ourselves, the 'we' he has in mind includes only those he considers capable of becoming his 'rightful readers': those, that is, who are in a position to understand the nature of the value that knowledge has for them. Thus, Nietzsche's repeated complaint that he lacks the readers he requires should be understood in the context of his insistence that the present age is virtually defined by an absence of culture. For Nietzsche, the existence of culture, surprisingly enough, depends upon there being readers of the sort he seeks. I suggest, then, that we cannot understand what Nietzsche believes *we* lack until we understand how *he* means to be read.

Though I am adapting my usage of the term 'culture' from Nietzsche's own in his *Untimely Meditations*, the term in the present context may mislead. In speaking on Nietzsche's behalf of an absence of culture, I am not talking about an absence of, for example, musical or intellectual culture. As I read him, Nietzsche is not claiming that we lack a culture in the sense of being untutored in the finer things of life.[21] Such a claim

[18] From Nietzsche's point of view, then, the task of learning how to read him properly cannot be divorced from the aim of understanding what he has to say. This, as we will see, is part of what it means for Nietzsche to say that pitiers make bad readers.

[19] See *On the Genealogy of Morals* III, sec. 27, part of which forms the epigraph of the Introduction.

[20] Or, rather, it turns on an appropriate understanding of the fact that we *have* a past at all.

[21] This is especially clear in the *Untimely Meditations*. Stanley Cavell has argued convincingly that Nietzsche's concerns there with the current state of 'culture' [*Cultur*] cannot be properly understood as the expression of a desire to promote some aspect of present literary, musical, or intellectual culture. See his *Conditions Handsome and Unhandsome* (Chicago: University of Chicago Press, 1990), esp. pp. 51–52.

may well be true, but this is not the particular complaint in which I am interested here. Nor do I take Nietzsche to be suggesting that we have no distinctly modern practices, customs, and institutions—something that we might try either to hand down to or to keep from future generations. We clearly do have such practices, and Nietzsche finds many of them repugnant. In the sense of the term that will concern us here, however, 'culture' refers neither to mental, institutional, or artistic cultivation, on the one hand, nor to any particular stage of, say, 'Western civilization', on the other. My usage is both broader and more specialized than these senses of the term suggest. Roughly, 'culture', in the sense in which I am using the term here, refers to a form of life in which sense is made. Accordingly, I mean to argue that, in Nietzsche's view, where our lives fail to be intelligible, we may be accused of lacking culture in this sense.

The notion of intelligibility to which I am appealing can hardly be clear at the outset, but it will be explained in due course. As I said, I argue that making sense is a matter of taking a certain sort of responsibility for what one says. For Nietzsche, where we fail to do *that*, we have no culture in the sense that concerns us here. As I read him, Nietzsche sets himself the difficult task of making clear to us both the fact of and the reasons for our failure to speak responsibly. Though my usage does not reflect everything he meant by the word 'culture', and I do not mean to suggest that he used that term in a systematic way, I do mean to draw attention to one particular way in which he used the word: to designate the fact of human intelligibility. That culture, in *this* sense, has something to do with the notion of taking responsibility for what one says, and that such responsibility is, for Nietzsche, a matter of reading, is the burden of Chapter 5 to demonstrate.[22]

It is in Chapter 1, however, that I most explicitly identify the concepts of culture and intelligibility. For reasons that will become clear, it seems to me that Nietzsche's criticism of Socratism licenses my doing so. Nietzsche believes that the kind of detachment from the ordinary condi-

---

[22] Nietzsche is sometimes said to be a philosopher of culture. By this it is usually meant, I take it, that he has much to say about the forms of life that define particular moments in history—and specifically, the present one. A philosophy of culture in this sense occupies itself with the various institutions, practices, and self-interpretations that constitute a given historical community. But I am suggesting that we may distinguish a different kind of philosophy of culture in Nietzsche's work. He is interested, as I put the point here, in our failure to amount to a culture, and it is with this latter view that we will be concerned. There are, of course, a variety of ways of bringing home to someone his or her failure to make sense—her failure to take responsibility for what she says—some of which constitute a philosophy of culture in the more common sense of the term.

tions of meaningful speech that Socratism advocates is impossible on the grounds, roughly, that the intelligibility of the philosophical demand for detachment requires those same conditions. On Nietzsche's view, then, meaningful—that is, in his sense, responsible—speech requires a willingness to submit oneself to precisely the sorts of conditions from which Socrates would try to detach us. In this sense, we cannot stand outside culture in the way Socratism supposes we must if we are to engage in rational criticism.

The identification of the notions of culture and intelligibility may, however, give rise to some confusion. For it seems perfectly reasonable to object that the former notion is in fact much narrower than the latter. That is to say, in at least one sense of the phrase, nothing might appear easier than to 'stand outside' one's culture. For example, it does not seem tremendously to tax our conceptual resources to try to imagine someone who no longer sees the sense of her culture's conception of femininity—or at least of some significant part of it—or someone who can no longer make sense of her culture's understanding of courage. Concepts, after all, do change and even go dead for us altogether. And if Nietzsche's attack on Socratism appears to legislate such possibilities out of existence, so much the worse, one might feel, for Nietzsche.

I have, however, employed the notion of culture in a much broader sense than this. And it is not part of Nietzsche's criticism of the specifically Socratic demand for reasons to suggest that *no* sense can be made of a request to justify some particular understanding of, for example, a moral concept. Nor, of course, do I mean to suggest that, on his view, conceptual change is impossible.[23] What I believe he means to deny is only—though, as I see it, he considers this to be quite a lot—that when we make and answer such requests or when we try to understand these sorts of changes, we do not do so from a Socratically neutral point of view. Though what is involved in the form of neutrality Nietzsche finds to be unintelligible cannot be made explicit outside the context of his attack on Socratism, I want to emphasize at the outset that it is not part of the view I attribute to him that no form of rational criticism is possible at all. It is Socratism alone that is under attack here.

In Nietzsche's view, our lives in the present age fail to make sense specifically with respect to the will to knowledge: as it stands, our commitment to the virtue of truthfulness is, he insists, incoherent. For we try, in effect, both to own and to disown it at the same time. And

---

[23] Clearly not. From Nietzsche's point of view, of course, nothing appears more significant that the sort of conceptual change involved in, for example, the shift from the values expressed by the opposition between good and bad to those expressed by the opposition between good and evil.

we fail, in this way, to understand the significance of the death of God. In this sense, we have not yet become what we are: men of knowledge.

Nietzsche is quite explicit, however, that it is difficult to see where there is room for a problem about the death of God. Indeed, far from thinking that the news of that event will disturb us, he expects his announcement of the unbelievability of Platonism to be greeted with complete indifference.[24] Nietzsche is clear that such indifference at least appears to be a wholly reasonable response to the death of God. Talking about the death of God is, as I have claimed, Nietzsche's way of talking about what it makes sense to believe. Yet if, as he maintains, the belief in God is indeed unbelievable, then it is not clear that we can intelligibly be troubled by talk of the death of God. Indeed, to the degree that we do let ourselves be disturbed by such talk, it would appear that we have simply failed to understand that the beliefs in question are in fact no longer believable. Nietzsche insists that good sense can no longer be made of what the death of God seems to deny us: namely, the idea of an external standpoint on life. It appears, then, that if we believe that God is dead, we cannot coherently pretend that it *matters* to us that God is dead.

But Nietzsche insists that the nihilist's indifference to the death of God represents a failure to take responsibility for what he has become.[25] From his point of view, nihilism represents a flawed or, as we might put it, 'weak' will to knowledge, a refusal to question the value the man of knowledge presently attaches to truthfulness. By claiming indifference to the consequences of the relentless pursuit of knowledge, the nihilist ultimately resists membership in what I call 'the community of knowers'. This form of nihilism is a form of self-blindness, a failure of

[24] Once again, this sort of indifference is the type of nihilism with which I will be most concerned. In an interesting paper, Alan White proposes a helpful taxonomy of the different forms of nihilism Nietzsche discusses in *The Will to Power*. White distinguishes in particular three fundamental levels of nihilism: 'religious', 'radical', and 'complete' nihilism. A complete nihilist is, according to White, someone who no longer either appreciates the importance nor feels the force of our 'highest values and ideals', someone who is, in some sense, free of them. See Alan White, "Nietzschean Nihilism: A Typology," *International Studies in Philosophy* 19/2 (1987): 29–44. The nihilism I associate with indifference to the announcement of the death of God might be a form of complete nihilism. This form of nihilism infects those Nietzsche calls 'the last men'. They no longer feel the force of our highest values, but they do not care that they do not. (Once again, this is the kind of nihilism about which Nietzsche warns us in sec. 5 of the preface to the *Genealogy*.) I will explore the sense in which such nihilists may be said not to be free of the values the special force of which they claim no longer to recognize.

[25] Consequently, that indifference represents a failure of self-consciousness about our commitment to truthfulness.

individuality. As I suggested at the outset, however, overcoming this failure would allow the individual finally to *achieve* a form of community, not to stand outside it.

To understand Nietzsche's conception of the special character of our contemporary commitment to truthfulness, as well as how he means to respond to the nihilism he associates with our present understanding of that commitment, we will need to understand his criticism of Socrates. This is where *Nietzsche's Genealogy* begins. It is by seeing what Nietzsche believes is wrong with the Socratic demand for reasons that we can best understand the conception of culture that underwrites his insistence that, as I put it, the present age fails to count as one. To this end, I propose in Chapter 1 a reading of Nietzsche's attack on Socratism in *The Birth of Tragedy*. This reading sets the stage for the account in Chapters 2, 3, and 4 of the development of the modern will to knowledge. Finally, in Chapter 5, I suggest how Nietzsche's response to the nihilist should best be understood. I would like now to say something a little more specific about each chapter, before briefly turning my attention to some general questions about the overall character of my reading of Nietzsche.

In Chapter 1, I explain the conception of culture that, in *The Birth of Tragedy*, underwrites Nietzsche's criticism of the moral impulse expressed by the Socratic demand for reasons.[26] At first blush, Nietzsche appears to believe that Greek tragedy provided a direct, nondiscursive grasp of the reality of nature that lies behind what he calls 'the lie of culture'. Such insight supposedly allowed the tragic Greeks to justify their lives to themselves in spite of the suffering to which Nietzsche thought them especially prone. But this reading does not allow us to understand in what sense life may, as he says, be 'justified as an aesthetic phenomenon'. I argue that we can make sense of *that* idea only by appreciating how tragedy might be seen to question the very intelligibility of the Socratic demand for reasons.

Though making sense of what Nietzsche says about tragedy in the light of his attack on Socratism requires that we ignore the actual histori-

[26] As I explain in Chapter 1, Nietzsche's reasons for considering the Socratic demand for reasons to be a form of morality are complicated. The basic idea here is that any way of life that seeks to justify the actual life we live in terms of something independent of that life counts as a 'moral' way of life in the ostensibly pejorative sense in which Nietzsche uses the term. Socratism counts as a form of morality on these grounds insofar as it seeks to uncover something, wholly independent of our practices of moral judgment, that makes those practices intelligible.

cal order of development as he recounts it,[27] I believe that substantial clarity is gained if we do so. In any event, nothing I say here about tragedy contradicts Nietzsche's insistence that Socratism was possible only on the basis of the collapse of tragic culture. Indeed, I think we stand the best chance of understanding this last claim if we proceed in the way I have suggested.

On the reading I propose, then, tragedy denies the intelligibility of the conceptual standpoint necessary to make sense of the Socratic demand for reasons. For, according to Nietzsche, Socrates asks what justifies interpreting one's concepts in the way one does—what, for example, justifies taking *these* actions to be courageous—and demands that the justification be articulated in terms wholly independent of the actual conditions of the interpretation in question. He is not asking an overtly skeptical question about how we know that such and such an action is courageous, but seeks rather to understand what guides our judgment that it is so. On Nietzsche's reading, then, Socrates figures, roughly, that unless we have good reason to rule out alternative interpretations, we cannot be said truly to mean anything at all by our moral judgments. In other words, without 'reasons', those judgments are guided, as Nietzsche has Socrates say, 'only by instinct'. And, Socrates maintains, instincts without the sorts of reasons he seeks are blind; they cannot 'guide' in the relevant sense at all. On Nietzsche's reading, however, tragedy denies that it makes good sense to say—in the way Socratism supposes we must—that, as I put the point, we *interpret* our concepts.[28]

These considerations suggest that, on Nietzsche's view, the intelligibility of Socratism turns on something I will call 'resistance to community'. Indeed, The Birth of Tragedy suggests that only someone who was not in the relevant sense a member of the cultural community in question could intelligibly ask the specifically Socratic question of what justifies interpreting one's concepts in the way members of that community

[27] Nietzsche does not treat tragedy as a response to Socratism but proceeds rather the other way around. It nevertheless remains true that a tragic culture is immune to Socratism, and we need to understand that immunity if we are to understand what Nietzsche thinks is incoherent about the Socratic demand for reasons.

[28] Nietzsche, it is important to point out, does not use the term 'interpretation' in this way. If we bear this in mind, however, we will be better able to understand how he does use it. My talk of interpretation here is suggested, on the one hand, by Nietzsche's attack on Socratism and, on the other, by a powerful but misleading reading of the doctrine of perspectivism. It seems to me that talking about interpretation in this context is the easiest way to get at the points Nietzsche wants to make. As we will see, whatever Nietzsche *does* mean in suggesting that the most fundamental ways in which we grasp the world may be understood as forms of interpretation, he does not mean that they are something we somehow 'project' onto that world.

do. (Once again, this reading does not entail that, on Nietzsche's view, no questions about those concepts can be posed at all. Nietzsche is concerned to understand only the nature of what he thinks of as specifically *philosophical* resistance to the ordinary conditions that govern the employment of any concepts at all. In attacking Socratism, then, he is not trying to rule out the possibility of all rational inquiry whatsoever. Indeed, to think so is precisely the error of Socratism itself.)

Though, on Nietzsche's view, Greek tragedy shows how Socratism is rooted in resistance to one's community, it neither calls on the audience to remain within the confines of culture nor urges them not to step outside them. Rather, it asks them to give up the Socratic picture of confinement altogether. I try to explain this last point by appealing to the notion of *authority*. The idea of authority seems pertinent in this context because, on Nietzsche's view, culture calls for a form of obedience. In effect, it is only by treating this kind of obedience as an act of interpretation that the Socratic demand for reasons can get off the ground. In other words, only if obedience is thought of as interpretation in this sense does the Socratic charge that instinct is blind make sense. But Nietzsche denies that there is any compelling reason to conceive obedience in such terms.

This reading of Nietzsche's attack on the demand for reasons allows us to see in what way he is concerned, in *The Birth of Tragedy*, to understand the relationship between individual and community. He wants to undermine the particular conception of that relationship that fuels Socratic inquiry. He rejects, in particular, the view that to be an individual member of a community is somehow to adopt that community's view of the world—sharing a world view or self-interpretation with it. The principal upshot of this reading, however, is that Nietzsche does not seek a philosophical account of that relationship, but rather tries to understand the drive to seek such an account at all. *The Birth of Tragedy* thus helps us to locate Nietzsche's interest in undermining philosophical motivations rather than in attacking worked-out philosophical views. I argue that, in general, his attack on so-called traditional philosophy is best understood in these terms.

Finally, my reading denies that Nietzsche sought a positive alternative to what, in the "Attempt at a Self-Criticism," he condemns as 'morality'. Given the sort of misunderstanding he claims to find at the root of Socratism, there is nothing left for such an alternative to be. The content of the concept of obedience to the authority of culture that I find in Nietzsche is simply exhausted by the uncovering of resistance to authority.

My claim that Nietzsche did not seek to articulate an alternative to morality may mislead. I mean simply that, given the kind of criticism he directs toward Socratism, he could not coherently understand himself to have been in the business of offering an alternative philosophical account of culture. The aim of his attack on the Socratic demand for reasons is to show that the demand is not intelligible independent of the particular historical context in which it is raised, which is to say that it is not intelligible on its own terms. Thus, Nietzsche cannot be trying in a philosophical vein to tell us what it is like to live without reasons. (Outside of philosophy, knowing what it is like to live without reasons is something that, as he sees it, we can hardly fail to understand.) I do not deny, of course, that he imagines a life immune from philosophy to be very different from one infected by it, but that difference does not suggest a difference of *philosophical* outlook.

My aim in Chapter 2 is to make explicit the positive role Socratism plays in Nietzsche's account of the rise of the modern will to knowledge. As I have suggested, it is in this context that we can best understand the point of his more explicit reflections on the nature and limits of knowledge. Nietzsche appears concerned to argue that, our Socratic pretensions notwithstanding, the philosophically privileged relationship of knowing the world is, in fact, an interpretation of the world, rather than a faithful representation of its nature. He is thus often understood to advocate a doctrine called 'perspectivism'. According to one helpful statement of this doctrine, every view of ourselves and of the world—that is, every system of belief, structure of desire, artistic creation, and so on—is an interpretation, something we create rather than discover. My goal in Chapter 2 is to try to understand the concept of interpretation that appears to underwrite such a doctrine. I argue that if that concept is not itself a version of the misused notion of interpretation Nietzsche diagnoses at the root of Socratism, then perspectivism cannot be a *view* with which Nietzsche intended to replace the traditional epistemology he rejected.

Perspectivism is a profoundly deflationary doctrine, and that is, I argue, all it *can* be. My concern in Chapter 2, however, is neither to articulate a defensible interpretation of Nietzsche's perspectivism for its own sake, nor to take issue with any particular commentator's version of that doctrine.[29] I am interested in those aspects of Nietzsche's think-

---

[29] See Nehamas's *Nietzsche: Life as Literature* for the most detailed defense of the doctrine of perspectivism. Nehamas characterizes perspectivism as the view that every view is an interpretation. The content of this view depends, of course, upon the content of the notion of interpretation. My aim here is to understand what this last notion comes to for Nietzsche. Though the formulation of perspectivism as the view that every view is an interpretation is due to Nehamas, I appeal to it here only

ing that seem to drive us to construct such a doctrine for him in the first place. Seen in their proper light, I argue, the claims that appear to support a perspectivist epistemology should undermine our confidence that such an epistemology answers to truly intelligible philosophical concerns.

More specifically, in this chapter, I endeavor to apply the conclusions of Chapter 1 to one of the two essential components of the perspectivist epistemology commonly attributed to Nietzsche: the idea that the world has no determinate character 'in itself'.[30] In Chapter 3, I go on to suggest how we should understand the other essential component of perspectivism: the idea that, because the world has no character in itself, we must *impose* one on it and so bear some sort of responsibility for the character the world appears to have. Once again, my goal in both chapters is to undermine the very idea that Nietzsche had an epistemology.

Nietzsche's denial of the thing-in-itself should, I argue, be understood to question the very intelligibility of philosophical talk about our relationship to the world. In his view, the notion of a thing-in-itself gives voice to a picture of interpretation, according to which our judgments about the world must be rooted in something wholly independent of our human, all too human interests and desires. The philosopher reasons that if our judgments are not in this way independent of our interests, we remain cut off from the world as it really is. But these fears of the groundlessness and contingency of our interpretations of the world are rooted in the same error Nietzsche believes he has diagnosed at the heart of Socratism: the idea that we apply our concepts to the world, that it makes interesting philosophical sense to say that we *interpret* them in one way rather than another.

In Chapter 3, I suggest how, given an adequate understanding of Nietzsche's denial of the thing-in-itself, we should understand the other idea that appears to motivate the doctrine of perspectivism: namely that, because we somehow impose interpretations on the world, we are

---

as a matter of convenience: the notion of interpretation is what interests me, not the accuracy of Nehamas's formulation of Nietzsche's doctrine.

[30] See Alexander Nehamas, "Immanent and Transcendent Perspectivism in Nietzsche," *Nietzsche-Studien* 12 (1983): 473–90. (See also Tracy Strong's interesting comment on this paper in the same volume, pp. 491–94.) Immanent perspectivism is the view that no view can claim a privileged relationship to the world as it is in itself. What in Nehamas's view keeps this doctrine from devolving into a form of skepticism is Nietzsche's attack on the very idea of 'the world as it is in itself'. It is to keep Nietzsche's doctrine from turning into skepticism that Nehamas distinguishes it from 'transcendent' perspectivism—a view that threatens to reintroduce the notion of 'the world as it is in itself'.

therefore responsible for the sense we make of the world. Properly understood, the denial of the thing-in-itself suggests that the philosophical idea that we impose meaning on the world is incoherent. Nietzsche denies that we can make good sense of the idea of the *object* of such an imposition, but then the concept of imposition itself makes no sense. This conclusion implies that, rather than claiming that we should take responsibility for the meaning we impose on the world, Nietzsche means to show us how—in a philosophical mood—we resist the meaning that we find in the world. Nietzsche thus seeks to replace the basically Socratic notion of responsibility, which in his view expresses philosophical dissatisfaction with life, with a notion of *responsiveness*. This notion allows us to see that dissatisfaction for what it is. 'Will to power', I argue, is one name he gives to this kind of responsiveness. However, this account of intelligibility is, I emphasize, a psychological not a philosophical one.

We must, therefore, distinguish two different senses of the notion of responsibility at work in Nietzsche's thinking. As we will see, this notion expresses in both cases a certain understanding of the nature of responsible *speech*. On the one hand, we may speak of Socratic responsibility. On this view, responsibility is a matter of articulating one's standards of judgment. Those standards, as I have said, must be sufficiently independent of one's actual practices of judgment to have the kind of objectivity and justificatory status that the Socratically minded philosopher seeks. This same Socratic sense of responsibility is expressed in the idea of acknowledging that, because there are no such standards, one must take responsibility for the judgments one makes in their absence. Here, in a roughly existentialist vein, one either owns up to or disowns responsibility for what one says just because there is no one and nothing else to bear that responsibility. Nietzsche, as I have said, finds this notion of responsibility incoherent, because he finds unintelligible the conception of 'standards' to which it appeals. On the other hand, however, he is indeed deeply concerned with what it means to take responsibility for what one says—specifically, for saying that God is dead. And, in this context, it is true that he encourages us to think in terms of responsibility—but only of the sort he thinks we can conceivably bear. I refer to this form of responsibility as 'responsiveness' in order to distinguish it from its Socratic counterpart. Responsiveness, I argue, suggests a form of passivity in contrast to the kind of activity apparently involved in 'taking responsibility' in the existentialist or Socratic sense. As I read him, Nietzsche finds that true activity is achieved only by means of such passivity.

This reading tends, I think, to support my claim that what appears to some readers as Nietzsche's positive alternative to what he rejects as morality—in the form, again, of philosophical demand for 'firm foundations'—is really only a further step in his ongoing diagnosis of the drive both to philosophical inquiry *and* to clear-cut alternatives to that form of questioning. Behind both the philosophical search for grounding our interpretations of the world and the opposed demand to give up such a search and instead acknowledge the so-called groundlessness or contingency of those interpretations lies the same resistance to the meaningfulness of the world.[31]

As I argue in Chapter 1, *The Birth of Tragedy*'s attack on Socratism is best understood as an extended meditation on the nature of such resistance. The force of the Socratic demand for reasons turns, Nietzsche argues, on a failure to understand the nature of membership in a culture.[32] The Greeks lose their tragic sense to the degree that they come to view *being* Greek as a matter of interpretation. But to make sense of this sort of claim as it applies to the *present* age, we need an example of the sort of resistance Nietzsche finds in *us*.[33]

In Chapter 4 I contend that we find the example we seek in Nietzsche's discussion of the form of contemporary nihilism with which this book is most concerned: in what he expects to be the man of knowl-

[31] I take the term 'contingency' from Richard Rorty. Rorty's recent work—most specifically the essays in *Contingency, Irony, and Solidarity* (Cambridge: Cambridge University Press, 1989)—articulates a position that is essentially a form of the nihilism with which I understand Nietzsche to be trying to come to terms. Rorty does, I take it, think that we should take responsibility for the sense we make of the world. Nietzsche, on the other hand, encourages us to be responsive to the sense the world makes to us. We do not go far wrong in taking Rorty to be the spokesperson for the 'last man'. But Nietzsche does not so much take issue with the considerations that lead to the last man's nihilism as with the conclusions the nihilist draws from them.

[32] As we shall see, however, Nietzsche's Greeks have no real choice in this matter, because their culture had become uninhabitable; Socratism merely offers them a way out of this situation. See, especially, *Twilight of the Idols*, "The Problem of Socrates," sec. 9: "Socrates . . . saw *behind* his aristocratic Athenians; he grasped that *his* case, the idiosyncrasy of his case, was already no longer exceptional. The same kind of degeneration was everywhere silently preparing itself: the old Athens was coming to an end.—And Socrates understood that all the world had need of him" (p. 32). This is a passage to which I will return later, but I want to suggest here that the seeds of the claim that Socratism is a response to and not a cause of corruption can already be found in *The Birth of Tragedy*.

[33] The sort of nonsense to which Nietzsche feels that we in the present age are prey is not exactly *philosophical* nonsense. And this fact can seem to distinguish Nietzsche's 'absurdly rational' Greeks from us. It is not clear, however, that Nietzsche believes that truly philosophical nonsense is possible after all. He presents the appeal of Socratism in terms of the appeal of talk about grounding or foundations, but he seeks a *psychological* account of that appeal in part precisely because he believes that no coherent *philosophical* account is forthcoming.

edge's resistance to the news of the death of God. What has authority for such a person, Nietzsche claims, is knowledge. This fact, however, is what he believes the man of knowledge resists. But unlike the Socratic demand for reasons, which appears to rest upon a felt need for justification, his resistance to the authority of knowledge is, for Nietzsche, a matter precisely of his apparent indifference to such a need. Here, as elsewhere, however, Nietzsche's diagnosis of resistance does not point to a positive philosophical alternative. Our distinctive indifference to the unbelievability of the belief in God simply signals our resistance to the imperative to truthfulness, to becoming what we are: men of knowledge. Overcoming that indifference is not, for Nietzsche, a matter of coming to have further beliefs about or attitudes toward the value of knowledge, nor does it free us up to adopt some other perspective on the present age.

Thus, whereas Chapter 2 is an attempt to understand what Nietzsche took to be the origins of the will to knowledge, in Chapters 3 and 4 I try to understand what he thought of as its chief consequence: namely, the death of God. Though the practice of *genealogy* is a direct descendant of the original Socratic demand for reasons, it is genealogy that contributes most to the unbelievability of the Platonism that once provided an answer to the Socratic demand. This claim suggests, in turn, that the nature of the nihilism Nietzsche diagnoses at the heart of the present age may be seen most clearly in our understanding of the consequences of genealogical investigation.

Nietzsche suggests that the practice of genealogy is responsible for the demise of what he calls 'Christianity as dogma'—that is, for rendering belief in God unbelievable. But he goes on to say that Christianity *as morality* will perish only when the will to truth at the heart of genealogy becomes 'self-conscious'. As I have remarked, this latter claim has often been taken to suggest that Nietzsche believed that our commitment to truthfulness—that is, the will to knowledge—is merely a contingent historical fact about us, something that might eventually be overcome in favor of some other commitment. Such a reading, however, is wholly at odds with the spirit of Nietzsche's critique of morality, because he would find the fantasy of overcoming the will to knowledge to be a form of resistance to its authority. Our commitment to truthfulness is, indeed, a fact about us, but, according to Nietzsche, just because it *is* a fact about us, there is no room to treat it either as something for which we should—in a Socratic sense—take responsibility or as something we might try to overcome. Rather, our responsiveness to that commitment is measured by our ability to overcome our resistance to it. As I have said, our resistance to the authority of knowledge takes the shape of a particular aversion to—and misunderstanding of—the *historical* character of that commitment.

My principal aim in the first four chapters is to try to make clear the ways in which, in Nietzsche's view, certain fundamental philosophical confusions express our resistance to intelligibility. Thus, the Socratic demand for reasons gives voice to the desire to find a basis for our practices of judgment that is independent of those very practices, somehow more basic than they are. As we will see in Chapter 2, the notion of a thing-in-itself similarly expresses a philosophical fantasy of an independent ground for our judgments about the world. I mean, in other words, to explain Nietzsche's insistence that, in philosophy, we respond to the fear that the life we actually live is wanting in some way by concocting a fantasy of a standard against which we then pretend to measure the value of our lives. Seeing through such fantasies would seem, for Nietzsche, to be a necessary condition of what he considers making sense to be. But as we will see in the subsequent chapters, he believes that, by and large, we in the present age (we 'men of knowledge') still fail to make sense—that we are, as I put it, inarticulate—even though we can no longer make sense of the philosophical illusions of the past.

My aim in the final chapter, in turn, is to see what the notion of intelligibility comes to in the context of this particular failure to make sense. More specifically, I mean in Chapter 5 to explore in greater detail Nietzsche's conception of individuality, and in particular to understand his conception of what I referred to above as the 'antagonism' between individual and community. As we will see, Nietzsche most consistently employs the notion of individuality in opposition to that of the herd. This reading allows me to put into perspective Nietzsche's claim that morality is hostile to individuality. *"Morality in Europe today,"* he says, *"is herd animal morality"* (BGE, sec. 202, p. 115). This form of morality is more or less defined by its opposition to the very possibility of individuality. As I have said, the specific form of herd morality at stake in Nietzsche's understanding of modernity involves resistance to the authority of knowledge by a refusal to acknowledge the historical character of the modern will to truth. Such resistance expresses our unwillingness to take responsibility for our commitment to truthfulness—for saying that God is dead. This unwillingness is, in turn, responsible for our failure, as men of knowledge, to count as a culture in the special sense in which I use the term here.

My emphasis on this picture of culture as Nietzschean responsibility (or as responsiveness) will surely strike some readers as foreign as Nietzsche's thought. But, as Chapter 5 makes clear, it is a picture that

Nietzsche himself stresses explicitly. This is especially true in the second essay of the *Genealogy*, where he claims that having the right to make promises is our true problem. As I read him, Nietzsche means here to say that being able to *speak* is our true problem: to say that someone has the right to make promises is, for Nietzsche, to say that he can take responsibility for what he says—that he has the right to give his word. The *Genealogy* calls such a person a 'sovereign individual'. We begin to see what Nietzsche thinks responsibility (and, hence, individuality) comes to in this context by understanding how he thinks morality—specifically, the morality of pity—tries to deny it. Understanding the obstacle Nietzsche believes morality represents for individuality is, I argue, a matter of seeing how, in his view, the morality of pity *silences* the individual. My aim, in sum, is to make clear in what Nietzsche believes making sense in the present age consists.

By way of bringing these introductory remarks to a close, I want to say something more about the notion of intelligibility employed in these pages. For Nietzsche, making sense is a fundamentally *practical* matter. Intelligibility, in other words, is something at which he believes one either fails or succeeds.[34] Success or failure in this context is indeed something for which he believes we bear, in his sense of the word, responsibility. We can in a preliminary fashion cast some light upon these claims by recalling a distinction that is absolutely fundamental to Nietzsche's thought, early and late: the distinction between activity and reactivity.[35] In *Schopenhauer as Educator*, this distinction appears as the difference between the individual and the herd, between my higher and my lower self.[36] In *Beyond Good and Evil*, it appears as the distinction between what is noble and what is common or plebeian.[37] In the first

[34] What it means to say that making sense is a *practical* matter is the subject of the last chapter of this book. I am, for the moment, concerned only to note a difference Nietzsche intends between treating intelligibility in this way and treating, as he believes philosophers do, the difference between sense and nonsense as a *theoretical* matter.

[35] Gilles Deleuze properly appreciates the centrality of this distinction to Nietzsche's thought as a whole. See his *Nietzsche and Philosophy*, trans. Hugh Tomlinson (New York: Columbia University Press, 1983).

[36] See *Schopenhauer as Educator* in Friedrich Nietzsche, *Untimely Meditations*, trans. R. J. Hollingdale (Cambridge: Cambridge University Press, 1983), pp. 125–94: "your true nature lies, not concealed deep within you, but immeasurably high above you, or at least above that which you usually take yourself to be" (p. 129).

[37] See, in particular, *Beyond Good and Evil*, sec. 287: "What is noble? What does the word 'noble' still mean to us today? What betrays, what allows one to recognize the noble human being, under this heavy, overcast sky of the beginning rule of the plebs that makes everything opaque and leaden? . . . *The noble soul has reverence for itself*" (pp. 227–28).

essay of the *Genealogy*, it appears as a distinction between certain character traits of Nietzsche's 'masters' and 'slaves'.[38] It is natural to think that this distinction must mark the difference between different classes of human action. Thus, Nietzsche appears to some readers to advocate, say, egoistic actions as expressive of activity, and correspondingly to condemn altruism as a form of reactivity. I want to suggest, however, that the distinction between activity and reactivity marks the distinction between sense and nonsense to which I have been appealing here. We might put this point by saying that the kind of 'human excellence' to which Nietzsche is most consistently committed is excellence at making sense. Let me explain.

As I have intimated, the distinction between activity and reactivity is drawn in the second essay of the *Genealogy* in terms of the difference between two forms of speaking—a difference Nietzsche describes as that between having and lacking the right to make promises, between being able and being unable to take responsibility for what one says. If this reading is correct, then the distinction between activity and reactivity does not refer us to two opposing sets of things we might say—'noble' things, for example, as opposed to 'base' things—but rather to the difference between success and failure in speaking at all. From this point of view, Nietzsche's question about what constitutes nobility or individuality in the present age is not a question about what marks or features serve to distinguish the individual from the herd, but rather a practical question about whether or not the words one has uttered have been uttered meaningfully. In other words, when he says that we in the present age fail to count as individuals—that we lack the right to make promises—he is not saying that we neglect to say the things individuals say, but rather that we fail to say anything at all.[39]

Because my account of Nietzsche's attack on Socratism goes against the grain both of what many find it attractive to think of as Nietzsche's early view, in particular, and, as I have suggested, of a fundamental presupposition many readers bring to their interpretation of Nietzsche's

---

[38] See *On the Genealogy of Morals* I, sec. 10: "[*ressentiment's*] action is fundamentally reaction" (p. 37).

[39] Once again, Nietzsche wants to know whether we have the right to make the *particular* claim that God is dead—whether, that is, we have the right to say that the truth matters to us. But here again, the distinction he has in mind is not that between saying that God is dead and saying something else, but between success and failure at meaning what one says when one claims to be committed to the truth.

work in general, it is pertinent to say something here about the general character of my interpretation as a whole.

I do my best here to understand Nietzsche on his own terms. Specifically, I try to work my way as carefully as I can through a handful of arguments that seem to me absolutely crucial to understanding Nietzsche's conception of the life of the man of knowledge in the present age. This does not mean, however, that I try everywhere to understand Nietzsche *in* his own terms. Thus, in Chapter 1 I employ the notions of authority and obedience in an attempt to illuminate that which, in a Socratic frame of mind, Nietzsche thinks we resist. Though 'authority' and 'obedience' are both words that Nietzsche himself sometimes employs in roughly the sense in which I use them here, I do not claim to offer an interpretation of *his* use of them. Thus, talk of obedience, as I use the term here, is meant merely as a helpful way of getting at what Nietzsche believes the Socratically minded philosopher tacitly treats as an interpretation—thus generating the demand for reasons. And though Nietzsche's usage of the term 'authority' suggests that we may understand the idea of obedience in these terms, he himself certainly does not do so everywhere and indeed often has little patience with those who, in a different sense, are unwilling to question authority.[40]

It seems to me that, at a very general level, Nietzsche is interested in what it means to find the world to be an intelligible place.[41] I do not mean by this that he has a philosophical interest in *explaining* the world's intelligibility, but rather that he is concerned with what we might think of as the very fact of it—the fact, for example, that doing *these* things (say) counts as acting courageously, as giving praise, and so forth.[42] My talk of the 'relation between community and individual' is meant to get at this central feature of his thought. These terms are recommended by his attack on Socratism, because that attack suggests that, in a philosophical mood, the Socratic interlocutor resists something it is very

[40] In sec. 188 of *Beyond Good and Evil*, for example, Nietzsche treats a certain kind of obedience as a precondition for the sort of obedience to authority that he believes is essential to fully human intelligibility. As will become clear in Chapter 5, the former sort of obedience is what the *Genealogy* refers to as 'calculability, regularity, and necessity'. The latter form of obedience, on the other hand, is expressed in a willingness to adopt the roles of creditor and debtor with respect to one's interlocutors.

[41] It might be more accurate to say that he is interested in various forms of the *failure* to find the world an intelligible place. It is, as we shall see, quite difficult to state at all clearly just what Nietzsche believes to be the upshot of his investigation of this failure.

[42] Or again, more precisely, with our human, all too human wish to avoid this fact. Putting the point of Nietzsche's attack on Socratism in these ostensibly Wittgensteinian tones does not seem to me to distort the spirit of either philosopher's thinking.

natural to think of as the fact of his membership in the cultural community whose authority Socrates calls on him to question.[43] Nietzsche's rejection of Socratism as unintelligible implies, in turn, that, for him, individuality is not a matter of rejecting membership in the community, but rather one of acknowledging it. This reading suggests that, for Nietzsche, we see what the world's intelligibility—or its 'authority'— comes to only by overcoming philosophical opposition to it.

On the other hand, as we shall see, there is a different sense of the term 'individual' according to which Nietzsche in fact rejects the idea that the individual should acknowledge membership in his or her community. But this sense of individuality makes sense only in terms of its opposition to the notion of a herd. And the herd is constituted precisely by its resistance to real community, by its lack of culture. Certainly, as far as the will to knowledge is concerned, the individual is not committed to something different from that to which what is most herdlike within (and without) her is committed. On the contrary, she is committed to precisely that to which the herd resists being committed: namely, to the value of truthfulness.

Such a reading is likely to encounter resistance at a number of levels, three of which I would like merely to identify here. First, as a reading of Nietzsche's very early work, *The Birth of Tragedy*, it appears to grant that work an overly proleptic status, and hence to suggest that Nietzsche's views about Socratism did not significantly develop over time. This is indeed a consequence of my interpretation. Nietzsche, in my view, maintains throughout his work an attack on the Socratic view of life in essentially the form I give it here, and draws essentially the same conclusions from it. This is not to suggest that he never changed his mind or modified his views on a wide variety of other matters— though, to my mind, the most significant developments in his thinking concern a changing conception of his readership and hence of his role as an author, and not his particular philosophical views.[44] Moreover, it

[43] Of course, Nietzsche's views about Socrates are more complex than my analysis here may appear to suggest. In particular, viewed under the aspect of the collapse of Greek culture, Socrates counts for Nietzsche as an individual—someone, that is, who points out the incoherence of the life of his particular community. For a fuller interpretation of this aspect of Nietzsche's relationship to Socrates, see Tracy Strong's *Friedrich Nietzsche and the Politics of Transfiguration* (Berkeley: University of California Press, 1975). I am, however, interested at this point primarily in only one aspect of his view of Socrates: namely, in the fate of the philosophical demand for reasons.

[44] Over the years, Nietzsche appears to devote more and more attention to the question of who his proper audience might be. See especially the various prefaces he adds to his works in 1886. In Chapter 5, I try to show why this question is wholly *internal* to the content of his thought. See Tracy Strong, "Nietzsche's Political Aesthetics," in *Nietzsche's New Seas*, ed. Michael Allen Gillespie and Tracy B. Strong

also seems to me that the distinction between individual and herd is central to Nietzsche's thought early and late. While not expressed in these terms in *The Birth of Tragedy*, that distinction nevertheless plays an important role in Nietzsche's early thinking about Socrates to the degree that the latter appears, even there, as something like the prototype of the individual who distinguishes himself from the herd.[45] Even in *The Birth of Tragedy*, that is, Socrates is presented not merely as the corrupter of Athenian youth; rather, he *responds* to their corruption— precisely by providing a model of what responsible speech might be. I think, then, that we may speak most helpfully of the development of Nietzsche's conception of the distinction between individual and herd to the extent that his views about the hostility of the latter to the former mature over time.[46] The distinction itself nevertheless remains central to his work, and is, in any case, crucial for understanding what Nietzsche has to say about the will to truth.

Second, my rejection of the idea that Nietzsche meant to provide an alternative to what he attacks as Socratism is likely to provoke resistance because it appears to deny so much. As I have said, Nietzsche's concerns with philosophy are, from the beginning, aimed at understanding and thereby, in his view, undermining its motivations. When the latter are seen for what they are, there is, for Nietzsche, nothing left for philosophical theorizing to be about. This reading appears to imply that the philosophical aim of Nietzsche's work is wholly critical or negative. I

(Chicago: University of Chicago Press, 1988), pp. 153–74, for an interesting suggestion about how to account for what we might call the 'unity' of Nietzsche's early and late thought. The introductory chapter of Strong's *Friedrich Nietzsche and the Politics of Transfiguration* contains an intriguing account of the development of Nietzsche's views. In any case, the all-important distinction he draws between the individual and the herd is central to his work, early *and* late, and this distinction is absolutely crucial to understanding his attack on morality, as well as to understanding his conception of the modern will to knowledge.

[45] This theme is, of course, made quite explicit in the *Twilight of the Idols*.

[46] In particular, Nietzsche deepens his account of the psychology of the spirit of revenge, and this allows us to understand more about the *source* of herd morality's hostility to the possibility of individuality. As far as our modern commitment to truthfulness is concerned, Nietzsche treats herd morality as an expression of our hatred of history. For only the individual acknowledges that the will to knowledge has a history and yet grants that commitment the status of fate. Even here, however, there is room to argue that substantial elements of *Zarathustra's* story about the will's "ill-will against time and its 'it was'" and of the doctrine of eternal recurrence are already present in the *Untimely Meditations*. Moreover, even *The Birth of Tragedy* carries the seeds of Nietzsche's ostensibly more mature views about the authority of truthfulness for the present age. See in particular sec. 15, from which the epigraph of Chapter 2 is taken. It is not my goal, however, to deny that Nietzsche's views on a variety of matters changed over time.

mean to show, however, that it is part of Nietzsche's goal to deny the intelligibility of the dichotomy we may wish to draw here. Of course, the case for this last claim is made only in the chapters that follow.

It is worth pointing out, however, that, from another point of view, Nietzsche's aims here are not *simply* deflationary. He seeks what he thinks of as a *psychological* diagnosis of the needs that lie behind our urge to philosophize. Indeed, this fact should help partly to account for the pertinence of my employment of the psychoanalytic notion of resistance in this context. As we will see, however, the sense in which Nietzsche's investigations can be said to be psychological is quite complicated. He recognizes that the Socratic response to such investigations is to treat them as simply irrelevant to properly philosophical concerns. At the very least, then, we must bear in mind that, on pain of irrelevance, Nietzsche cannot simply oppose psychological thinking to reflection of a more strictly philosophical variety. And though, as we will see, he wants to call that distinction into question, from the point of view of *philosophy*, the only ostensibly relevant means for doing so—philosophical means, that is—can in principle never do the job Nietzsche would ask of them.

Third, and finally, by drawing attention to the role of community in Nietzsche's thought and by trying to show how his attack on Socratism is aimed at that which undermines obedience to the authority of community, I do not wish to appear to provide an antidote to the (correct) assumption that some form of individualism underwrites Nietzsche's criticism of morality. On the contrary, Nietzsche means to defend the individual against the demands of herd morality. My aim, however, is to understand precisely *which* conception of individuality underwrites his criticism of the latter, and I hope to show that the notions of individuality and community in Nietzsche's work are not opposed in the way they can quite naturally seem on a first reading.[47] In any case, this distinction is—as is the related distinction between the individual and the herd—of paramount importance for our understanding of Nietzsche's thought, in general, and of his critique of morality, in particular.

As I have indicated, a primary goal of this book is to cast doubt upon the very basic assumption that Nietzsche's thought can be divided into

---

[47] Recently Leslie Paul Thiele has devoted a good deal of attention to the question of the relationship between individual and community in Nietzsche's work. See his *Friedrich Nietzsche and the Politics of the Soul* (Princeton: Princeton University Press, 1990). Misled by Nietzsche's often strident declamations against the herd, however, Thiele treats these notions as simply opposed to one another, thus missing the important consequences of the Nietzschean attack on Socratism.

positive and negative (or merely critical) aspects. Almost every reader gets around to complaining, for example, that though Nietzsche's criticism of traditional morality is in many respects compelling, he does not do enough to spell out the alternative he supposedly recommends.[48] And though the assumption that Nietzsche wished to propose alternatives to the views he rejects does indeed guide many interpretations of his work, it is more important to notice how *natural* an assumption it is—one, in fact, that Nietzsche himself struggles to overcome in his readers. But just because such a response to his work is indeed so natural, I have found it best to address the response head-on, and to try to uncover its motivations and consequences, rather than to take a detour through the secondary literature that seems to me to rely upon it. I therefore confine the bulk of my references to the scholarly literature on Nietzsche to footnotes.

Giving up the presupposition that we may distinguish the constructive from the destructive or critical moments of Nietzsche's thought involves a kind of aspect shift in one's reading. For one thing, neglected and misunderstood passages can be seen in a new light. Nowhere, I think, is this so evident as in the case of Nietzsche's early work, *The Birth of Tragedy*. But, as I have suggested, the issue of perspectivism is also seen quite differently once we take seriously the character of Nietzsche's attack on Socratism. Finally, a text that, to my knowledge, has received far too little attention—the second essay of the *Genealogy*— emerges as one of the most important for understanding Nietzsche's conception of life in the present age.

[48] Or to defending him from that charge. At the end of the second essay of the *Genealogy*, Nietzsche himself makes an ironical reference to the worry that he is merely destroying something without offering to set up anything in its place. In that context, however, the point of mentioning such worries appears to be to get us to question our assurance that we understand the distinction in question.

CHAPTER 1

THE PHILOSOPHICAL SIGNIFICANCE OF
NIETZSCHE'S ATTACK ON SOCRATISM

The Birth of Tragedy *and the Concept of Culture*

'Socratism', as I use the term in this book, refers to the philosophical demand that one provide a certain kind of reason for interpreting concepts in the ways one does. Specifically, Socrates asks that one say what all actions of a given type have in common in virtue of which they are actions of that type. If one can do that, he supposes, one will have given the appropriate sort of reasons for one's judgments about such actions. Though the exact nature of the reasons he seeks will become clear only as we go along,[1] my aim in this chapter is to articulate my sense that Nietzsche's criticism of the specifically *Socratic* demand for reasons is underwritten by a particular understanding of the notion of culture, an understanding first deployed in *The Birth of Tragedy*.[2] His attack on Socratism suggests that culture, in the special sense in which I am using that term here, is a form of community—a form, in particular, of what he gives us reason to think of as linguistic community.

---

[1] Hereafter, when I use the expression 'the demand for reasons', I mean to refer to the specifically Socratic form of that demand.

[2] Though the term 'culture' is used in this sense much more explicitly in the *Untimely Meditations*—and especially in *Schopenhauer as Educator*—than it is in *The Birth of Tragedy*, I think Nietzsche's investigations in the latter work underpin his later, more explicit usage. In *The Birth of Tragedy*, Nietzsche tries to resist the philosophical wedge Socrates wants to drive between culture and nature; he wants to recover the sense in which what the Socratic spectator of life insists is merely cultural can in fact only be something natural to us. Culture, as Nietzsche says in the *Untimely Meditations*, is the *perfection* of nature, the refinement—not the replacement—of instinct. For a thought-provoking discussion of Nietzsche's treatment of the idea of culture in *Schopenhauer as Educator*, see Stanley Cavell's *Conditions Handsome and Unhandsome* (Chicago: University of Chicago Press, 1990), especially the introduction and chap. 1.

On Nietzsche's account, the demand for reasons is born of what I call 'resistance' to such community.[3] An adequate assessment of his attack on the demand for reasons turns, therefore, on a proper understanding of this form of resistance.

A natural but, as I will argue, misleading approach to understanding Socratism's resistance to community is to take it to express a desire to achieve a vantage point on the world radically independent of the terms one has inherited from the culture in which one finds oneself. Socratism, however, gives voice to a special understanding of the kind of independence that is sought here. The form of critical independence from one's tradition that Socratism requires is not simply that which is presupposed in asking whether this or that judgment or range of judgments reflects our most considered understanding of the concepts in question. Rather, as Nietzsche sees it, Socratism presupposes a standpoint that is *completely* external to culture as a whole. Its aim is not to achieve critical independence from this or that tradition in particular, but rather from any and all tradition whatsoever. In other words, from the Socratic point of view, the problem with us in our prereflective state is not that our judgments about this or that are made from the standpoint of this or that particular cultural tradition. It is not that we fail to realize, for example, that someone else might employ his or her concepts differently. Rather, the difficulty is that we fail to draw the proper conclusion from this very possibility. For, in Socrates' view, we fail adopt what he considers to be a specifically philosophical standpoint that is independent from any tradition at all. Nietzsche does not believe, however, that this is a standpoint we *can* adopt—though, as we will see, he does not consider our inability to achieve properly Socratic neutrality to reflect cognitive limitations on our part.

[3] In the late preface to *The Birth of Tragedy*, Nietzsche refers to Socratism as a form of morality, and claims that his hostility to Socratism should be understood as part of his broader hostility to morality in general. As I noted in the Introduction, Nietzsche often uses the term 'morality' in a very broad sense—broad enough, indeed, to encompass philosophy itself. It is reasonable to wonder, however, whether the meaning of the term 'morality' has somehow been violated if philosophical inquiry itself is thereby made to count as a form of morality. But Nietzsche treats philosophy as a way of life, not as a body of theories. As a way of life, philosophy embodies a range of attitudes toward the world and toward ourselves and each other, and in particular a certain understanding of the relationship between individual and culture. Though his use of the term 'morality' is far from systematic, in general Nietzsche calls 'moral' those of our attitudes toward the world and toward each other that he condemns as 'life-denying'. The goal of this chapter, then, is to explain in what sense philosophy—specifically, in the form of Socratism—is one such attitude. But, once again, the target of attack is Socratism alone. Nietzsche's rejection of this attitude does not imply a similar rejection of all rational criticism whatsoever.

According to the sort of reading we are considering, however, by attacking Socratism, Nietzsche meant to urge his readers to forego philosophical attempts to step outside culture and instead to work within it to give sense or 'style' to their lives. But such readings sidestep Nietzsche's most important insight about Socratism: namely, that the intelligibility of calls to remain within the bounds of community stands or falls with the intelligibility of the Socratic attempt to stand outside it. Nietzsche's criticism of the demand for reasons is meant to deny just this dichotomy between standing inside and standing outside culture. Of course, I may revise or reject some aspect of the particular tradition in or against which I live. On Nietzsche's view, however, I do not and cannot occupy a position of Socratic impartiality in doing so. But if Nietzsche is not saying that all rational criticism is impossible, how shall we understand the concept of culture that underwrites his attack on *Socratic* criticism in particular? More specifically, what understanding of the idea of community emerges from *The Birth of Tragedy*?

The relevant conception of community emerges most clearly when we take seriously Nietzsche's suggestion that the distinction he draws between Apollonian and Dionysian art is like that between culture and nature. While the latter distinction may appear not to exhaust the content of the former, it nevertheless allows us to understand what Nietzsche finds objectionable about the demand for reasons in a way that an apparently more straightforward interpretation of his talk of Apollonian and Dionysian 'artistic tendencies' threatens to obscure for us.[4] Or so I mean to argue. For, contrary to the sort of reading we have

[4] There are, of course, other ways to flesh out Nietzsche's concepts of the Apollonian and the Dionysian than, as I do here, in terms of the distinction between culture and nature. But this is certainly one way to do so, and indeed a way that is suggested by Nietzsche himself. We should in any case not let our preconceptions about what the opposition between culture and nature *must* be—in particular that the distinction is somehow too intellectual to encompass the apparently more basic notion of 'art forces' in nature—obscure its importance for understanding Nietzsche's attack on Socratism. There is certainly room to speculate further—both in this context and in the context of an interpretation of the second essay of the *Genealogy*—about what Nietzsche thought nature might be. In particular, it does not seem unreasonable in this regard to explore a psychoanalytic approach to the question of the relation between the notions of culture and nature as they appear in Nietzsche's work. See, in this connection, Eric Blondel, *Nietzsche: The Body and Culture,* trans. Seán Hand (Stanford: Stanford University Press, 1991). What interests me here, however, are the constraints that Nietzsche's attack on Socratism places on his understanding of both nature and culture. It is true that in the *Genealogy*, Nietzsche is much more interested than he is in *The Birth of Tragedy* in understanding what is involved in the production of culture. Even in that work, however, his primary aim is to understand our philosophical, religious, and moral misconceptions about the character of what is achieved in that production; and those investigations, I contend, are meant to have a practical, not a theoretical, upshot.

considered so far, the deepest aspect of his criticism of Socratism is not that the demand for reasons insists that we give sense to our lives independent of the community or culture in which we happen to find ourselves, but rather that this demand stems from a desire not to see ourselves as members of a community at all.[5] Nietzsche diagnoses, behind this desire, a wish to fail to make sense altogether. His attack on Socratism turns, then, on a particular understanding of the relationship between individual and community; my immediate purpose here is to see what light the distinction between culture and nature as it is used in *The Birth of Tragedy* sheds upon this relationship.

To begin, it will help to understand in a general way the sense in which Nietzsche considers Socratism a form of morality. This will enable us properly to ask what sort of alternative to morality he sought. Once we have sketched an answer to this question, we can turn our attention in the remaining sections of the chapter to the specific details of Nietzsche's attack on Socratism and to the conception of culture that underlies it.

In the late preface to *The Birth of Tragedy*, he says that "it was *against* morality that [his] instinct turned" in that book (*BT*, "An Attempt at a Self-Criticism," sec. 5, p. 24). In general, his antipathy toward what he calls 'moral values' is aimed at those ways of life that seek, as he puts it, to deny life.[6] In the context of his attack on Socratism in particular, the term 'morality' seems to refer to whatever it is in our religion, philosophy, and ethical life that, according to him, gives voice to our need for reasons. If, therefore, we are to understand what it means to treat Socratism as a form of morality, we need to know in what sense such a way of life could be said to strive to deny life. What, that is, does Nietzsche mean in saying that to insist that one provide a certain sort of reason for interpreting one's concepts in one way rather than another amounts to a denial of life? It is the principal goal of this chapter to

[5] To say that Socratism demands that we 'give sense' to our lives in terms of something independent of them is only to say that for Socrates we must make sense of our practices of judgment in terms of something wholly independent of those practices. Thus, a Socratic definition must express what we 'know' about the virtue in question, not merely what we believe to be true about it. It is this notion of independence (of our practices of judgment) whose intelligibility Nietzsche means to question. He insists that the notion *appears* to make sense only in a very specific context, and that it is not independently intelligible.

[6] That speaking of a way of life that denies life has a semiparadoxical air is part of Nietzsche's point about the ascetic ideal generally. See *On the Genealogy of Morals* III, sec. 13.

offer an answer to this question. But as I indicated in the Introduction, I will also be trying to show that there are good reasons to doubt that Nietzsche sought, in *The Birth of Tragedy*, an alternative to what he calls 'morality'. Let me once again suggest briefly why it might appear tempting to think otherwise.

Some readers find it attractive to maintain that Nietzsche believed that morality in this sense—marked by the need to justify one's judgments—is a sign of an inability to take responsibility for one's own evaluations of the world. This reading makes it natural to think that Nietzsche meant to hold open the possibility of some sort of alternative to morality: the ability not to give in to the demand for reasons is taken to signify a different, more affirmative, attitude toward life. Now there is a sense in which such a reading does indeed do justice to Nietzsche's views about morality. I mean to argue, however, that a proper understanding of his claim that morality denies life does not leave room for one very natural way of understanding that purportedly affirmative alternative. As we will see, there is, in short, nothing in *this* sense for 'taking responsibility for one's evaluations of the world' to be.

In one of his own critical assessments of his first book, Nietzsche says that the 'gravest question' with which *The Birth of Tragedy* had burdened itself was "What, seen in the perspective of *life*, is the significance of morality?" (*BT*, sec. 4, p. 22). The connection Nietzsche sees between the general Socratic demand for reasons and what we might more commonly think of as properly *moral* concerns is complicated, but nothing in *The Birth of Tragedy* exactly entails that, for example, a Kantian demand that one be able to justify the fairness of one's actions is itself somehow a form of Socratism, nor does anything suggest that a specifically Christian conception of morality must also be construed as a form of Socratism.[7] Nevertheless, Nietzsche does appear to believe that each of these three very different ways of life share the following characteristic: they all try to make sense of the life we actually live in terms of another life that is somehow better (more stable, more worthy, more pure) than this one.[8] We might, therefore, be able to make sense of a connection between Kantian morality and Socratism in terms of a shared demand that one's actions be justified by appeal to something

---

[7] I suppose we might say that, just as Socrates asks what all courageous actions have in common and answers that they all reflect a knowledge of what to fear and what not to fear, so Kant asks what all moral actions have in common and answers that they all satisfy the test of the categorical imperative. But ultimately this is not the aspect of the connection between Socratism and our more ordinary sense of morality that most interests Nietzsche.

[8] See, for example, sec. 6 of "'Reason' in Philosophy," in *Twilight of the Idols*.

both independent of our interests and opinions, and available to everyone just insofar as he or she is rational.[9] For my purposes here, however, to say that Socratism is a form of morality is simply to say that it represents a way of life—a life-denying one—that seeks to understand the life we live in terms of something independent of it. This claim suggests that Nietzsche takes himself already in *The Birth of Tragedy* to have been trying—as later on in the *Genealogy* he was trying—to understand how something like 'life-denial' was possible.[10] In what follows, then, when I refer to Socratism as a form of morality, all that is meant is that the Socratic life of reason is a way of life that has this particular shape.

As I explained in the Introduction, my suggestion that Nietzsche did not mean to offer a philosophical alternative to Socratism is at odds with a common understanding of the spirit of his writing, both early and late. For it is indeed natural to want to analyze his thought into its negative or critical elements, on the one hand, and a more positive—though perhaps more sketchy—alternative, on the other. Indeed, he seems quite obviously to advocate life-affirmative attitudes and practices, on the one hand, and to oppose these to what, under the rubric of morality, he condemns as life-denying, on the other. I aim to show, however, that an apparently natural interpretation of this opposition—an interpretation that Nietzsche himself invites—in fact obscures the real character and point of his criticism of morality. To this end, I will lay out the principal features of his criticism of the Socratic demand that one justify one's standards of judgment. While Nietzsche's criticism of this demand is sustained throughout his work as a whole, I will generally restrict my discussion in this chapter to what he says about it in and in connection with *The Birth of Tragedy*.

My interpretative strategy in this chapter will be to ask in what tragic insight *must* consist if it is to do the job Nietzsche gives it to do: namely, to silence the Socratic demand for reasons, to show what it might be like to be in some sense *entitled* not to take that demand seriously. My aim, however, is not to demonstrate that in fact we *are* so entitled. In any event, Nietzsche did not believe that arguments for that conclusion were either forthcoming or appropriate. What in his view clouds the

---

[9] Thus, in both cases, to think of our practices (say, of moral judgment) in 'moral' terms means that we see them as standing in need of a justification in terms of something radically independent of them, and that we think of that justification as being something that everyone can be expected to provide.

[10] See *On the Genealogy of Morals* III, sec. 13: "But let us return to our problem. It will be immediately obvious that such a self-contradiction as the ascetic appears to represent, 'life *against* life', is, physiologically considered and not merely psychologically, a simple absurdity. It can only be *apparent*" (p. 120).

vision of the Socratically minded philosopher is not merely faulty rea-
soning, but, more basically, prejudices that must be given up if he is
to see the world aright. And no argument, in Nietzsche's view, can
compel one to give up those prejudices as long as one has need of
them.[11]

To some extent, of course, my approach inverts the historical order
of the development of Socratism as Nietzsche recounts it. For, by and
large, he construes the demand for reasons as a response to the death
of tragedy, not the other way around.[12] Nevertheless, it was their ability
not to be tempted by the demand for reasons that allows us to count
the Greeks as a culture in the special sense of the term that concerns
us here. Tragedy, as Nietzsche sees it, functioned to keep them safe
from that temptation.[13] Thus, I will in the following exposition speak
as though tragedy defended the Greeks against the power of Socratic
dialectic, even though, as Nietzsche sees it, dialectic was not taken

[11] For the Socratically minded philosopher, the absence of argument here may
provide an overwhelming obstacle to taking Nietzsche seriously. This, indeed, is to
be expected. For Nietzsche has, of course, no properly philosophical argument that
no argument can undo the philosopher's attachment to argument in the first place.
There are plenty of psychological considerations that Nietzsche can bring to bear on
the philosopher's resistance here, but it will always be open to the philosopher to
question their relevance.

[12] I will not comment further here on this aspect of Nietzsche's treatment of Socrates except to say that, from the point of view of Nietzsche's conception of the role of
the philosopher as the bad conscience of his time, Socrates functions as a prototype
of the individual. That is to say, it is Socrates' role to point out that the practices of
his culture have become incoherent: "He saw *behind* his aristocratic Athenians; he
grasped that *his* case, the idiosyncrasy of his case, was already no longer exceptional.
The same kind of degeneration was everywhere silently preparing itself: the old
Athens was coming to an end.—And Socrates understood that all the world had
need of him—his expedient, his cure, his personal art of self-preservation" (*TI*, "The
Problem of Socrates," sec. 9, p. 32). We should not fail to notice that, like Wittgenstein, Nietzsche does not believe that the Socratic question is intelligible in itself.
Something has to *happen*—the context in which it is asked must change in some
way—for the philosophical demand for reasons to appear to make sense. Thus,
Nietzsche writes, "Before Socrates, the dialectical manner was repudiated in good
society: it was regarded as a form of bad manners, one was compromised by it" (*TI*,
sec. 5, p. 31). My aim in this chapter is to come to terms with what Nietzsche says
about tragedy by way of trying to understand what has to happen to Greek culture
to make the Socratic demand for reasons appear intelligible. In Chapter 2, I take up
the question of what might be called 'the Socratic response to the death of tragedy',
thus returning to the historical order of development as Nietzsche recounts it.

[13] It remains true, however, that once they give in to that temptation, tragedy is
powerless to help them. Nietzsche, I think, does not mean to offer a historical or
psychological account of *why* the Greeks eventually succumbed to the temptation to
think of themselves in Socratic terms. As we will see, he says that their relation to
pain changed radically, but he does not say why it did.

seriously until tragic culture began to collapse.[14] As I have claimed, proceeding in this fashion allows us to appreciate what Nietzsche imagines tragic culture really to have been like in a way that a more straightforward examination of the notions of Dionysian and Apollonian art renders much more difficult.

Given the extent of *The Birth of Tragedy*'s Schopenhauerian vocabulary, many commentators insist that Nietzsche's earliest thinking must be deeply indebted to Schopenhauer's views. Thus, according to one recent account, the early Nietzsche, like Schopenhauer, found life to be unbearable because—our Socratic pretensions notwithstanding—human suffering is both pointless and inevitable. On this reading, art—specifically, tragic art—provides a non-Socratic solution to the problem of suffering by offering a glimpse of the reality behind what he calls 'the lie of culture'. The destruction of the tragic hero permits the audience to identify itself with this deeper reality, thus providing what Nietzsche calls 'metaphysical comfort' from the 'horror and terror' of existence.[15] As we will see, however, focusing our attention on Nietzsche's criticism of Socrates generates a reading of *The Birth of Tragedy* that appears diametrically opposed to this interpretation. It is unclear whether the discrepancy between these two readings indicates an important tension in Nietzsche's early thinking, or whether it directs us to reassess the nature of Schopenhauer's influence on his first book. I incline toward the latter view, but I am not concerned to decide the issue here. I am interested only to see what light Nietzsche's rejection of Socratism sheds on his understanding of culture.

In *Ecce Homo*, Nietzsche refers to *The Birth of Tragedy*'s conception of the Socratic demand as one of that work's "decisive innovations." "Socrates," he writes, "is recognized for the first time as an instrument of Greek disintegration, as a typical decadent. 'Rationality' against instinct. 'Rationality' at any price as a dangerous force that undermines

[14] See *Twilight of the Idols*, "The Problem of Socrates," sec. 9, pp. 32–33. It is worth remarking, however, that much of Nietzsche's account of the death of tragedy in secs. 11–15 of *The Birth of Tragedy* depicts it as the result of a struggle between Socratism and tragedy. Rhetorically anyway, he often seems to want to hold Socrates responsible for the demise of tragic art. For the reasons we are exploring here, however, such rhetoric cannot represent Nietzsche's considered opinion about the relationship between tragedy and Socratism. Once again, the latter, in his view, simply makes no sense on its own terms, and is itself therefore powerless against tragedy. Thus, even in *The Birth of Tragedy*, Nietzsche says that "we must . . . assume an anti-Dionysian tendency operating even prior to Socrates, which merely received in him an unprecedentedly magnificent expression" (*BT*, sec. 14, p. 92).
[15] See Julian Young, *Nietzsche's Philosophy of Art* (Cambridge: Cambridge University Press, 1992).

life" (*EH*, "*The Birth of Tragedy*," sec. 1, p. 271). It is often pointed out—
and rightly—that the central features of Nietzsche's criticism of Socratism are rooted in his conviction that 'rationality at any price' is itself
a form of instinct.[16] Thus, according to Nietzsche, someone committed
'at any price' to a life of rationality only mistakenly thinks of himself
as standing in fundamental opposition to what he condemns as instinct.
But we fail fully to appreciate the force of Nietzsche's chief claim that
rationality at any price is hostile to life if we do not understand the
properly Socratic conception of instinct that underwrites the contrast
Nietzsche means to call into question between it and rationality. We
will need, therefore, to clarify the conception of instinct that, on
Nietzsche's view, undermines life.

My thesis is that, in *The Birth of Tragedy*, Nietzsche is concerned to
articulate a particular conception of culture. It is this conception that
underwrites his attack on the intelligibility of the Socratic demand for
reasons.[17] His chief conclusion about culture, however, appears to be
largely negative. For though, on his account, the Socratic demand for
reasons turns on a misunderstanding of what it means to belong to a
culture, appreciating the fact of this misunderstanding does not leave

[16] For the idea of Socratic reason as a form of instinct, see *The Birth of Tragedy*, sec.
13, p. 88. Nietzsche's attack on the demand for reasons is, of course, an objection to
what has been called Socrates' 'intellectualism', to his faith that virtue is a form of
knowledge. As Alexander Nehamas points out in a recent essay, Socratic intellectualism also involves the idea that virtue alone is both necessary and sufficient for the
good life. Both aspects of the Socratic approach to the good life (that virtue is knowledge and that such knowledge is the only thing that can make us happy) seem to
many readers to ignore, on the one hand, the wider human context in which rational
activity normally takes place, and, on the other, what has been called the 'fragility'
of virtue's relationship to happiness. While Nietzsche would, I believe, agree with
both of these complaints, when he maintains that virtue should stem from happiness
rather than the other way around and that virtue is not a form of knowledge, I think
that we should understand him differently. With respect to the second claim, in
particular, he does not—like Aristotle, perhaps—take himself to be correcting a mis-
·take he thought Socrates had made, as though, in Nietzsche's view, he had simply
overestimated the importance of giving reasons (wanting, for example, to do so in a
context where it cannot be done). Nietzsche's complaint, rather, is that the demand
for reasons depends upon a confusion that renders it incoherent. For a helpful discussion of the issue of Socrates' intellectualism, see Alexander Nehamas, "What Did
Socrates Teach and to Whom Did He Teach It?" *Review of Metaphysics* 46 (December
1992): 279–306.
[17] More specifically, I think, Nietzsche means to ask whether modern Europe
counts as a culture. He wants, that is to say, to understand what the tragic Greeks
had that his (Nietzsche's) audience lacks. At first blush anyway, this is why he is so
concerned with what Wagnerian opera might be able to promise modern Europeans.
We should, in any case, not let the fact that the bulk of *The Birth of Tragedy* is ostensibly
about the past distract us from its overarching concern with the present.

us with a positive philosophical account with which to replace it. As I hope to show, Nietzsche believes that the Socratic demand makes sense only if membership in one's culture is conceived in terms of partaking in a shared interpretation or world view, and, though he rejects this picture of culture, he does not propose to replace it with another.

Thus, it is nearly impossible to say anything in a positive vein that is at all philosophically satisfying about what Nietzsche took culture to be. From Nietzsche's standpoint, however, the difficulty in saying anything satisfying about culture is very much to be expected. Let me try to make clear why I believe this to be so. As I suggested, we do not go far wrong if we think of culture—in the sense in which I am using the term here—as a form of linguistic community. Nietzsche pictures human life as a struggle to make sense, and, as the second essay of the *Genealogy* makes clear, this is the struggle to speak intelligibly.[18] Consequently, we may imagine community, as he thinks of it, as individuals who succeed in making sense—to themselves and to one another. This concern with what it means to make sense, to be intelligible, lies behind Nietzsche's repeated complaints that he lacks readers (and that he himself is not responsible for his lacking them). He believes that there is room to speak of success and failure here because he thinks that, in a variety of ways, human beings tend to resist making sense. Life-denial stems, as I have said, from such resistance. To affirm life, on the other hand, means to affirm one's membership in culture. But this, as I shall argue, is simply to make sense, to speak intelligibly. Thus, for Nietzsche, because there is nothing to say about making sense beyond demonstrating the fact of our resistance to doing so, there will be nothing to say about what culture is either, beyond demonstrating the fact of resistance to it.

My talk of linguistic community and my suggestion that Nietzsche thinks of human life as a struggle to make sense, to speak intelligibly, may seem to express an overly intellectualized approach toward the notions of life-denial and life-affirmation.[19] Life-affirmation seems after

[18] My employment of the notion of linguistic community will mislead if it is understood to imply that Nietzsche sought anything like a philosophical account of, say, semantic content. The insight into life that the ancient tragedies afforded Greek audiences did not consist in an *explanation* of the relationship of community and individual. Indeed, on the view I am trying to articulate here, Nietzsche condemns Socratism precisely for trying to offer such an account. Nevertheless, as I argue in Chapter 5, the *Genealogy* makes clear that Nietzsche considers the capacity to make sense to be man's true problem. He considers that capacity to be the capacity for speech.

[19] This objection has been made to me by Professor Raymond Geuss in private correspondence.

all, for Nietzsche, to be much more a matter of, say, affirming those passions, affects, and drives that are condemned by morality than it is of merely speaking. But though it is true that Nietzsche often writes in these sorts of tones and often appears to believe that a moral self-conception is achieved only by means of what he portrays as the repression and exploitation of our human, all too human, passions, and so on, this objection rests on a failure to appreciate the importance Nietzsche attaches to the very fact of human intelligibility. It is, one might say, an overly intellectualized notion of *speaking* that prevents us from understanding the sense in which life-denial represents, for Nietzsche, a failure of intelligibility, a failure, as he sees it, to speak responsibly. And as we will see in Chapter 5, talk of making sense and of being responsible for what one says are precisely the terms that Nietzsche himself suggests we use to understand the distinction he draws between ascending and descending forms of life. Moreover, he argues at some length in the second essay of the *Genealogy* that the capacity to make sense is something that is achieved only through a great deal of just the sort of repression that he is mistakenly thought by some readers to condemn. In any event, if my interpretation of his attack on Socratism is at all correct, then where he ostensibly encourages his readers to enjoy and celebrate their passions, he is not in any way encouraging them to step outside the achievement that he considers intelligibility to represent.[20] For this is not the kind of intimacy with the world he sought. Consequently, I do not think that there is anything particularly bloodless about my use of the idea of linguistic community in this context. Intelligibility is achieved and maintained by just the sorts of immoral means appropriate to any discipline.[21]

Ultimately, the sort of culture or community with which we will be concerned in this book is the community of *knowers*. And, on Nietzsche's view, that culture—if, indeed, there is one—depends on the willingness of men of knowledge to take responsibility for their commitment to truthfulness. Taking responsibility for that commitment, however, is something Nietzsche understands as a matter of hav-

[20] Nietzsche's thinking here bears an obvious affinity with Freud's.

[21] Thus, in an important passage to which I will return in a moment, Nietzsche writes, "Every morality is, as opposed to *laisser aller,* a bit of tyranny against 'nature'; also against 'reason'; but this in itself is no objection, as long as we do not have some other morality which permits us to decree that every kind of tyranny and unreason is impermissible. What is essential and inestimable in every morality is that it constitutes a long compulsion. . . . What is essential 'in heaven and on earth' seems to be . . . that there should be *obedience* over a long period of time and in a *single* direction" (*BGE*, sec. 188, pp. 100–101).

ing the right to say that God is dead.[22] I begin, however, with Nietzsche's attack on Socratism because, on the one hand, it is easiest to see what culture or community comes to in the context of Socratic resistance to it and because, on the other hand, the attack on Socratism is a crucial part of Nietzsche's account of the rise of the modern will to knowledge. I am therefore less interested in Nietzsche's criticisms of worked-out philosophical views than I am in those philosophical prejudices that seem to him to motivate the questions that give rise to such views. For, as I read him, Nietzsche means to attack the philosophical impulse at its roots.

In any event, as what he thinks it means to deny life becomes clearer to us, our grip on the question of what he thought it might mean to affirm life and to articulate a positive alternative to the morality he rejects should begin to dissolve. Ultimately, I think, Nietzsche would have found a desire for such an articulation to be of a piece with the very morality he rejects.

The Problem of Socrates

In speaking of Socrates as a problem, Nietzsche is asking how the Socratic enterprise is possible at all. How, in other words, is the specifically *Socratic* form of detachment from our ordinary practices of judgment and justification possible? What must be true if we can so much as make sense of the Socratic demand for reasons? It is absolutely essential, however, to try to keep alive one's sense of just how peculiar a question this is. Indeed, as I suggested in the Introduction, it is not at all obvious what sort of question Nietzsche might be asking here. He himself fully expects the Socratically minded philosopher to dismiss it as merely psychological. From the latter's point of view, it is difficult to see that there is a real philosophical question to be asked here. As the Socratic philosopher sees it, the sort of metaphilosophy Nietzsche practices is simply not philosophy at all. But because Nietzsche finds ill conceived the contrast between philosophical questions, on the one hand, and psychological questions, on the other, he is deeply suspicious of the philosopher's 'merely' here. In any case, in asking how Socratic philosophy is possible, Nietzsche is not simply asking why this form of philosophical endeavor took hold of a particular civilization at

[22] Once again, there is, for Nietzsche, nothing bloodless about such community: in sec. 344 of *The Gay Science* he writes, "'[truth] at any price': how well we understand these words once we have offered and slaughtered one faith after another on this altar!" (p. 281).

a certain moment in history. In other words, he is not asking why these people finally grasped something that had (or anyway would have) escaped their predecessors. For he does not take it for granted that the Socratic demand for reasons makes sense on its own terms. This is not to deny that the demand came to appear to make sense. On the contrary, he insists that people came to have *need* of Socratism as a way of making sense of their lives. But the Socratic demand for reasons is not a demand he considers to be intelligible independent of those needs: it makes sense only in the context they provide. "With Socrates Greek taste undergoes a change in favor of dialectics: what is really happening when that happens? It is above all the defeat of a *nobler* taste; with dialectics the rabble gets on top. . . . [T]he dialectician is a kind of buffoon: he is laughed at, he is not taken seriously.—Socrates was the buffoon who *got himself taken seriously:* what was really happening when that happened?" (*TI*, "The Problem of Socrates," sec. 5, p. 31). As Nietzsche sees it, by giving voice to a particular understanding of the status of culture, tragedy functioned to keep the Greeks safe from the misunderstanding that gave rise to Socratism. As they lose their grip on this understanding of themselves, however, they come to have need of Socrates—of "his expedient, his cure, his personal art of self-preservation" (*TI*, "The Problem of Socrates," sec. 9, p. 32). In Nietzsche's view, then, the Socratic demand for reasons makes sense only in the context of the collapse of culture. This is the claim that we most need to understand.

Let us begin, then, with an overview of *The Birth of Tragedy's* critique of Socratism. The aim of that critique, once again, is to understand how Socratism is possible at all. As Nietzsche portrays him, Socrates demanded of his interlocutors that they justify their application of moral concepts. He asked, in other words, that they give reasons for interpreting their concepts in *this* way rather than that. Nietzsche is convinced, however, that the intelligibility of the demand for reasons turns on Socrates' failure properly to understand the role that the authority of culture played in the practices of judgment whose justification he sought. For, properly understood, authority silences the demand for reasons, allows one not to take it seriously. "Wherever authority is still part of accepted usage . . . one does not 'give reasons'" (*TI*, "The Problem of Socrates," sec. 5, p. 31).[23]

But, as Nietzsche well knows, our response to such an appeal to

---

[23] For more on the role the notion of authority plays in Nietzsche's writing, see Tracy B. Strong, "Aesthetic Authority and Tradition: Nietzsche and the Greeks," *History of European Ideas* 11 (1989): 989–1007.

authority is likely be one of Socratic offense, for "that which makes institutions institutions," he says, "is despised, hated, rejected: whenever the word 'authority' is so much as heard, one believes oneself in danger of a new slavery" (*TI*, "Expeditions of an Untimely Man," sec. 39, p. 94). Indeed, precisely what the Socratic philosopher believes he is calling for is a justification of *obedience* to such authority; mere obedience, he insists, is never enough to guarantee intelligibility. I want to argue, however, that the error that Nietzsche diagnoses at the root of Socratism is a matter of treating obedience as interpretation, as (say) accepting one's culture's interpretation of itself, of its members, its world, as something, in short, that presents itself as a candidate for philosophical justification.

In Nietzsche's view, the notion of obedience has become difficult for us to understand, and my use of it in this context may occasion some confusion. Moreover, as I noted in the Introduction, unlike the notion of authority, Nietzsche does not consistently apply it in the way in which I mean to here. For him, obedience most often refers to the sort of training and discipline that produce what he sometimes calls 'the morality of mores'.[24] Obedience, in this sense of the term, is part of what Nietzsche thinks of as the long prehistory of any form of obedience to authority, in the sense in which I am using the term 'obedience' here. As I use it, however, obedience simply refers to the fact that we go on intelligibly with our concepts in the ways that we do.

One might, however, object to this reading that Nietzsche in fact reviles obedience—that he condemns it as thoughtless slavishness. After all, one might ask, did he not mean for individuals and 'higher men' to forge new values to replace the decayed values of the past? I suggest, however, that Nietzsche means in general—and in his attack on Socratism in particular—to underscore what he takes to be our dis-

---

[24] As we will see in Chapter 5, however, there is nevertheless room to speak of the form of obedience to authority Nietzsche counts as human intelligibility even in the context of the 'morality of mores'. There is a tendency in the literature to want to relegate Nietzsche's view of morality as a form of custom or tradition to his early philosophy on the grounds that he eventually recognized that such a view cannot explain the more complex and, as it were, introspective features of modern morality. See, in particular, Maudemarie Clark's unpublished dissertation, *Nietzsche's Attack on Morality* (University of Wisconsin–Madison, 1976). Whether mere obedience can account for our sense of moral responsibility depends, of course, upon what one understands by both obedience and responsibility. I would suggest that Nietzsche's understanding of both notions deepened over time. As he recognized before Freud, only in a certain psychic context does fear of reprisal amount to fear of transgression. In any event, the *Genealogy* quite explicitly directs our attention back to that view as an integral part of his mature thought, and I will try in the last chapter to make clear the role that view plays.

tinctively modern unwillingness to distinguish obedience from slav-ishness.[25] As he reminds us about the sort of obedience that constitutes a precondition to genuine human intelligibility, "What is essential and inestimable in every morality is that it constitutes a long compul-sion. . . . What is essential 'in heaven and on earth' seems to be . . . that there should be *obedience* over a long period of time and in a *single* direction: given that, something always develops, and has developed, for whose sake it is worth while to live on earth" (*BGE*, sec. 188, pp. 100–101). Mere slavishness, on the other hand, does not tend to produce 'something for whose sake it is worth while to live on earth'.

Nietzsche means quite generally to rehabilitate the notions of obedi-ence and authority—to make manifest what he considers to be our moral misunderstanding of these notions. Such a rehabilitation is in large part what is at stake in his attack on Socratism. For from the point of view of Socratism, the sort of obedience in question in section 188 is, in fact, mere slavishness. That is to say, from the Socratic standpoint, what Nietzsche calls 'obedience' looks like blind, unthinking repetition, and nothing intelligible can be achieved by means of the mere repetition of something unintelligible. As Nietzsche sees it, however, the Socratic difficulty here stems from an unwillingness to draw the crucial distinc-tion between obedience and slavish repetition. If one fails to draw that distinction, it is small wonder that one cannot understand how obedi-ence in the first sense can lead to the sort of obedience—or intelligibil-ity—recommended by Nietzsche's attack on the Socratic demand for reasons.

I suggest, then, that when Nietzsche claims that one does not give reasons as long as authority remains part of 'accepted usage', we ought to read him somewhat more strongly than might initially seem war-ranted. For he is not here insisting merely that, as long as an appeal to 'what is done' is an intelligible and appropriate response to the demand for reasons, one will not take seriously the special Socratic version of that demand, but rather that something about authority actually *permits* one to ignore it.

A weaker reading than the one I am proposing makes it seem that Nietzsche is insisting merely that as long as one refuses—or is for some reason simply unable—to distance oneself from one's cultural norms and practices, one cannot make good sense of Socrates' question. This amounts to the claim that from our engaged perspective an appeal to

[25] Once again, that Nietzsche seeks to defend obedience in this sense in the face of Socratic challenges to authority should not be taken to imply that he resists any and all forms of rational inquiry.

tradition or to precedent will seem the only intelligible sort of reply to make in response to a demand for reasons.

Now it may well, as a matter of psychological fact, be impossible for someone who is actively engaged in the practices of his or her culture to make good sense of the Socratic question. But there is nothing in this fact with which the Socratically minded philosopher will be in the least inclined to disagree. For he will insist that it is indeed a condition of properly philosophical questioning that one stand back from one's practices in such a way as to permit an appropriately critical examination of them.[26] He knows that *this*—for example, calling these sorts of things virtuous—is 'what is done'. But he wants to know why this is so; he wants to understand that in virtue of which these practices are intelligible. And the sort of account of their intelligibility he seeks should, he supposes, justify those practices of judgment whose 'reason' he hopes to uncover. According to Nietzsche, however, something is lost sight of in this sort of philosophical detachment: our life with concepts in question.

'Authority', in the passage I quoted above from *Twilight of the Idols*, refers to something we might call the 'constraint' that one's culture exercises on one's judgments. Nietzsche refers to this kind of constraint in a variety of ways—as we will see, his use of the notion of power is the most famous. Thus, in a passage I will discuss at some length later, he refers to the distinctively modern estimation of the value of knowledge as a power in just this sense.

> Thus knowledge became a piece of life itself, and hence a continually growing power—until eventually knowledge collided with those primeval basic errors: two lives, two powers, both in the same human being. A thinker is now that being in whom the impulse for truth and those life-preserving errors clash for their first fight, after the impulse for truth has proved to be also a life-preserving power. (*GS*, sec. 110, p. 171)

As we will see, part of the reason for talking about constraint in this context is that such talk helps to undercut the idea that Nietzsche meant in any way to suggest that our obedience is something for which it

---

[26] Similarly, the Cartesian skeptic knows that we are not ordinarily inclined to ask his version of the 'how do I know?' question and that ordinarily the fact that I have no good grounds for a given belief does not serve to impugn my capacities as a knower in general. 'But', he asks, 'why should I concern myself with what we ordinarily say? Indeed, how can I do so without begging the important epistemological question of whether what we ordinarily say is true?'

makes philosophical sense to hold us responsible. For we do not choose or otherwise decide what constrains us. As we will see, the freedom Nietzsche associates with obedience to this sort of constraint has nothing to do with freedom of choice. He says, "Every artist knows how far from any feeling of letting himself go his 'most natural' state is—the free ordering, placing, disposing, giving form in the moment of 'inspiration'—and how strictly and subtly he obeys thousandfold laws precisely then, laws that precisely on account of their hardness and determination defy all formulation through concepts" (*BGE*, sec. 188, p. 100). To think otherwise is what we might think of as the existentialist equivalent of the Socratic demand for reasons.[27]

Throughout his writing, Nietzsche maintains that the force of the Socratic demand rests on a misunderstanding of the nature of this form of obedience. The Socratically minded philosopher, he insists, thinks of such obedience merely as a fact about us, as something of no more than anthropological significance. In other words, the philosopher would like to insist that the fact that we count these things as virtuous and those as vicious is, until suitably grounded in reasons, merely an artifact of how the world strikes *us*. It is important to stress that Nietzsche thinks that there is indeed some sort of misunderstanding here, for, as I have said, a central feature of his conception of culture is that membership in it makes one immune to the Socratic demand. Thus, on his view, the notions of culture and authority or power are in this way conceptually intertwined: where there is no immunity from the demand for reasons, there is no culture in Nietzsche's sense of the term.

But we must also try to determine the specific sort of misunderstanding of which Nietzsche claims Socratism is guilty. My interpretative hypothesis has been that an examination of his conception of Greek tragedy will shed light on the specific nature of the Socratic misunderstanding of obedience. Let us see, then, where this hypothesis leads us.

To begin, we should notice that Nietzsche is not likely to have held

---

[27] In what strikes me as a Nietzschean moment of *The Sovereignty of Good*, Iris Murdoch writes, "If I attend properly [to the world] I will have no choices and this is the ultimate condition to be aimed at. This is in a way the reverse of Hampshire's picture, where our efforts are supposed to be directed to increasing our freedom by conceptualizing as many different possibilities of action as possible: having as many goods as possible in the shop. The ideal situation, on the contrary, is rather to be represented as a kind of 'necessity'. This is something of which saints speak and which any artist will readily understand. The idea of a patient, loving regard, directed upon a person, a thing, a situation, presents the will not as unimpeded movement but as something very much more like 'obedience'" (Iris Murdoch, *The Sovereignty of Good* [New York: Ark Paperbacks, 1985], p. 40).

that Socratism is ignorant of some *philosophically* relevant piece of information to which membership in their culture somehow made the tragic Greeks privy, or to have believed that tragedy afforded them access to such information. As we shall see, any such information would only too understandably become the object of Socratic inquiry. This is one reason we should not expect to find a positive philosophical account of constraint in Nietzsche's work. But the absence of such an account does not imply that authority is an ineffable something of which such an account simply cannot be given. Indeed, to view tragedy as providing ineffable insight embodies the same misunderstanding Nietzsche believes he finds at the root of the philosophical demand for reasons.[28]

In *The Birth of Tragedy*, Nietzsche maintains that it was the function of tragic drama—specifically, of the works of Aeschylus and Sophocles—to present the authority of Greek culture in such a way that the Socratic demand for reasons was not taken up.[29] It is along these lines, I mean to argue, that Nietzsche understands the significance of the dramatic destruction of the tragic hero. Presented in this context, the hero's destruction conveys something about the status of Greek culture as a whole. (I want for the moment to postpone the question of whether Nietzsche believed that what the tragedies showed their audiences was that their culture was in some way 'merely' cultural. As we shall see, this reading, though a natural one, does not allow us to understand in what Nietzsche believes the relationship between tragedy and Socratism consists.) On Nietzsche's view, tragedy allowed the Greeks to live—or, anyway, celebrated their ability to live—without the sorts of reasons that Socrates thought necessary if their aesthetic and ethical behavior was to be fully intelligible. But he thought that it allowed them to do so without simply ignoring the Socratic demand. Rather, tragedy enabled them, or so Nietzsche supposes, in some way to see through that demand. In other words, by denying the intelligibility of the Socratic starting point, tragedy provided the Greeks with a kind of justification for not taking Socrates' demand seriously.[30] How could this be?

[28] As we will see, it is precisely in this context that Nietzsche's usage of a Schopenhauerian vocabulary is most misleading.

[29] What I have to say here about *The Birth of Tragedy* does not depend upon the accuracy of Nietzsche's claims about the genre of tragedy. In other words, I mean simply to bracket the question of whether or not what he says about, for example, *Prometheus Bound* and *Oedipus at Colonus* can be taken with any plausibility as readings of those plays. What I am concerned with here is rather the very general picture of culture that first emerges in *The Birth of Tragedy* and is refined in subsequent writings.

[30] Of course, if this reading is correct, then the use of the word 'justification' in this context is ironic at best, for they will, in effect, have seen that the Socratically minded philosopher has simply failed to provide them with the grounds for real doubt about the authority of their culture.

Nietzsche twice says that Socrates failed to comprehend and therefore to esteem tragedy. I think that, from the point of view of Nietzsche's attack on Socratism, this is the central claim of *The Birth of Tragedy*. The more famous idea, twice articulated as well, that life can be justified only as an aesthetic phenomenon can best be understood, I think, in the light of the claim that Socrates failed to understand tragedy. According to Nietzsche, understanding Greek tragedy is, as I have suggested, a sign of knowing what it means to be Greek, for the tragedies express a particular understanding of the status of Greek culture as a whole. In saying that Socrates failed to understand tragedy, then, Nietzsche suggests that he failed properly to understand what it meant to be Greek—what it meant to be a member of this particular linguistic community. This is the misunderstanding at the root of his demand for reasons.

This point is, however, easily misunderstood because nothing Nietzsche says implies that the Socratically minded philosopher does not understand the specific conventions governing the employment of his interlocutors' aesthetic and ethical vocabulary. He knows, in other words, which actions the Greeks call courageous. Whatever Socratic confusion about the authority of Greek culture really comes to, then, it is not confusion about that. Where, then, does his confusion lie?

It is important to remember that the Socratically minded philosopher need not find unintelligible Nietzsche's ostensibly psychological question about why the demand for reasons was taken seriously. He will, however, think that question orthogonal to his own. The philosopher agrees that the Socratic demand for reasons requires a shift of focus away from the local practices of judgment on whose authority particular judgments about this or that depends, to a standpoint of detachment from which the legitimacy of those practices themselves might be questioned. Certainly from the point of view Nietzsche means to criticize, an investigation into the state of mind of the individual capable of understanding the philosophical request for justification can only be a psychological one; as such, it cannot shed light, in the way Nietzsche seems to suppose it does, on the very intelligibility of the Socratic request itself.

As I have claimed, however, the force of the Socratic demand for reasons turns, for Nietzsche, on a misconstrual of the nature of obedience to authority. The shift of focus necessary for making sense of the philosophical demand for reasons involves, according to him, a distortion in one's view of the very nature of those judgments whose justification is sought. More specifically, in order that the philosophical demand for a justification of our judgments make sense, the philosopher must construe our way of going on with our concepts as, so to speak, 'merely' our way of going on with them. Nietzsche suggests, however, that tragedy served to call into question the intelligibility of this prephilosophical move.

Now if the insight afforded by ancient tragedy is at all relevant to the problem of Socratism—that is, if, as Nietzsche suggests, tragedy and Socratism are *fundamentally* at odds—then, I think, tragedy must be understood as an expression of the fact of the culture's authority for its members. As such, tragedy allows the Greeks to see through Socratic confusion about obedience. The effect of tragedy must, Nietzsche suggests, be somehow to remind the audience that good sense cannot be made of the idea that their membership in this particular culture is—in a philosophically relevant sense—'merely' a fact about them. Only this effect would silence the Socratic demand for reasons in a way that did not amount simply to ignoring it. And only if this demand is silenced do the Greeks count as a culture.[31]

This conclusion may seem unexpected. But though my interpretation of the effect of tragedy flies in the face of what is arguably the most tempting way to understand Nietzsche's talk of 'metaphysical comfort', I think it is strongly urged upon us by the peculiar opposition he erects between tragedy and Socratism. We need, above all, to see how these address the same human problem. And, as we will see, the ostensibly straightforward way of understanding Nietzsche's description of tragic insight simply recapitulates the basic Socratic conception of culture as a fundamentally arbitrary imposition upon nature. An uncritical acceptance of this first blush reading of the idea of metaphysical comfort fails, in short, to account for the peculiar opposition Nietzsche sets up between Socratism and tragic insight between, if we like, philosophy and poetry. For reasons that should become clear, the problem they both address cannot be anxiety about the contingency of their culture, with tragedy saying that we should accept this fact and Socratism urging us to seek firmer ground.[32]

On Nietzsche's view, then, to esteem tragedy is to understand what it means to be Greek, to understand what it means to be a member of

---

[31] Again, this appears to be a surprising point only if we fail to recall that Nietzsche believes that Socratism only makes sense to people who *need* it—as the posttragic Greeks needed it. That is to say, only once tragic culture has collapsed can the Greeks make any sense of Socrates' question. At that point, Nietzsche says, "one had only *one* choice: either to perish or—be *absurdly rational*" (*TI*, "The Problem of Socrates," sec. 10, p. 33). Prior to that point, however, the Socratic demand for reasons is only a sign of bad taste.

[32] The phrase 'contingency of culture' is due to Richard Rorty.

this particular culture. This is the picture of culture that underwrites his suggestion that in fact Socrates was *not* Greek. "Socrates belonged, in his origins, to the lowest orders: Socrates was rabble. One knows, one sees for oneself, how ugly he was. But ugliness, an objection in itself, is among Greeks almost a refutation. Was Socrates a Greek at all?" (*TI*, "The Problem of Socrates," sec. 3, p. 30). The suggestion here is that only someone who was not, in the relevant sense, a member of Greek culture could either ask the Socratic question or find it intelligible when asked of him. Nietzsche, in other words, accounts for the idea of membership in culture—and, hence, of culture itself—in terms of the intelligibility (or lack thereof) of the Socratic question. I think we may begin to untangle some of these claims if we look at Nietzsche's criticism of the Socratic project in a bit more detail.

As we have seen, the broader outlines of Nietzsche's description of that project are not especially startling. Socrates confronts those who claim to know what some virtue is—or who claim anyway to know that this or that is virtuous—with the demand that they say what they know, that they articulate the standard according to which they pick out persons and their actions as virtuous. He finds, however, that no one can do so; and his interlocutors are left 'benumbed'. Nietzsche puts the point this way: "What did [Socrates] do his life long but laugh at the awkward incapacity of noble Athenians who, like all noblemen, were men of instinct and never could give sufficient information about the reasons for their actions?" (*BGE*, sec. 191, p. 104).[33] More specifically, Socrates requires that his interlocutors provide *definitions* of their concepts. He is confident that only such definitions will allow them to explain either their present judgments or how it is that they are able to go on applying those concepts in new and unforeseen circumstances. Only in this way will they be able either to justify the confidence they place in their culture or to reject those categories for truer ones. And Socrates insists that, until they provide the appropriate definitions, their claim to know what they are doing in calling someone, say, just or courageous is at best pretense—something inherently unstable, sub-

---

[33] Note that in this passage Nietzsche brackets the issue of the decay of Greek culture: from the point of view of a healthy Greek culture, the inability to give sufficient information about the reasons for one's actions is a sign of nobility. From the point of view of a declining culture, however, that inability is more or less what Socrates said it was: a sign of his interlocutors' unwillingness to take responsibility for what they said. Of course, from Nietzsche's point of view, Socrates seriously misinterprets that unwillingness just insofar as he fails to understand what responsibility really comes to in this context. I will return to these topics in Chapter 2.

ject to sophistry and the vagaries of rhetoric. To find the demand for reasons binding, therefore, is to find something puzzling or mysterious about one's behavior with one's concepts until such standards have been unearthed. In other words, until a suitable definition of the concept has been articulated, one seems to be operating, as Nietzsche has Socrates put it, 'only by instinct'.

But this talk of instinct denigrates one's practices with those concepts. Nietzsche writes, " 'Only by instinct': *with this phrase we touch upon the heart and core of the Socratic tendency*. With it Socratism condemns existing art as well as existing ethics. . . . *Basing himself on this point*, Socrates conceives it to be his duty to correct existence" (*BT*, sec. 13, p. 87, my emphasis).[34] From Socrates' point of view, by nature instincts are—as is any practice founded upon them—unintelligible, blind. Nietzsche's point in the passage at hand, however, is that Socrates *starts* with this presupposition about the nature of judgment. He 'bases himself on this point'; it is the 'heart and core of the Socratic tendency'. In other words, the Socratic demand is grounded on—makes sense in terms of—a particular conception of the nature of judgment. Nietzsche's attack on Socratism aims to call the intelligibility of this conception into question.

When Nietzsche says that, with the phrase 'only by instinct', Socrates condemns existing art and existing ethics, he suggests that Socrates somehow succeeds in making activity without such standards as the philosopher seeks seem unintelligible. This seems to be how Nietzsche thinks of Socrates' ability to benumb his interlocutors. Furthermore, Nietzsche treats such benumbedness as a condemnation of life, at least in part because he believes that it represents not the result of a *discovery* about our life with concepts but rather an imposition upon it. This, then, is the character of the specifically Socratic condemnation of existing art and existing ethics: it makes those forms of life seem mysterious. This, as we shall see, is why it makes sense to speak of the Socratic conception of instinct as a form of *resistance*.

[34] Nietzsche says 'existing art' because he believes that Aeschylus and, perhaps to a lesser extent, Sophocles had created tragic drama by instinct and without the use of reason. He speaks of 'existing ethics' because, in his view, the practices of moral judgment Socrates wants to call into question had hitherto operated on the basis of instinct and in the absence of Socratic definitions. Because Nietzsche maintains so adamantly that Socrates is wrong in believing that knowledge can make us happy, it is tempting to understand him—as does Julian Young—to be taking issue only with the Socratic pretense that human reason can plumb the depths of (and thus correct the faults of) nature. See Julian Young, *Nietzsche's Philosophy of Art*. It seems to me, however, that Nietzsche's complaint is primarily with the Socratic equation of virtue and knowledge. This equation, he finds, gets the connection between virtue and happiness backward. Nietzsche's fundamental difficulty with Socratism is with its separation of reason and instinct, not with what it erects on this basis.

It is important to remember that Nietzsche does not believe that Socrates' question is intelligible in itself, but rather that it appears to make sense only in a particular context. This is why he is much more skeptical about Socrates' actual ability to corrupt his interlocutors than my reconstruction here may appear to allow. Indeed, to grant Socrates this ability would be to countenance the possibility that the demand for reasons might makes sense on its own terms—something Nietzsche clearly denies. For, as we have seen, on his account something must happen to Greek culture if Socratic questioning is to appear to be anything more than bad taste.

As a rough approximation, then, we might say that it was the essence of tragedy, as Nietzsche saw it, to allow the Greeks to comprehend how they could speak intelligibly without supplying the sorts of definitions Socratism seeks.[35] But this idea, too, is easily misunderstood. For Nietzsche is often thought to have believed that the tragic Greeks lived with an awareness of something like the contingency or groundlessness of their culture, and that the tragedies served to give voice to that awareness. But Nietzsche's criticism of Socratism suggests that tragedy allowed the Greeks to be intelligible to themselves by permitting them to see for what they were the needs to which the Socratic demand for reasons gives voice, by seeing how Socratic talk of contingency is motivated. The implication is that to be intelligible without giving reasons is, for Nietzsche, a matter of overcoming the misunderstanding that drives one to seek such reasons in the first place, rather than simply a matter of learning to live without them.

Thus, though Nietzsche thought of the tragic Greeks as unphilosophical, it is precisely his point that they were not philosophically *naive* in the way that someone who simply refuses to consider the Socratic demand may be accused of being. We can understand Nietzsche's claim in section 8 of *The Birth of Tragedy* that the Greeks allowed themselves to be represented by the satyr chorus as suggesting that they were, as we might now put the point, *identified* with their culture, and that they

---

[35] As I have claimed, however, once the Greeks become unintelligible to themselves, Nietzsche considers the Socratic response to be the only effective one. Thus, he writes, "Rationality was at that time divined as a saviour; neither Socrates nor his 'invalids' were free to be rational or not, as they wished. . . . The fanaticism with which the whole of Greek thought throws itself at rationality betrays a state of emergency: one was in peril, one had only *one* choice: either to perish or—be *absurdly rational*" (*TI*, "The Problem of Socrates," p. 33). Tragedy is an expression of the Greeks' intelligibility to themselves. Nietzsche describes the need for tragedy as a 'neurosis of health'. In effect, however, the role of tragedy is to render unintelligible the misunderstanding that Nietzsche believes underwrites the Socratic demand for reasons.

found the demand for reasons compelling only as that identification faltered. And although a simple refusal to question seems as arbitrary to Nietzsche as it does to Socrates, such 'identification' does not.[36]

From the point of view suggested by Nietzsche's Schopenhauerian vocabulary, to say that in letting themselves be represented by the satyr chorus, the audience is identifying itself with its culture sounds, to say the least, counterintuitive. Nietzsche says that the tragic chorus was the voice of Dionysian nature. That, after all, is why they were disguised as satyrs! But we must not forget what the chorus witnesses: the destruction of the tragic hero. On the reading I am proposing, it is *this* spectacle that presents the authority of Greek culture. If we are to understand what Nietzsche says about tragedy, we must try to see how this could be so. How, in other words, could the *destruction* of culture come to reinforce the *authority* of culture? However paradoxical the idea may seem on the surface, something like this must represent Nietzsche's view, because, as we have seen, *The Birth of Tragedy*'s attack on Socratism implies that the destruction of the tragic hero somehow celebrates the tragic audience's immunity to the demand for reasons. The point of tragedy must be to convey to them not the illusoriness of their culture with respect to nature, but rather the illusoriness of these categories altogether.

To say that the members of the tragic audience were identified with their culture is, however, merely another way of saying that they were obedient to its authority, that they let themselves be constrained by it. Though for Nietzsche the intelligibility of the demand for reasons turns on the failure to understand obedience, he does not provide, as I have insisted, a positive philosophical account of such obedience. At a specifically philosophical level, we learn all there is to learn about obedience only by seeing how Socratism—and, indeed, morality more generally—resists it. Putatively philosophical claims about the nature of obedience can have only this sort of content. If we try to give them more content than that, we will tend to talk about the 'special connection' between the tragic audience and its culture, and about the 'special internal relationship' their ethical and aesthetic judgments bear to the world. From Nietzsche's point of view, talk of special internal relationships only too understandably and justifiably invites the Socratic demand. This is why I said that tragedy does not make the audience privy

[36] I borrow the term 'identification' from Harry Frankfurt. The parallels between Frankfurt's notion of identification and Nietzsche's discussion of what I have been calling 'membership in culture' are, I think, suggestive. See, for example, "Identification and Wholeheartedness," in *The Importance of What We Care About* (Cambridge: Cambridge University Press, 1988), pp. 159–76.

to any philosophically relevant information about membership in Greek culture of which Socrates remains ignorant. Any such information would be the proper object of philosophical inquiry and, as such, could not accomplish what Nietzsche suggests it is supposed to accomplish.

Thus far, I have been considering in a very general way in what tragic insight *must* consist if it is to do the work Nietzsche gives it to do. Of course, putting the point in this way leaves open the possibility that nothing *could* do this work, but at least we can see what it would mean for Nietzsche's claims about tragedy to be mistaken.[37] I will try now to be a bit more specific about the picture of tragedy articulated in his first book.

The Concept of Culture: Authority and Obedience

We should take seriously Nietzsche's claim that "a public of *spectators* as we know it was unknown to the Greeks" (*BT*, sec. 8, pp. 62–63, my emphasis). On his view, the audience of the tragedies 'permitted themselves to be represented by' the tragic chorus and 'from that point of view witnessed the actual drama unfold. We might be able to understand the importance of a tragic presentation of the authority of culture if we could understand the difference between being a spectator and letting oneself be represented by the chorus in this way. What, then, did the audience 'see' when it permitted itself to be represented by the chorus? What, that is, does Nietzsche think the tragedies are really about?

In one way or another, he says, the significance of any good Greek tragedy—the content, so to speak, of the dramatic action—is the suffering of Dionysus. The "tradition," he writes, "is undisputed that Greek tragedy in its earliest form had for its sole theme the sufferings of Dionysus. . . . But it may be claimed with equal confidence that until Euripides, Dionysus never ceased to be the tragic hero; that . . . Prometheus, Oedipus, etc. . . . are mere masks of this original hero" (*BT*, sec. 10, p. 73).

> Thus, [he writes,] the choral parts with which tragedy is interlaced are, as it were, the womb that gave birth to the whole of the so-called

[37] Nietzsche, it seems to me, does not exactly have an *argument* against the Socratic distinction between instinct and reason. He does, however, mean to make very explicit in what the Socratic presupposition behind this distinction consists, and to ask us whether we can in fact make good sense of it. I think he supposes most of us at least believe that we can, and, though he considers us much mistaken in this belief, he does not suppose that arguments here will be decisive.

dialogue, that is, the entire world of the stage, the real drama. . . .
Thus the drama is the Dionysian embodiment of Dionysian insights
and effects and thereby separated, as by a tremendous chasm, from
the epic. . . . [N]ow we realize that the scene, complete with the action, was basically and originally thought of merely as a *vision;* the
chorus is the only "reality" and generates the vision, speaking of it
with the entire symbolism of dance, tone, and words. . . . [O]riginally
tragedy was only "chorus" and not yet "drama." (*BT,* sec. 8,
pp. 65–66)

For Nietzsche, the Dionysian destruction of the individual is always
only an expression of the status of culture as a whole—thought of, for
the moment, in terms of its relationship to nature. On the surface, the
suggestion here seems to be that in witnessing the destruction of the
tragic hero (the rending of the god Dionysus) the tragic audience gains
insight into something like the tenuousness of their culture.[38] In their
properly tragic form, however, such Dionysian effects must convey insight into the nature of the authority of Greek culture, into what it
means to be a member of this community. For this, as we have seen, is
the work Nietzsche's criticism of Socratism gives such effects to do.

Allowing themselves to be represented by the chorus—in other
words, not being spectators—the members of the audience of such
tragedies do not see their culture standing in opposition to nature. They
have no sense that what they are witnessing is a portrayal of the ways
in which they—the members of this particular culture—happen to approach the world. And we should not let an arguably unhappy use of
Schopenhauerian vocabulary mislead us into thinking otherwise. Paradoxically enough, the effect of witnessing the destruction of the tragic
hero must be to strengthen the audience's confidence in its culture. We
can make no sense of such confidence in terms of an opposition between culture and nature.

Nietzsche reproaches both Socrates and Euripides for failing to
understand and properly value tragedy on the grounds that they misunderstand and neglect the importance of the chorus. They misconstrue

---

[38] To put the point in the sort of Schopenhauerian terms that (for reasons that will
become apparent) I have been studiously avoiding, by witnessing the destruction of
the tragic hero, the audience comes to appreciate the fragility of the so-called principle
of individuation. The audience comes to appreciate, in other words, that the apparent
order of things does not reach below the surface of reality. The question I have been
trying to ask, however, is in what way such insight might be at all relevant to the
Socratic demand for reasons, and my suggestion has been that its only relevance
would be to reinforce the point of view from which that demand issues.

the destruction of the tragic hero as a sign of the need to provide rational grounding for the culture in which he lives, to find a rational way
out of the dilemma confronting him. As spectators, however, neither
Socrates nor Euripides understands what I have called the audience's
'identification' with its culture. They cannot understand the chorists'
view of the world and hence cannot understand what tragedy has to
teach about the meaning of culture.

This last claim, however, must be handled with care, for it might
seem to suggest that Nietzsche thought tragedy provided the Greek
audience with what we might call an 'internal perspective' on its culture.
Such a reading would, indeed, allow us to make some sense of
Nietzsche's insistence that, as long as tragedy functioned properly, the
tragic Greeks were immune to the force of the Socratic demand for
reasons. However, as I have argued, I think we should resist the temptation to construe Nietzsche's Greeks in this fashion, for this interpretation would not show that Socrates had indeed *failed* to understand
tragedy. The point of tragedy, as Nietzsche sees it anyway, is to drive
the audience away from the temptation to think of membership in their
culture in terms of internal and external perspectives on that culture.
Talk of an internal perspective, on the other hand, retains precisely the
picture of confinement to culture that Nietzsche must reject if he wants
to maintain that the tragic Greeks were justifiably immune to the demand for reasons.

The claim that, in allowing itself to be represented by the chorus,
the audience of the tragedies of Aeschylus and Sophocles acknowledged the authority of its culture sounds extremely odd to most readers
of *The Birth of Tragedy*, and I do not mean to minimize the unorthodox
character of the reading we are now considering. As I have tried to
show, however, this is precisely the interpretation to which we are
driven by Nietzsche's criticism of Socrates. The more customary reading, on the other hand, finds that, by presenting the Greeks with a
kind of immediate, nondiscursive grasp of a truth about *nature*, tragedy
taught them something about their culture in only an indirect fashion
at best. Nevertheless, we have seen that Nietzsche thought that tragedy
functioned, in effect, to undermine the intelligibility of the standpoint
from which Socratism issued its demand for reasons.[39] He believed that

[39] Once again, I say functioned *in effect* to undermine the intelligibility of this standpoint because Nietzsche insists that once Socrates *had* become a problem—once his
case was no longer exceptional but in fact representative of Athenians generally—
tragedy was helpless to stop him. Nevertheless, as long as tragedy functioned properly, the Greeks were indeed immune to Socratism, and Nietzsche's account of tragedy is meant to explain why this is so.

the audience of the tragedies understood that belonging to a culture cannot properly be thought of as a matter of adopting a particular point of view on the world. Insofar as the very intelligibility of the Socratic demand rests on this conception of culture, clearing up this confusion is meant to rid the refusal to countenance that demand of its appearance of arbitrariness.

According to the most common reading of *The Birth of Tragedy*, by presenting the audience with an immediate truth about nature, identification with the chorus taught the following lesson about its culture: that it was an illusion and a lie.[40] The point of this lesson, however, was to provide the tragic Greeks with metaphysical comfort. In this way tragedy could justify life by showing it to be an aesthetic phenomenon. On this reading, to claim as I do that the audience *identifies* with its culture appears to be nearly the opposite of Nietzsche's intention, because what the audience of these tragedies is supposed to come to appreciate is that that which 'really is' is something wholly natural—something, as Nietzsche says, Dionysian—and not at all something cultural—or, as he says, Apollonian. Culture, on this reading, is an illusion, and tragedy helps the audience overcome the temptation to think otherwise. What motivates this reading?

Nietzsche twice claims, as I noted above, that it is only as an aesthetic phenomenon that life can be justified, and in *The Birth of Tragedy* he argues that tragic drama showed the Greeks in what respect life might be said to be an aesthetic phenomenon. Our lives require some kind of justification, he says, because, though human suffering is unavoidable, there appears to be no point to it. The most common reading maintains, in effect, that the audience of a tragedy took metaphysical comfort from insight into the fact that, at bottom, one's life as a suffering individual is somehow a dream or an illusion. Thus, in a representative passage, Nietzsche writes:

just as tragedy, with its metaphysical comfort, points to the eternal life of this core of existence which abides through the perpetual destruction of appearance, [so] the symbolism of the satyr chorus proclaims this primordial relationship between the thing-in-itself and appearance. The idyllic shepherd of modern man is merely a counter-

[40] Though I think that many readers do indeed subscribe to some version of this interpretation, I do not mean here primarily to take issue with any particular commentary on *The Birth of Tragedy*. Rather, as I claimed in the Introduction, it is my hope that, by seeing clearly what is wrong with a reading Nietzsche's text so clearly seems to invite, we will be forced to confront squarely the uncritical assumption that Nietzsche meant to offer a positive alternative to that which he rejects as morality.

feit of the sum of cultural illusions that are allegedly nature; the Dionysian Greek wants truth and nature in their most forceful form—and sees himself changed, as by magic, into a satyr. . . . Such transformation is the presupposition of all dramatic art. In this magic transformation the Dionysian reveler sees himself as a satyr, and as a satyr, in turn, he sees the god, which means that in his metamorphosis he beholds another vision outside himself, as the Apollonian complement of his own state. With this new vision the drama is complete. (*BT*, sec. 8, pp. 61–64)

Given the Schopenhauerian-Kantian vocabulary Nietzsche employs here to describe the tragic synthesis of the Dionysian and Apollonian (of the natural and the cultural), it is small wonder that the metaphysical comfort he says that the synthesis provides is most often taken to be a matter of understanding that culture is simply an illusion. M. S. Silk and J. P. Stern, for example, write that "tragedy . . . presents us with the destruction of individuals in a way which is exalting, because it gives us a glimpse of the underlying deeper power of life . . . in which we have a share, but which is only glimpsed when individuality is transcended."[41] Much of what Nietzsche says appears at first blush to support this sort of reading. Thus, Alexander Nehamas writes:

tragedy, primarily through the musically inspired "Dionysian" chorus, can intimate the final truth that the ultimate nature of the world is to have no orderly structure: in itself the world is chaos, with no laws, no reason, and no purpose. Tragedy gives a nondiscursive glimpse of the contrast between "the real truth of nature and the lie of a culture that poses as if it were the only reality," a contrast that "is similar to that between the eternal core of things, the thing-in-itself, and whole world of appearances." (*BT*, sec.8) It shows that the orderly, apparently purposeful world within which we live is a creation we have placed between ourselves and the real world, which pursues its course without any regard for our view, our values, and our desires. But . . . in the very process of revealing this painful truth, it offers a consolation for the negative and desperate reaction this is bound to generate. It shows that ultimately we are not different from the rest of nature, that we are part and parcel of it, and belong totally

---

[41] M. S. Silk and J. P. Stern, *Nietzsche on Tragedy*, (Cambridge: Cambridge University Press, 1981), p. 267.

to it . . . and that its blind, purposeless, constant ebb and flow is to be admired and celebrated.[42]

On this interpretation, tragic insight is the result of grasping a truth that lies, so to speak, *behind* appearances. The audience sees that the whole of culture—the sense they make of the world—is nothing more than an illusion.

Here, then, is the situation as we find it on the most common reading: the life of which we can make sense in terms of the concepts and categories with which our culture presents us is a source of some as yet unspecified sort of suffering. Because there seems to be no way to avoid such suffering and because it lacks any ultimate point, life seems to require some other sort of justification. At first blush, the point of tragedy seems to be simply to deny that there *is* any such justification, and it thereby appears to confirm our worst fears: namely, that our suffering is senseless and unavoidable. But on the standard reading, this is only half the story, because tragedy also reminds us that the life of which we can make sense is only an illusion and that at bottom what we really are is of a piece with chaotic and unfathomable nature. Thus, the world of which we can make sense (culture) is only an expression—an artistic expression, if one likes—of the world of which we can make *no* sense (that is, nature). This insight, though acknowledging that there is no justification, properly so called, of suffering, is supposed to provide metaphysical comfort.

It is, as I have said, *The Birth of Tragedy*'s employment of a Schopenhauerian vocabulary to describe the tragic synthesis of the Dionysian and Apollonian that appears to provide the strongest support for this sort of interpretation. By equating the Dionysian and the Apollonian with the Schopenhauerian world will and the realm of appearances governed by the *principium individuationis*, respectively, Nietzsche suggests that tragedy showed the Greek audiences that the intelligible order of things is merely an illusion laid over the deeper reality of nature. Because there is, as we will see presently, no obvious way to make sense of a straightforwardly Schopenhauerian description of tragedy in the context of Nietzsche's attack on Socratism, we appear to be left with two interpretative options: either Nietzsche uses a misleading philosophical terminology to press his attack on Socratism, or there is a fundamental tension in *The Birth of Tragedy* between his conception of Socratism and his ostensibly Schopenhauerian description of tragedy.

[42] Alexander Nehamas, *Nietzsche: Life as Literature* (Cambridge: Harvard University Press, 1985), pp. 42–43.

The latter option is certainly possible, but because I find Nietzsche's relationship with Schopenhauer in general to be far from straightforward, I recommend the former reading.[43] We need, in any case, to know what, from the point of view of Nietzsche's attack on Socratism, is wrong with the Schopenhauerian reading's account of tragedy.

It is, indeed, Nietzsche's view that the tragic Greeks were able to live without Socratic justification, and it is his view as well that they were especially susceptible to some sort of suffering. He also believed that the Socratic demand for reasons reflected a misunderstanding and denial of life. Finally, he believed that it was to their credit that the tragic Greeks were for a while able to resist the Socratic demand, and that it is in some sense to Socrates' interlocutors' *dis*credit that they were unable to do so. But though he is fairly clear about the kind of justification without which they were able to live, Nietzsche is nowhere in *The Birth of Tragedy* terribly clear about the sort of suffering to which he believed them especially prone. The chief shortcoming of the standard reading, I want to argue, is that it takes the nature of that suffering for granted.[44]

---

[43] A number of recent commentators have found the relationship between Schopenhauer and Nietzsche to be remarkably straightforward—as though early on Nietzsche had simply adopted a few key Schopenhauerian theses and then later in life struggled (mostly unsuccessfully) to distance himself from his first philosophical teacher. There is not room here to address the complicated issue of Nietzsche's relationship to Schopenhauer. I would suggest, at the very least, that the relationship must be assessed in the light of *Schopenhauer as Educator*, but that, of course, is not an uncontentious point either. In any event, it seems to me that if we want to know what Nietzsche made of Schopenhauer's views, we should indeed look to the *The Birth of Tragedy*. But I see no compelling reason to suppose that we must use Schopenhauer's views to assess the use Nietzsche there made of them. For the reader who is nevertheless inclined to believe Nietzsche must have straightforwardly adopted Schopenhauerian views in *The Birth of Tragedy*, I think the first interpretative option is the appropriate one. In either case, however, my point remains the same: properly understood, Nietzsche's attack on Socratism does not leave room for a Schopenhauerian alternative.

[44] See, for example, Ivan Soll, "Pessimism and the Tragic View of Life: Reconsiderations of Nietzsche's *Birth of Tragedy*," in *Reading Nietzsche*, ed. Robert C. Solomon and Kathleen M. Higgins (New York: Oxford University Press, 1988), pp. 104–31. Soll understands the 'terror and horror of existence' that Nietzsche claims the Greeks felt to be a recognition of the unavoidable and irredeemable character of human misery. On Soll's reading, Nietzsche unreflectively took over this conception of life from Schopenhauer, 'found' it again in the tragic Greeks, and indeed maintained it in one form or another throughout his career. "The Greeks," Soll writes, "despite their acceptance of the same view of life, had affirmed the value of life and advocated living as intensely as possible" ("Pessimism," p. 113). I have argued, however, that there is no compelling reason to attribute such a view to Nietzsche, even in *The Birth of Tragedy*. Silenus's message that "what is best of all is utterly beyond your reach, not to be born, not to *be*, to be *nothing*. But second best for you is to die soon," is indeed presented by Nietzsche as a piece of folk wisdom, but hardly, as Soll would have us believe, "in any event, as true" ("Pessimism," p. 108). *The Birth of Tragedy* is

Nietzsche understands tragedy, on the one hand, and the demand for reasons, on the other, to represent two different kinds of response to the same basic problem: something he calls 'suffering'. If, following Schopenhauer, we understand the kind of suffering in question here to be nothing more than ordinary human misery, then, when Nietzsche repudiates the Socratic attempt to 'correct existence', we will conclude that he means primarily to reject any attempt to do away with that kind of suffering.[45] But we have seen that Socrates' complaint with 'existence' is that his interlocutors form moral judgments in the absence of reasons. The happiness he connects with the virtuous life can only be achieved with the aid of such reasons, but this form of knowledge does not attempt to correct the problem of human misery per se. It is, in other words, difficult to see how the Socratic demand for reasons could be understood as a demand for something to justify life in the face of ordinary misfortune. It is true that Socrates is portrayed both by Plato and by Nietzsche as someone who has succeeded in detaching himself from his body's perceptions, needs, and desires and who therefore bears physical suffering with greater equanimity than the nonphilosopher can ever hope to achieve. But this sort of immunity to misery is presented both by Plato and by Nietzsche not as the goal of philosophy but rather as its side effect. And insofar as such detachment is indeed a goal of philosophy, it is something like a necessary feature of an unclouded view of the world, rather than an independently desirable end to which philosophical inquiry might be seen as the means.

As we have seen, according to Nietzsche, those who find compelling Socrates' demand for definitions do in fact suffer from something. But Nietzsche does not portray Socrates as trying to provide a justification for the suffering caused by everyday misfortune, however great this might be. Giving reasons of the sort Socrates seeks is simply irrelevant to the fact of that kind of suffering. Nevertheless, Nietzsche insists that "the question of the Greek's relation to pain, his degree of sensibility, is basic: did this relation remain constant? or did it change radically?" (BT, "Attempt at a Self-Criticism," sec. 4, p. 21). From what, then, did they suffer?

Because the form of the solution to the problem of suffering that, on Nietzsche's account, Socratism represents is that one should give rea-

---

an attempt—as Nietzsche thought tragedy was an attempt—to *understand* this piece of wisdom, to interpret it. My suggestion is that we can best understand Nietzsche's interpretation of such wisdom—and understand what is true about it—by seeing how tragic insight could silence the Socratic demand for reasons.

[45] This seems to be how Julian Young reads him. See, again, his *Nietzsche's Philosophy of Art*.

sons for one's interpretation of one's concepts, it might appear that the problem confronting Nietzsche's Greeks was that they suffered from a lack of reasons. But Nietzsche denies this. For though the problem they faced appears to have been that they were in some way tempted to think of membership in their culture in such a way as to *invite* the Socratic demand, it was Socrates who succeeded in redescribing *this* problem as one of lacking reasons. This redescription represents his contribution. As we have seen, it is only on the basis of this redescription of the problem facing the Greeks that Socrates' solution or 'cure' came to seem appropriate.

This account suggests that the problem confronting the Greeks was one that presented itself to *Socratism* as a fear of contingency, a fear that there might be no connection between the way they thought about things and the way things themselves really were.[46] Further, if this idea is on the right track, then the Schopenhauerian reading is guilty of the same misunderstanding of tragedy of which Nietzsche accuses Socratism. The insistence that tragedy functions by showing the audience that the world of which it can make sense is only an illusion—a mere appearance—could only serve to *reinforce* their sense of the contingency of its culture. Contingency, that is to say, is not the disease for which it is its own cure.

It might seem more accurate, then, to say that the problem confronting Nietzsche's Greeks was the temptation to describe their situation in terms that invite the Socratic demand. In other words, the problem to which tragedy functioned as a solution might be said to be that the tragic Greeks were somehow tempted to conceive of membership in their culture as a matter of *looking* at the world in a certain way, of seeing it as Greeks see it. For it is precisely this way of thinking that invites the Socratic question of what justifies one in looking at the world in one particular way (as opposed to some other). Once they are able to make sense of *that* description of what it means to belong to a culture, all appeals to the authority of their culture can express only an arbitrary refusal to entertain the Socratic question. But tragedy functions, on Nietzsche's account, by showing the tragic audience the world *simpliciter*. The special tragic synthesis of culture and nature achieves the *dissolution* of the opposition upon which the intelligibility of Socratism depends.

Ultimately, however, talk of temptation here is worthless as a diagnosis of why the Socratic demand was taken seriously. Trivially, the diffi-

---

[46] It does not seem to me to distort Nietzsche's intentions here to express these worries in Rortyian tones.

culty is that this use of the notion of temptation is empty. We wanted to know why the demand for reasons was taken seriously, and to say that those who so took it were 'tempted' to do so is simply uninformative. (This is, however, not quite the claim I made. I said that they were tempted to think of their culture *in such a way* as to invite the Socratic demand. But this refinement only pushes the problem back a step.) More seriously, however, the problem with talk of temptation in this context is that it does not help us understand the sort of suffering to which Nietzsche says the tragic Greeks were especially susceptible. According to his historical reconstruction, pretragic Greece was a dominantly Apollonian culture that began to lose confidence in itself when Dionysian cults began to reemerge. Nietzsche describes the problem confronting these Greeks as one of a fear of the 'excess of nature'. Though such a fear might appear to express a worry about the groundlessness or contingency of culture, this cannot really be the right way to describe what Nietzsche believed the Greeks suffered from, just because talk of contingency accepts the Socratic account of the problem facing the Greeks. Such talk fails, in short, to treat Socrates *as a problem*.

I claimed a moment ago that, on Nietzsche's view, tragedy and Socratism both represent solutions to the problem of suffering. But now it seems that I need to modify that claim because *The Birth of Tragedy* says that, as long as tragedy functioned properly, the Greeks were simply immune to Socratic temptations. The demand for reasons, we have seen, is not independently intelligible and becomes compelling, on Nietzsche's view, only once one has need of it. But the tragic Greeks, it seems, simply had no such need. Thus, one might object that my reading distorts Nietzsche's meaning inasmuch as that reading treats tragedy as a solution to a problem. What we should say instead, it seems, is that tragedy is possible only as long as the Greeks remain immune to philosophy. It is not clear that there is room to give tragedy a role in actually preserving that immunity.

I think, therefore, that we have no real choice but to acknowledge that, unlike Socrates, Nietzsche's Greeks did not seek in tragedy anything that can helpfully be called a 'solution to a problem'. Nevertheless, Nietzsche does say that the tragic Greeks suffered, and he considers tragedy to have been *some* sort of response to that suffering, even if not precisely a solution to a problem. They suffered specifically from what the late preface to *The Birth of Tragedy* calls the 'overfullness' of life. In the context of his criticism of Socratism, it does not seem to me to do injustice to Nietzsche's account of tragedy to say that the tragic Greeks suffered from life in the sense that they were open— 'responsive'—to the authority of their culture. The attack on Socratism implies precisely this sort of connection between intelligibility and a form of affliction. This, I suggest, is the kind of suffering tragedy celebrates.[47]

I have argued that the suffering to which Nietzsche suggests Socratism functioned as a response is not that which is connected with everyday misfortune. Nor may those to whose suffering Socratism provides a solution be said to suffer from the 'contingency of human convention'. For this sort of 'existential' suffering turns out to be a misinterpretation of the kind of suffering that is truly at stake in tragedy. I am therefore inclined to believe that, odd though it may sound to put the point in this way, Nietzsche believed that the tragic Greeks suffered from the meaning*ful*ness of life, for this seems to be what Socratism *resists* by saying that life stands in need of justification. But once we have appreciated that claims about contingency or groundlessness represent *interpretations* of the problem confronting the Greeks rather than simple presentations of it, the sort of suffering Nietzsche seems to think is so basic to life appears to lack a distinct object. Though they interpret their suffering very differently, Nietzsche's tragic Greeks and their Socratic counterparts simply suffer from *life*. This, I think, is what is implied by saying that the tragic Greeks suffered from the overfullness of life.[48]

In later works, Nietzsche says that we suffer from time—from, so to speak, the fact of history.[49] The claim that we suffer from the past is as

---

[47] I am not sure how best to respond to someone who still insists that the sort of suffering I associate here with intelligibility can be called suffering only in a metaphorical sense. I have not meant to suggest on Nietzsche's behalf that the tragic Greeks found making sense to be *physically* painful. But surely physical pain is only one sort of suffering. In any case, there is certainly nothing unusual—nor, perhaps, terribly original—in Nietzsche's thinking of responsiveness or receptivity as a kind of suffering: it is, we might say, something undergone or endured, something with which we might be said to be afflicted. And as we shall see, Nietzsche comes to think of making sense as something that demands a kind of effort on our part, something of which he does not find many of us to be capable.

[48] Another way to think about the idea that Socratism and tragedy were responding to the same problem has been suggested by Martha Nussbaum in *The Fragility of Goodness* (Cambridge: Cambridge University Press, 1986). She begins with the recognition that the tragic Greeks had, as Bernard Williams has put it, "a sense . . . that what is great is fragile and that what is necessary may be destructive" (in *The Legacy of Greece: A New Appraisal*, ed. M. I. Finley [Oxford: Clarendon Press, 1981], p. 253) and argues that Plato sought a way to avoid the vagaries of 'moral luck' by seeking to guarantee the connection between virtue and happiness by means of knowledge. One way to put the problem with the Schopenhauerian reading of tragedy, on this reading, would be to say that it can make no compelling sense of the tragic Greeks' concerns with the always potential *lack* of connection between virtue and happiness.

[49] See especially *Thus Spoke Zarathustra*, "On Redemption," but also *Twilight of the Idols*, "'Reason' in Philosophy," sec. 1.

central to Nietzsche's thinking as is the doctrine of eternal recurrence, but the idea that we suffer from time is a difficult one to assess. At a more or less flat-footed level of analysis, we can say that the Platonist, for example, suffers from time in the sense that he believes that the world's intelligibility can be accounted for only in terms of something that lies wholly outside the world. From Nietzsche's point of view, as we will see, the Platonist is motivated by a desire to speak without consequences—to speak without having to rely upon our human, all too human, willingness to go on with our words in the particular ways we do. As I suggested in the Introduction and will explain in greater detail in Chapters 3 and 4, Nietzsche believes that our suffering from history drives us to entertain what he considers to be the 'pious' and ascetic fantasy that the will to truth represents a decisive break with the past. This fantasy prevents us from questioning the value of truth.[50]

It should by now be clear in what, on Nietzsche's view, the Socratic misunderstanding of tragedy consists. For Socrates, either tragedy is in the business of providing grounds for culture and fails to do so, or its point is radically to underscore the absence of all such grounds. Socrates' misunderstanding is therefore not so much about *how* tragedy does what it does as it is about *what* tragedy is supposed to do in the first place. Socrates, in short, understands tragedy as *competing* with his own form of rationalism. And, as we have seen, this is precisely what Nietzsche wants most to deny.

We might put these points in the following terms: Socrates understands what I have called 'membership in culture' to be a matter of applying one's culture's standards to the world. In other words, he takes membership to be a matter of *interpreting* the concepts of that culture as one's fellow members do. The intelligibility of the Socratic spectator's stance depends upon our being able to make sense of this idea of interpretation. Nietzsche believes, however, that tragedy had the effect of showing that this picture of membership is unintelligible, precisely by denying that it makes good sense to speak of interpretation in this

[50] It might appear that Nietzsche is largely mute about the subject of history in *The Birth of Tragedy*, but we should not ignore the fact that the story he tells about tragedy is a historical one. More important, however, is the fact that, insofar as it is centrally concerned with what is unique about the present age and with whether modern Germany has a future, the book as a whole may be read as an extended reflection on what it is to be historical at all. It is hard to know how much is reasonable to make of this fact. I do not want to go so far as to suggest that *The Birth of Tragedy* considers Wagnerian opera as a means for the Germans to overcome their ill will against time. It seems pretty clear, in fact, that Nietzsche himself comes to reject such a suggestion. Nevertheless, Socratism, as he treats it in his first book, is manifestly an expression of such ill will, and tragedy, I think, treats it as such.

context. From the tragic point of view, when I call something courageous, it makes no sense to say that I am interpreting the concept in a particular way. Or rather, whatever sense it does make does not serve to motivate the specifically *Socratic* version of the question 'But why this way rather than that?'.[51] From the tragic point of view, I no longer see my culture as standing over against nature; I am simply obedient to its authority—where that means nothing more or less than that, for example, I let this or that count as courageous for me.

It is illuminating to compare what Nietzsche says about Socratism with his complaint about the other great spectator of Greek culture: Euripides. Nietzsche accuses Euripides of trying to prove by means of reasons what he—Euripides—mistakenly believed his public had so far accepted on faith: "[Euripides] put the prologue even before the exposition, and placed it in the mouth of a person who could be trusted: often some deity had to guarantee the plot of the tragedy to the public, to remove every doubt as to the reality of the myth—somewhat as Descartes could prove the reality of the empirical world only by appealing to the truthfulness of God and his inability to utter falsehood" (*BT*, sec. 12, p. 88). Like Socrates, in other words, Euripides fails to understand and properly to value tragedy. He tries, in effect, to *explain* what it means to be Greek to an audience that sees no force in such explanations. Euripides does not understand that explanations always come too late and insists that the authority of Greek culture can be, as it were, demonstrated.

To sum up, then, Socratism depends upon the ability to imagine that the authority of culture is somehow not enough to justify the judgments one makes. That *this* is what one calls courageous, for example, is not enough to justify the claim that it really *is* courageous.[52] The intelligibility of the demand for reasons depends, in other words, upon our being able to make sense of the claim that the actual practices of judgment— the very claims one is inclined to make—are not enough to show that

[51] See, in this connection, Edward H. Minar, "Paradox and Privacy: On §§201–202 of Wittgenstein's Philosophical Investigations." I am suggesting that the 'tragic Greeks' can make only what in the Introduction I called 'practical' sense of the Socratic question, answering it: 'Because this is the *right* way to "interpret" it'. They can make no sense of the philosophical question of why this is the right way to do so. But this suggests that the notion of interpretation idles here.

[52] The point, of course, is not that whatever one calls courageous is courageous, that one can never be mistaken. Rather, I understand the implication of Nietzsche's rejection of Socratism to be that Socrates has given us no reason to believe that the possibility of being mistaken by itself provides reasons to worry whether one has somehow gone astray from the beginning. The possibility of error, in other words, does not give one reason, in this sense, to distrust one's instincts.

this way of applying these concepts is any better off—any less arbitrary—than any other. What one does is, in short, simply *not good enough* for Socrates. Unless we have something better as grounds for going on with our concepts than the mere fact that we do go in these very ways, our application of those concepts seems to Socrates simply arbitrary or, as the Schopenhauerian reading would have it, contingent. That we have no real choice but to apply these concepts in the ways we do is, on Socrates' view, merely a fact about this particular community of speakers and reflects nothing about the way the world is anyway.

Nietzsche thinks of this Socratic fantasy, broadly, as a matter of wanting to think that we are better than we are. In philosophy, in other words, we have managed somehow to turn on ourselves by in this way denouncing what we do as worthless. He insists, however, that we have succeeded in doing so only because instinct has been construed as 'the application of concepts'. Nietzsche's point in talking here about instinct is therefore to deny the sense of the philosophical 'merely about us'. Thus, Nietzsche's point about tragedy's response to Socratism is not to show that what philosophy considers to be merely a fact about us is anything *more* than that, but rather that the philosopher has failed to draw a real contrast here. Indeed, Nietzsche claims that, ultimately, the philosopher's desire for something more than our human, all too human practices is a desire for something less than what we have already got.

The Question of Aesthetic Justification

Nietzsche claimed to be the first philosopher ever to have treated morality as a problem.[53] He might have come to consider himself the only philosopher ever to do so. Much of the subsequent critical effort to come to terms with his attack on morality has taken his goal to be to show that our moral values answer to nothing in the world itself, but rather reflect in one way or another only our own human, all too human psychology. But to treat morality as a problem is to see that that psychology is shot through with what Nietzsche considers to be specifically moral prejudices.

What, then, does Nietzsche's early account of tragedy suggest about his conception of psychology? To begin, our obedience to the authority of culture is not guaranteed by anything other than our willingness to go on. For Nietzsche, as I have claimed, it is indeed a fact about us that

[53] See sec. 345 of *The Gay Science,* "Morality as a Problem."

we go on in the ways we do with our concepts. I have called this the fact of our obedience in part precisely because it *can* fail. And the fact that it can fail in ways that seem to support the intelligibility of the Socratic demand for reasons is what is most deeply puzzling to Nietzsche. We may say, then, that a *psychological* investigation, as he conceives it, is an inquiry into the possibility of such failure. Such an inquiry is what he carries out under the title of a 'genealogy of morals'.

It is, for Nietzsche, a very basic fact about human beings that we must struggle to make sense. He believes that there is room to talk about struggle here, because, he finds, we tend to resist making sense. The struggle to make sense is a struggle to overcome this kind of resistance. Nietzsche's attack on Socratism suggests that tragedy may be seen to function as a tool of such overcoming.

But the sense in which such claims may be said to be 'psychological' is complicated. On the one hand, the fact of obedience, as I have used that notion here, is a psychological fact about us in the sense that going on in these ways with our concepts is only a fact about us not underwritten by anything more basic than our life with them. In this sense, we do indeed employ our concepts in these ways 'only by instinct'. On the other hand, however, because Nietzsche feels entitled to reject the philosophical opposition between reason and instinct, he does not think we are licensed to treat our instincts as, in any philosophically troubling sense, only facts about us. Our instincts are crucial to the sense we make of the world, but there is, Nietzsche insists, no conceptual room to treat the sense we make as of anything *less* than the world. For this same reason, I think, there is no conceptual room to treat sense as anything other than something we make—in the way, that is, we say of a speaker that he or she 'makes sense'. In particular, I shall argue, there is, in Nietzsche's view, no room to treat it as something we *create*— not anyway in the sense of it being something that we impose upon or project into the world.

Finally, Nietzsche does indeed say that life—more precisely, 'existence and the world'—is justified only as an aesthetic phenomenon, and, though a full discussion of Nietzsche's complicated views about art lies well beyond the scope of this book, I should say something about this most famous claim of *The Birth of Tragedy*. Clearly, Nietzsche cannot mean by 'aesthetic justification' a justification that somehow competes with the Socratic justification that he denies is forthcoming. For he would have us acknowledge that our lives simply do not stand in need of justification in the Socratic sense of the word. Indeed, in this sense, seeing that our lives do not stand in need of that kind of justification is all the justification we need. The question, then, is what if anything *art* has to do with any of this: in what way may making sense—being intelligible—be said to be an aesthetic matter?

Briefly, we will get nowhere with Nietzsche's talk of aesthetic justification if we think of art in terms of the imposition of form upon content, because this is yet another version of the basic philosophical dichotomy he asks us to give up. Very roughly, he believes that whatever we might be inclined to call content of anything that we could count as a work of art is only a function of that work's form, and vice versa. So we need to know how Nietzsche would understand aestheticist talk of form. My suggestion is that form must be whatever Nietzsche considers what I have here called culture to be. As my reading of *The Birth of Tragedy* should lead us to expect, the latter cannot be something that we somehow impose upon something else. Culture is rather something to which we are called upon to be responsive, our resistance to which we are called upon to overcome. As we shall see in Chapter 3, that there is something to be done here might be one thing Nietzsche's idea of artistic *activity* comes to in this context.

Nietzsche calls on us to transform our lives, and, in this sense, to make something of ourselves. The intuitive picture behind so-called aestheticist readings of Nietzsche is roughly that we are to do this by realizing that our natures are not discovered but remain rather to be invented.[54] The problem such readings tend to confront, however, is that of specifying the identity of the inventor, who must, it seems, invent him or herself.

I think we need to be able to make sense of this idea of self-creation in substantially different terms. I suggest that what Nietzsche has in mind when he talks, for example, of giving one's life style is that one should overcome resistance to recognizing the particular life one has. What is to be 'invented' here, therefore, is a kind of self-recognition. In other words, becoming what we are is a matter of properly understanding what we have become. *The Birth of Tragedy*'s attack on Socratism tends to support this suggestion.

As we will see in Chapter 4, Nietzsche appears to believe that reading the *Genealogy* can be for a certain sort of individual—a man of knowledge—an artistic exercise in self-recognition in this sense. It is in this way that we might speak of making sense as an aesthetic matter. This interpretation suggests that the Nietzschean idea of 'inventing oneself' is not so much a matter of doing something to what one is, but rather

[54] Nehamas's *Nietzsche: Life as Literature* provides the best articulation of this sort of reading.

of ceasing to do anything to what one has become. It is, as Nietzsche says in the preface to the *Genealogy*, a matter of *finding* oneself.[55]

Nietzsche's criticism of Socratism implies, as I have said, that he depicts human life as a struggle to make sense, which, perhaps surprisingly, means for him a struggle against our *unwillingness* to let ourselves be intelligible. That aspect of our morality to which he most objects gives voice to this unwillingness. This happens in a variety of ways, only one of which we have been considering here: Socratism.[56] This reading suggests, as I claimed in the Introduction, that the tempting dichotomy between the negative and positive aspects of Nietzsche's work is merely apparent. The distinction he draws between ascending and descending forms of life marks the difference between success and failure at making sense. Though this last distinction cannot, of course, be understood on the model of two different ways of making sense, Nietzsche's criticism of the Socratic demand for reasons does not appear to leave room for an ostensibly positive philosophical account of intelligibility.[57]

[55] "We are unknown to ourselves, we men of knowledge—and with good reason. We have never sought ourselves—how could it happen that we should ever *find* ourselves?" (*GM*, preface, sec. 1, p. 15).

[56] In Chapter 5, we will explore another way in which our morality expresses our unwillingness to let ourselves be intelligible: the 'morality of pity' prevents us—in a very particular way—from recognizing the historical character of the will to knowledge.

[57] An earlier version of the main argument of this chapter was read to the philosophy departments at Princeton University and at Johns Hopkins University. I thank the audiences at those talks, and especially Alexander Nehamas. Special thanks are due to David Cerbone, who commented at length on earlier drafts of this material.

CHAPTER 2

KNOWLEDGE AND INTERPRETATION

In the spirit of these last suggestive questions it must now be said how the influence of Socrates, down to the present moment and even into all future time, has spread over posterity like a shadow that keeps growing in the evening sun, and how it again and again prompts a regeneration of *art*—of art in the metaphysical, broadest and profoundest sense—how its own infinity also guarantees the infinity of art.

The Birth of Tragedy, sec. 15, p. 93

The Death of Tragedy and the Rise of the Will to Knowledge

I have until now focused my attention largely on Nietzsche's account of the Socratic misunderstanding of tragedy. But we should not ignore his conviction that, misunderstanding or not, Socratism eventually triumphed over tragedy. In the light of our discussion so far, this means that once the tragic Greek has been made to appreciate the force of the Socratic demand for justification, he cannot simply leave that request unanswered. If that demand is taken to heart, then—in the absence of such a justification—the conclusion that he has no substantial reason for going on with his concepts as he does seems to follow naturally.

But there is more at stake in Nietzsche's discussion of the demise of tragedy than this reading suggests. He believes that a certain form of Socratism represents a positive human possibility in its own right, one that is decisive for the present age. Refined into the unconditional will to truth, Socratism in fact becomes our distinctively modern form of will to power. Indeed, Nietzsche's claim that, unlike the tragic Greeks, modern Europeans do not have an adequate sense of who they are reflects to a great extent an assessment of what he takes to be their failure to understand their Socratic inheritance.

The goal of the rest of this book is to understand Nietzsche's conception of the *value* that those he calls 'men of knowledge' place upon truthfulness, and in this way to understand what he took to be the consequences of Socratism's triumph over tragedy. My aim, in short, is to understand the death of God. I want in the rest of this introductory section first to explain why such an approach to Nietzsche's work is not implausibly monolithic, and then briefly to present the genealogy of the modern will to knowledge that *The Birth of Tragedy* allows us to reconstruct.[1] In the next section, I want to present what strikes me as substantially the same genealogy as it occurs in some central passages in *The Gay Science*. In the third section, I will explore Nietzsche's denial of the thing-in-itself. The aim of these two sections together is to make clear just what sort of interest Nietzsche might really have had in what are commonly thought of as epistemological questions. As I read him, he means primarily to get us to ask whether we have any good idea of what we are talking about when we ask such questions, but he himself does not seek to provide answers to them. Epistemological questions are, for him, symptomatic of a kind of dissatisfaction with our lives—a dissatisfaction that tends to disguise itself as a fear of being cut off from the world, of being confined to appearances. Such dissatisfaction, however, is neither acknowledged nor overcome by proving either that we are or that we are not in fact 'in touch' with the world. Talk of dissatisfaction, in turn, suggests that Nietzsche's ostensibly epistemological reflections have a primarily psychological aim, and in the concluding section of this chapter I will try to make clear the nature of that aim.

———

It is one of Nietzsche's most intriguing claims that nothing more than a certain form of intellectual honesty is required to undermine our faith in what he calls 'Christianity as dogma':[2] "You see what it was that

---

[1] A properly Nietzschean genealogy, as I understand it, is a historical inquiry into the origins of a given set of our values, which aims to bring home to us the fact that those particular values have become binding upon us. It should be clear that this understanding of the aim of the practice of genealogy is sharply at odds with a common interpretation according to which the genealogist's goal is to demonstrate the historical and psychological *contingency* of the values in question.

[2] In *The Antichrist*, Nietzsche suggests that truth-telling is an inherent good—good, as it were, for its own sake. But he also seems to hold, both in that work and elsewhere, that we should reject a belief not simply on the grounds that it is false, but rather because it is harmful. See, for example, sec. 4 of *Beyond Good and Evil*. These two suggestions can seem to be at odds with one another, and the way in which Nietzsche expresses himself is sometimes confusing. For if we reject false beliefs because we hold them to be harmful, then it seems that, in doing so, we are appealing

really triumphed over the Christian god: Christian morality itself, the concept of truthfulness that was understood ever more rigorously, the father confessor's refinement of the Christian conscience, translated and sublimated into a scientific conscience, into intellectual cleanliness at any price" (GS, sec. 357, p. 307). Anyone, that is, who is committed to the truth more than to any other value will eventually be forced to recognize the falsity of those religious, philosophical, and moral beliefs that formerly allowed him to make his way about the world. And, as I will argue, the commitment to truthfulness undermines those beliefs most basically by bringing home to us the mendacity of our interpretation of the human, all too human needs to which they answer. Moreover, anyone who is committed to those values is, in virtue of that very fact, committed to the truth. Thus, no external criticism of those beliefs is either needed or indeed conceivable.[3] Nietzsche does not consider everyone to be honest with himself to this degree, nor does he believe that everyone can become so. But anyone with sufficient 'intellectual cleanliness' must recognize that he is not entitled to his old religious, philosophical, and moral beliefs. The question for us here is this: how does Nietzsche think we should conceive such recognition?

Nietzsche believes that honesty is a necessary condition for being one of his 'rightful readers'—for understanding him properly.[4] Furthermore, he believes, as I will argue, that understanding him properly is not different from recognizing that one is no longer entitled to the beliefs that are incompatible with one's commitment to truthfulness.

---

to a different standard from that of their mere falsity. But, as we will see, Nietzsche considers some falsehoods to be *inherently* harmful. And *these* beliefs are rejected on the grounds of their falsity alone. As far as Socratism is concerned, truthfulness, I mean to argue, is Nietzsche's only standard. To put the point in terms closer to his own, Nietzsche means, in the name of truth, to defend life against the falsehoods directed against it precisely in the name of (philosophical) truth. I mean, therefore, to take issue with Barry Allen's suggestion that Nietzsche means to deny the idea that truth is a good. See Allen's *Truth in Philosophy* (Cambridge: Harvard University Press, 1993). For an independent defense of the claim that truth-telling is an end in itself, see Cora Diamond, "Truth: Defenders, Debunkers, Despisers," in *Commitment in Reflection*, ed. Leona Toker (Hamden: Garland Press, 1993).

[3] To say that no external criticism of 'Christianity as dogma' is *conceivable* is to say that anyone committed to truthfulness is not in a position to imagine some other commitment. Nietzsche is, once again, talking about what it makes sense to *believe*. Because what we believe is what we hold to be true, we are not in a position to believe something we take to be false. Truth is, in this sense, the final court of appeal for belief. I am grateful to Richard Moran for helpful discussion of these matters and for allowing me to read his unpublished manuscript, "The Undoing of Self-Knowledge."

[4] See, for example, sec. 27 of the third essay of *On the Genealogy of Morals*, and the foreword to *The Antichrist*.

But he also suggests that a dedication to the truth may in fact prevent one from reading him in the right way, and thus cloud one's understanding of the death of God. We must, therefore, understand the distinction he draws between having the modern virtue of truthfulness and only appearing to have it, if we are to understand this aspect of his conception of life in the present age. My principal interpretative hypothesis will be that we can best understand that distinction in terms of what Nietzsche thinks reading his own work properly might be like. We will turn to this topic in some detail in the last chapter.

Whatever one makes of this last suggestion, however, it is likely to be objected at the outset that such a single-minded focus on the will to knowledge distorts our vision of Nietzsche's work as a whole. Surely, it might be said, Nietzsche has more to say about modernity than that to be a modern European is to be committed to the value of knowledge. At the very least, one might complain, more matters to us—and perhaps matters more—than mere knowledge.[5]

By way of reply, I want to emphasize, first, that it is not my intention to deny any of these claims. Nietzsche does indeed have a great deal to say about modern Europe—about Germany especially—that I will not discuss here and that appears at best only tangentially related to the issue of the virtues and vices of truthfulness. Second, I think it is fairly clear that, as I said above, Nietzsche considers a commitment to truthfulness to be at least a *necessary* condition for understanding him in the right way. It may not be the only condition for such understanding. Humor, irony, wickedness, and so on, spring immediately to mind as other such conditions. But honesty is the one that interests me here, and, as we will see, that particular virtue has a complicated genealogy— one Nietzsche aims to articulate in the passages we will examine. Finally, as I noted in the Preface, I think it is clear enough that the problem

[5] One might also object that in talking of a specifically modern will to knowledge, Nietzsche meant to draw our attention to the distinctively modern ways in which our lives in society are presently governed by a concern with gathering and manipulating knowledge. This may well be how Michel Foucault, for example, read Nietzsche. Along lines that he saw running back to Nietzsche, Foucault struggled to articulate a conception of modern political power according to which an obsession with the mere fact of human life, as it were, as an object of knowledge—with what we can know about ourselves—governs our activity, determines its significance, and rules out alternative ways of life. I do not think that a Foucaultian concern with the normalizing effects of knowledge lay at the heart of Nietzsche's interest in the will to knowledge, but nothing I say here is incompatible with such a concern. For a thought-provoking discussion of Foucault and his relationship to Nietzsche, see Barry Allen, "Government in Foucault," *Canadian Journal of Philosophy* 21 (December 1991): 421–40. I am indebted to Hubert Dreyfus for bringing this article to my attention. Allen has given a fresh formulation to his ideas in *Truth in Philosophy*.

of the value of truth—of the value of the value we place upon knowledge—is as central to Nietzsche's thinking as is the idea of the death
of God.

Nietzsche was overwhelmingly concerned with the sort of resistance
he felt he would encounter in readers who were already inclined to
agree with his claim that God is dead. These are readers who share the
value he places upon truthfulness. Christians and idealists, on the other
hand, are blind to themselves and are unable or unwilling to read his
work in ways that both Nietzsche and the man of knowledge will want
to account for in terms of their not wanting to face up to difficult truths.
But that the man of *knowledge* is somehow blind to himself and unable
or unwilling to read Nietzsche is more difficult to demonstrate, and
represents something that it is perhaps both more difficult and more
pressing to overcome.

When I claim, therefore, that Nietzsche has something to tell us about
what it means to be human in the present age—about what it means
to be a modern European—I am interested only in his assessment of
the modern will to knowledge. The 'us' to whom Nietzsche means to
offer that assessment must be, at least, readers dedicated to the value
of truthfulness. This assessment is not by any means all that Nietzsche
has to say about Europe or about Europeans, but it is the substance of
what he has to say about what it means in this sense to *be* a good
European.

The parallel that might be drawn here between Nietzsche's conception of our commitment to truthfulness and his treatment of ancient
Greece should be fairly obvious: he is much more interested in what
the tragedies of Aeschylus and Sophocles showed their audiences about
the nature of *membership* in Greek culture than he is in the actual content
of any particular tragedy. Indeed, he thinks that the issue of what I
have called 'membership in culture' just *is* the content of any good
tragedy. Nietzsche is, in other words, much more interested in the
question of what it means for Greek—or European—culture to be binding on its members than he is in the specific ways in which those
members confront the world. While his thinking about life in the present age is not restricted to these very abstract questions about the nature of community, his insights into what we might think of as the
specifics of modern life are not the subject of this book. I want rather
to understand the character of that which Nietzsche suggests is a precondition of a proper understanding of such insights: namely, the will
to knowledge.

Nietzsche believes that there is something about the *character* of our
commitment to truthfulness that is blind to itself, something in our will

that is weak. The value we presently place on knowledge, he says, is unconditional, and he insists that that value must in some way be called into question. The temptation here is to think that calling the value of truth into question must be a way of undermining its authority. But, as I have suggested, Nietzsche's aim is rather to do the opposite, for he thinks that the unconditionality of our commitment to the truth is a sign of our *resistance* to the authority of the will to knowledge, a sign of our failure properly to have inherited our Socratic legacy.

Nietzsche seeks to establish a properly tragic understanding of that inheritance: it is in this sense, I will argue, that he says that the influence of Socrates eventually prompts a regeneration of art.[6] As I will try to make clear in Chapter 4, it is the practice of *genealogy* that best expresses such understanding, because that practice is obedience—in the tragic sense—to the authority of knowledge.[7] As we saw in the last chapter, Nietzsche thinks that such obedience can be understood in aesthetic terms. Genealogy would be an artistic endeavor in this sense, not because it represents a creative selection and arrangement of the details of our history, but because it is responsive to the past in a way that makes it our own, in a way that allows us—the men of knowledge—to be at home in the present.

According to the genealogy of our commitment to truthfulness that Nietzsche offers in *The Birth of Tragedy*, the form of Socratic inquiry that began as a way of life for those unable any longer to understand the idea of membership in a culture eventually develops into the modern will to knowledge. Nietzsche claims, therefore, that "we cannot fail to see in Socrates the one turning point and vortex of so-called world history" (*BT*, sec. 15, p. 96). In other words, even though the intelligibility of Socratism depends, initially, upon understanding membership in Greek culture in terms that present such membership as a candidate for justification, that misunderstanding nevertheless becomes decisive for subsequent history. Socratism, in short, is more than just a misunderstanding. On the one hand, it provides those Nietzsche considers 'spectators' of their culture with a way to make sense of their situation, and, on the other, it eventually becomes a force to be reckoned with in its own right. In the remainder of this introductory section, I will very briefly sketch the outlines of this development.

Let us turn our attention first to the way in which Socratism allowed the Greeks to make sense of their lives. I will then examine the way in

---

[6] See *The Birth of Tragedy*, sec. 15, p. 93; quoted as an epigraph to this chapter.

[7] By 'practice of genealogy' I mean reading *Nietzsche* in a particular way. *This* activity is artistic in the relevant sense.

which Nietzsche tries in *The Birth of Tragedy* to account for the significance of Socratism for the present age. As we will see, these two features
of Nietzsche's account of the will to knowledge together amount to a
brief genealogy of that commitment. Once we have this material before
us, we will be in a position in the next section of this chapter to understand the parallel account of the will to knowledge Nietzsche offers in
The Gay Science.

Socratism as a 'Cure'

As I have explained, Nietzsche does not think that the Socratic demand for reasons can justify itself. In Chapter 1, therefore, we examined
his account of the context in which that demand comes to seem to make
sense: we concluded that it is only if obedience to the authority of one's
culture is treated as a matter of interpretation that the demand for the
reasons for one's obedience seems so much as intelligible. But this account does not explain why that demand was taken seriously. In other
words, it does not explain what work taking it seriously does for someone who does so. All it does is allow us to begin to make some sense
of someone who *does* take it seriously: in order to take it seriously, one
must be confused about the nature of what I have called obedience.

Nietzsche does not seek to explain the appeal of Socratism in properly
historical, sociological, or economic terms. He does, however, offer what
he thinks of as a *psychological* account of the force of the demand for
reasons. He says, roughly, that it allows someone whose instincts are
in disarray to make sense of his situation. Socratism, in other words,
provides an interpretation of philosophical confusion.

In *The Twilight of the Idols* Nietzsche insists quite explicitly that the
Socratic request for justification is only felt to be a demand if tragic
instinct falters. In a passage that we have examined before, he writes:

> With Socrates Greek taste undergoes a change in favour of dialectics:
> what is really happening when that happens? It is above all the defeat
> of a nobler taste. . . . Before Socrates, the dialectical manner was repu-
> diated in good society: it was regarded as a form of bad manners,
> one was compromised against it. Young people were warned against
> it. . . . Wherever authority is still part of accepted usage and one does
> not 'give reasons' but commands, the dialectician is a kind of buffoon:
> he is laughed at, he is not taken seriously.—Socrates was the buffoon
> who *got himself taken seriously:* what was really happening when that
> happened? (*TI*, "The Problem of Socrates," sec. 5, p. 31)

"Dialectics," Nietzsche claims, "can be only a last-ditch weapon in the hands of those who have no other weapon left" (*TI*, "The Problem of Socrates," sec. 6, pp. 31–32).

Precisely because he finds such dialectics repellent, Nietzsche says that "it is therefore all the more necessary to explain the fact *that* [Socrates] exercised fascination" (*TI*, "The Problem of Socrates," sec. 8, p. 32). And although Socratic dialectic has, he admits, an 'erotic' appeal, insofar as struggling to win an argument appealed to the agonal instincts of Athenian youth, this is, so to speak, merely the healthy side of Socrates' appeal. Nietzsche insists instead upon the general decay of aristocratic instinct as the disease to which Socrates' success really points: Socrates

> saw *behind* his aristocratic Athenians; he grasped that his case, the idiosyncrasy of *his* case, was already no longer exceptional. The same kind of degeneration was everywhere silently preparing itself: the old Athens was coming to an end.—And Socrates understood that all the world had need of him—his expedient, his cure, his personal art of self-preservation. . . . Everywhere the instincts were in anarchy; everywhere people were but five steps from excess. . . . His case was after all only the extreme case, only the most obvious instance of what had at that time begun to be the universal exigency: that no one was any longer master of himself, that the instincts were becoming mutually *antagonistic*. He exercised fascination as this extreme case— his fear-inspiring ugliness expressed it for every eye to see: he fascinated even more, it goes without saying, as the answer, as the solution, as the apparent *cure* for this case.—(*TI*, "The Problem of Socrates," sec. 9, pp. 32–33)

Later in this chapter, we will explore in greater detail Nietzsche's psychological account of the appeal of Socratism. But we can already see why, even as a *solution* to the problem of decadence, Socratism must represent, from Nietzsche's point of view, a tremendous misunderstanding. He writes, "It is self-deception on the part of philosophers and moralists to imagine that by making war on *décadence* they therewith elude *décadence* themselves. This is beyond their powers: what they select as an expedient, as a deliverance, is itself only another expression of *décadence*—they *alter* its expression, they do not abolish the thing itself." (*TI*, "The Problem of Socrates," sec. 11, p. 34). In Nietzsche's view, aristocratic Athenians around the time of Socrates began to lose confidence in their culture. They began, in other words, to feel themselves prey to worries about the groundlessness or contingency of their culture. But the expedient or cure for those worries presented by Socratism was itself infected with the same misunderstanding of Greek practices that Nietzsche calls 'decadence'. In this way, the philosophical search for rational grounding tends to perpetuate the problem for which it takes itself to be the cure.[8] Finally, because the intelligibility of Socratism as a way of life depends in this way upon and indeed perpetuates the misunderstanding of tragic instinct that fuels the demand for reasons, Nietzsche can claim that what has become our highest value—in this case, the premium we put upon truthfulness—is rooted in *error*.[9]

"Socrates," Nietzsche concludes, "exercised fascination [because] he seemed to be a physician, a saviour" (ibid., p. 33). When it came to seem that obedience to the authority of Greek culture was really an ingrained unwillingness to question that authority, a *refusal* to seek its grounds, membership in that culture appeared to stand in need of the kind of grounding that dialectics promised. Nietzsche believes that the presence of this need helps to explain why Socrates was taken seriously. For it was a need that demanded satisfaction.

Socratism in the Present Age

> It is not the victory of science that distinguishes our nineteenth
> century, but the victory of scientific method over science.
> (The Will to Power, sec. 466, p. 261)

Let us turn now to our second question: what is the significance of Socratism in the present age? What has it become? In *The Birth of Tragedy*, Nietzsche says that "anyone who has ever experienced the pleasure of Socratic insight and felt how, spreading in ever-widening circles, it seeks to embrace the whole world of appearances, will never again find

[8] Notice that the structure of this claim exactly parallels the corresponding claim Nietzsche makes about Christian morality: like Socrates, the 'priests' employ 'sick' means to combat weariness with life. The line of thought I am pursuing here suggests that Christianity is definitely *not* the disease for which it is its own cure, but rather something more like the reverse.

[9] What Nietzsche is describing in the passages I am considering here is the overcoming of one configuration of the will to power by another. In general, I think these examples of his claims about the origins of whatever is great and noble in its opposite—in this case how the will to knowledge grows out of what might be called 'the will to ignorance'—are more illuminating than the sorts of examples that can be retrieved from passages that appear to support a reading of Nietzsche as, for example, a protophenomenalist.

any stimulus toward existence more violent than the craving to complete this conquest and to weave the net impenetrably tight" (BT, sec. 15, p. 97). Even while rooted in and indeed perpetuating philosophical confusions about the relationship between individual and community, Socratism, in Nietzsche's view, nevertheless becomes decisive for the present age. It comes, in other words, to represent a positive alternative to the understanding of life expressed by ancient tragedy: the modern will to knowledge. Our question is: how does Nietzsche conceive of this development?

In the late preface to The Birth of Tragedy, Nietzsche says that in that book he had stumbled onto the 'problem of science'. For Nietzsche, the problem of science is, roughly, the problem of determining the value of science in the present age. What, in other words, does science mean to us? This, I submit, is yet another way of asking about the character of our commitment to truthfulness, and, hence, about the significance of the death of God. I am suggesting, in other words, that we accept Nietzsche's contention that The Birth of Tragedy was already trying to pose the question of the character of the modern will to knowledge, a question that appears to emerge explicitly only in his later works. He is, that is to say, already trying to pose the question of the value of truth.[10]

As we will see in some detail in the next chapter, when Nietzsche talks about questioning the will to truth—about its becoming 'self-conscious'—we should resist the temptation to take him to be trying in any way to undermine our devotion to honesty.[11] But, as we will also see, making the will to truth self-conscious in Nietzsche's sense is not exactly a matter of learning more about it. More knowledge about our commitment to truthfulness will not help overcome our resistance to that commitment. What is required here instead is something to which, as we saw at the end of the last chapter, Nietzsche sometimes refers in aestheticist terms: obedience. It is in this sense that he speaks already in The Birth of Tragedy of the influence of Socrates prompting a 'regeneration of art'.

In the "Attempt at a Self-Criticism," Nietzsche remarks cryptically that "the problem of science cannot be recognized in the context of science" (BT, "Attempt at a Self-Criticism," sec. 2, p. 18). I think that what he has in mind here is this: a proper understanding of the special

---

[10] Once again, we should not let the Schopenhauerian vocabulary of that early work cloud our vision of its chief concerns and claims.

[11] See On the Genealogy of Morals III, sec. 27, p. 161. For a succinct version of the standard reading of these passages according to which Nietzsche means to undermine our commitment to truth, see Barry Allen, "Nietzsche's Question, 'What Good Is Truth?'," History of Philosophy Quarterly 9 (April 1992): 225–40.

character of our contemporary commitment to scientific knowledge will not be achieved by means of scientific knowledge itself.[12] Because Nietzsche is using the term 'science' very broadly here, his claim is easily misunderstood. His point is not that there is nothing more to learn about the will to knowledge. Quite the contrary: it is the goal of much of the *Genealogy*, for example, to provide just such knowledge.[13] Nietzsche aims, that is, to tell us something about the history of our contemporary commitment to truthfulness. But he insists that that commitment—the *will* to knowledge—is not itself a matter of knowledge. To put the point in his own terms, we might say that the 'self-conscious' man of knowledge does not know more about his commitment to truth than does the 'pious' man of knowledge. The latter, however, labors under an illusion of which Nietzsche understands the former to be free.

In a passage that we have already examined, Nietzsche says, "We are unknown to ourselves, we men of knowledge. . . . [W]e are necessarily strangers to ourselves, we do not comprehend ourselves, we have to misunderstand ourselves, for us the law 'Each is furthest from himself' applies to all eternity—we are not 'men of knowledge' with respect to ourselves" (*GM*, preface, sec. 1, p. 15). Broadly, Nietzsche's point here is that we in the present age fail—as Socratism failed—to recognize the 'life of reason' as a form of will to power. That is, just as Socratism failed to understand itself as a last expedient, so we men of knowledge fail to understand the ways in which the modern form of the will to knowledge conditions us. This is not to suggest that the Socratic and the modern forms of will to knowledge are identical configurations of will to power, but rather to indicate that in both cases—albeit in different ways—the will to knowledge tends to cover up its character *as* will to power.

Now, appearances notwithstanding, to say that we are not men of knowledge with respect to ourselves also suggests that to grant that

[12] Here, as with so much else, Nietzsche shows himself to have been a precursor to Heidegger. Heidegger likes to say of modern technology that its essence is nothing on the order of a machine, that is to say, technology—or anyway that aspect of it that is most of interest to Heidegger—cannot be understood in what he thinks of as technological terms. By 'understood' here, I mean what Heidegger calls a 'free relationship'—something that is a matter of responsiveness or receptivity, and not merely one of intellectual comprehension or instrumental use. As we will see in the next chapter, Heidegger's vocabulary of responsiveness or receptivity is wholly pertinent to Nietzsche's thinking about the modern will to knowledge.

[13] As we will see presently, Nietzsche provides a related genealogy of the modern will to knowledge in *The Gay Science*. I have suggested that the first such genealogy he offers can be found in *The Birth of Tragedy*'s discussion of the death of tragedy and the rise of the will to knowledge.

we are conditioned by the will to knowledge—in Nietzsche's terms, to acknowledge it as will to power—is also not to come to possess further information about *ourselves*. Tragic insight into the authority that knowledge has for us is not, in *this* sense, a matter of self-knowledge. The significance of this claim will become clearer when we turn our attention to *The Gay Science* and the *Genealogy*, but it should already be evident that here—as in *The Birth of Tragedy*—Nietzsche wants to get his readers over their tendency to adopt a spectator's stance with respect to what they have become.

Because we will be asking in what Nietzsche thinks the commitment to truthfulness consists, we must be careful to distinguish two different questions that can be asked about knowledge: roughly, in what does knowledge itself consist? and in what does our commitment to it consist? Nietzsche, I argue, does not propose a substantive answer to the former question, but means rather to undermine our confidence that we can make good philosophical sense of it. In the next chapter, we will investigate more closely the answer he provides to the second question.

As we have seen, Nietzsche claims that *The Birth of Tragedy* raises the problem of science—the problem, that is, of determining the character of our current commitment to scientific knowledge. Some commentators are reluctant to acknowledge the authority of the various prefaces Nietzsche added to his works in the second half of the 1880s, accusing him of a certain amount of anachronism and indeed, in some cases, of self-deception.[14] In the present case, however, it seems relatively clear that one of the central points of *The Birth of Tragedy* was indeed to draw precisely the distinction on which an investigation into the character of our commitment to truthfulness rests. In fact, Nietzsche credits Lessing with the distinction in question. In section 15, he writes, "Lessing, the most honest theoretical man, dared to announce that he cared more for the search after truth than for truth itself—and thus revealed the fundamental secret of science, to the astonishment, and indeed the anger, of the scientific community" (*BT*, sec. 15, p. 95). As we will see, *The Gay Science* makes a great deal of this basic distinction by way of accounting for what Nietzsche considers to be the piety of our commitment to the value of knowledge, our failure to recognize it as a form of will to power. For the moment, however, we need note only that in these remarks about Lessing he is stressing that 'caring for the search after truth' is not itself a *scientific* motive. But although he seeks a better

[14] See, once again, Julian Young, *Nietzsche's Philosophy of Art* (Cambridge: Cambridge University Press, 1992), especially the introduction and the epilogue, for a recent example of this sort of suspicion.

psychological understanding of that motive, nothing indicates that Nietzsche wishes in any way to impugn it. In itself, it is no better and no worse a motive than any other. He does, however, wish to remind us that, as a motive for engaging in scientific inquiry, an interest in the pursuit of truth, even for its own sake, is itself not yet *part* of such inquiry.

Being clear about the contrast between these two questions about knowledge is of crucial importance for our understanding of the will to knowledge generally. If we fail to recognize the distinction Nietzsche recommends here, we are likely, on the one hand, to miss the centrality of his concern with the virtue of honesty, and, on the other, to overestimate his interest in so-called epistemological questions in general. Among other things, we may be tempted to believe that his skepticism about the intelligibility of questions about the nature of knowledge somehow implies grounds for skepticism about the strength of his commitment to it. As we will see presently, it is precisely to such confusion that Nietzsche considers the 'Socratic optimist' to be prone. It is worth examining briefly his discussion of this form of 'optimism', if we want better to understand the distinction he urges us to draw between questions about the *nature* of knowledge and questions about our *commitment* to it.

Nietzsche writes, "Beside [Lessing's] isolated insight, born of an excess of honesty if not of exuberance, there is, to be sure, a profound *illusion* that first saw the light of the world in the person of Socrates: the unshakable faith that thought, using the thread of causality, can penetrate the deepest abysses of being, and that thought is capable not only of knowing being but even of *correcting* it" (ibid.).[15] This illusion lies behind what Nietzsche calls 'theoretical optimism'. Such optimism, he maintains, is contrasted with the 'pessimism of strength' he attributes to the tragic Greeks. This form of pessimism rejects the Socratic view that knowledge can make us happy. It is not clear, however, which *version* of that view the tragic pessimist really means to deny: that

---

[15] Julian Young argues that in rejecting Socratism Nietzsche means to reject the view that knowledge can 'correct' being. More specifically, he suggests that Nietzsche's early Schopenhauerian pessimism pits him against the Socratic conviction that scientific knowledge can relieve the kind of pointless and inevitable suffering that is our lot as human beings. This, according to Young, is what 'correcting' being means. On the Schopenhauerian view, knowledge in this sense cannot make us happy. While this is not the place to discuss the question of Nietzsche's pessimism, I think it is important to point out that his objections to theoretical optimism rest upon his more basic criticism of the Socratic separation of reason and instinct. Theoretical or Socratic optimism—the view that we, as knowers, can correct being—rests upon what Nietzsche finds to be this bogus distinction.

knowledge of *virtue* can make us happy or that, roughly, scientific knowledge of *nature* can do so. It would be odd, to say the least, to credit Socrates with the latter version. But, because Nietzsche contrasts pessimism with Socratic optimism, it might nevertheless appear tempting to suppose that the tragic Greeks were pessimistic only in the sense that they denied that human thought can correct being. In other words, we might suppose that the tragic Greeks were pessimistic only in the apparently straightforward sense that they deny that a human solution to the problem of suffering is possible. We might call this form of the view 'Schopenhauerian' pessimism. Nietzsche's point, however, is deeper than this reading suggests. For, as we have seen, the tragic Greeks were not in the grip of the sort of illusion that gave rise to Socratism in the first place. This, indeed, is what made them 'tragic' in Nietzsche's special sense of the term. So I think we have reason to want to resist an interpretation of their brand of pessimism according to which their concern with suffering is restricted to a conviction that human misery is somehow inevitable. The unavoidability of pain and suffering is not the problem with our lives as the Socratist sees it, nor is it the problem as the tragic Greeks see it. Rather, the problem seems to be that our lives make sense. This is what tragedy celebrates, on the one hand, and what Socratism resists, on the other. And although both tragedy and Socratism suffer from the world's intelligibility, they do not understand their suffering in the same way.

To put this point in the terms I introduced in the last chapter, we may say that Nietzsche's criticism of Socratism implies that the tragic Greeks were pessimistic only in the sense that they found unintelligible the Socratic tendency to treat obedience to the authority of culture as a matter of interpretation. If such a view does not seem properly pessimistic, we should recall that Nietzsche believed that these individuals suffered from an overfullness of life and that theirs was a pessimism of *strength*.

Nietzsche's tragic Greeks, then, were pessimistic just insofar as they were able to avoid treating obedience as interpretation, to forego the temptation to try, as Nietzsche puts it elsewhere, to look around their own corner. Theoretical optimism, on the other hand, tries to respond to this temptation directly by seeking firm and unequivocal foundations for judgment.

The suggestion in the passage at hand is that a certain conception of the nature of knowledge infects the way in which the Socratic theoretical optimist cares for the search after truth. He expects knowledge to be of firm foundations, to be of something lying relevantly *outside* the circle of his inherited opinions. If the accumulation of beliefs does not afford us access to such foundations, then, from the theoretical optimist's point of view, they are worthless. Thus, if rational inquiry provides nothing more than further information about our practices with our concepts, then it will be of no interest to the theoretical optimist. For if one is troubled—in the way Nietzsche thinks the Socratic optimist is troubled—by the so-called contingency of culture, then the accumulation of further facts about the ways in which members of the culture in question happen to confront the world will simply be irrelevant.

For Socratic optimism, then, the questions of the nature of knowledge itself and of our drive to acquire knowledge are inextricably intertwined. Indeed, the faith in the powers of reason that Nietzsche attributes to the theoretical optimist depends upon a certain robust conception of the nature of knowledge. Thus, giving up a certain picture of knowledge imperils the optimist's interest in its acquisition. Lessing's insight about the separability of the drive to truth and the character of truth itself stands in sharp contrast to this sort of optimism. He suggests that an interest in the *pursuit* of truth can in fact survive philosophical disillusion about its *nature*.

Nietzsche shares with Lessing this conviction that, despite the intimate connection upon which the theoretical optimist insists between a particular philosophical conception of knowledge and his commitment to the acquisition of knowledge, the commitment can—and in fact does—survive the unmasking of philosophical illusions about the status of knowledge itself. Unlike Lessing, however, Nietzsche maintains that the commitment that survives this unmasking remains fundamentally moral in character. Our will to truth, he says, is still pious. These considerations strongly suggest that Nietzsche does not believe that such piety necessarily depends upon a metaphysical conception of truth. This is a point to which I will return in the next chapter.

In *The Birth of Tragedy*, Nietzsche maintains that theoretical optimism comes to grief upon the collapse of the illusion that human cognition can plumb the depths of being:

Science, spurred by its powerful illusion, speeds irresistibly toward its limits where its optimism, concealed in the essence of logic, suffers shipwreck. For the periphery of the circle of science has an infinite number of points; and while there is no telling how this circle could ever be surveyed completely, noble and gifted men nevertheless reach, e'er half their time and inevitably, such boundary points on the periphery from which one gazes into what defies illumination. When they see to their horror how logic coils up at these boundaries and finally bites its own tail—suddenly the new form of insight breaks through, *tragic insight* which, merely to be endured, needs art as a protection and remedy. (*BT*, sec. 15, pp. 97–98)

Nietzsche, clearly enough, has Kant in mind here. Not surprisingly, he credits him with bringing home to us what we should not be too quick to call 'the limits of human cognition'. Both Kant and Nietzsche hold that scientific knowledge does not have to be surveyed as a whole for us to understand its character and limits. The optimism concealed in the essence of logic of which Nietzsche speaks here is the promise of reaching a final cause, some ultimate antecedent condition of all phenomena. To put the point in properly Kantian terms, human reason is structured in such a fashion as to outstrip the understanding in this way. Thus, Nietzsche believes, by having shown that the promise of a final cause is a hollow one—except perhaps insofar as it can be understood as a regulative fiction or ideal—Kant demonstrated that what Socratic optimism believes it needs cannot in fact be secured.

Now, as we will see later in this chapter, Nietzsche gives a distinctive twist to these ideas. In particular, his denial of the coherence of the notion of a thing-in-itself leads him to a rather unusual conception of the so-called limits of knowledge. For though he argues that the theoretical optimism falls prey to the illusion that human reason can plumb the depths of being, recognizing this illusion does not mean acknowledging that anything must go unknown, that a thing-in-itself lies somehow outside the bounds of sense. Rather, overcoming the illusions involved in theoretic optimism is a matter of recognizing the confusion expressed by the very idea of such a thing.

The Birth of Tragedy thus offers the following genealogy of the development of the modern will to knowledge: Socratism is originally rooted in an error about the nature of obedience. Because, according to Socrates, the danger confronting us is that of the arbitrariness or groundlessness of that obedience, no fact about the latter can possibly ensure its necessity. In other words, no fact about the way we go on with our concepts can guarantee that ours is the right way of going on with them. Socrates, therefore, seeks something completely independent of the fact of obedience—something utterly distinct from our practices with the concept in question—that could serve to provide those practices with adequate rational foundation.[16] And, as we have seen, if the Socratic philosopher were to decide that in fact we do not have access

---

[16] Socratic optimism, I have argued, consists in the conviction that in fact there *is* some such thing and that we have access to it—access, that is, to something completely independent of our practices which would provide those practices with suitably rational foundations.

to anything that is in this way independent of our practices, he would be reduced to despair. Nietzsche insists, however, that such despair is unnecessary and misguided, for he is convinced that our commitment to truthfulness can survive insight into the limits of human reason.

Nietzsche's Conception of Knowledge: The Gay Science, Sections 108–25

In this section, I want to begin to discuss what Nietzsche takes to be the chief consequence of our modern commitment to truthfulness: what *The Gay Science* calls 'the unbelievability of belief in the Christian god'.[17] He says that a commitment to truthfulness makes certain beliefs unbelievable; I want to suggest that it does so primarily by showing that the problems to which those beliefs functioned as solutions cannot be understood on their own terms. Thus, if we take Platonism as our example of a body of beliefs that, in Nietzsche's view, a commitment to truthfulness renders unbelievable, then we may put his claim about the unbelievability of those beliefs in the following terms: rather than attempting to show that the Platonist's views are false, the modern will to knowledge calls into question the intelligibility of the questions that give rise to such views in the first place. He means, that is, to question the tenability of our interpretation of the needs to which, to stick with our example, Platonism answers.

I will restrict my attention in this section to the aphorisms that open the third book of *The Gay Science*. These passages, however, are emblematic of Nietzsche's later reflections on knowledge in general.[18] As we will see, the account of the will to knowledge that Nietzsche sketches in book III refines *The Birth of Tragedy*'s account of the development of Socratism. In the next section, then, I will try to articulate in much more general terms the conception of knowledge that seems to me to underwrite this genealogy. It is, I will argue, a conception that is as much a consequence of the latter as it is a presupposition of it.

[17] See *The Gay Science*, sec. 343.

[18] The justification for taking these passages as emblematic of Nietzsche's mature conception of the will to knowledge will become apparent only in the context of my interpretation of these remarks. At the level of the text itself, however, the centrality of the opening sections of book III of *The Gay Science* is signaled by the fact that passages in question are bracketed by Nietzsche's saying both in sec. 108 and in sec. 125 that God is dead. I suggest that the sections that lie between these aphorisms are meant to explain what that claim means, and that sec. 125 comments on the fact and nature of our unwillingness to acknowledge something that Nietzsche thinks we can now hardly fail to know.

How, then, shall we understand the effect of our current commitment to truthfulness? To begin, we need to understand the *kind* of error the will to knowledge uncovers. And this, as I have suggested, is not at all a straightforward matter. Nietzsche sums up the results of the *Genealogy* by claiming to have shown how Christianity comes to grief at the hands of its own morality.[19] More precisely, he claims that it is the beliefs that constitute what he calls 'Christianity as dogma' that are gradually undermined by the Christian-moral imperative to be truthful.[20] Thus, in a passage I quoted above, he writes, "You see what it was that really triumphed over the Christian god: Christian morality itself, the concept of truthfulness that was understood ever more rigorously, the father confessor's refinement of the Christian conscience, translated and sublimated into a scientific conscience, into intellectual cleanliness at any price" (*GS*, sec. 357, p. 307). Nietzsche goes on to list some of these newly unbelievable beliefs: "Looking at nature as if it were proof of the goodness and governance of a god; interpreting history in honor of some divine reason, as a continual testimony of a moral world order and ultimate moral purposes; interpreting one's own experiences as pious people have long enough interpreted theirs, as if everything were providential, a hint, designed and ordained for the sake of the salvation of the soul". Such beliefs, he says, are *all over* now, they have "man's conscience *against* [them], [they are] considered indecent and dishonest by every more refined conscience—mendaciousness, feminism, weakness, and cowardice" (ibid.).

It is important to notice, however, that this sort of intellectual cleanliness refuses itself only "the *lie involved in belief in God*" (*GM* III, sec. 27, p. 160). The faith itself remains intact—indeed, principally in the form of the modern imperative to truthfulness. Thus, although Christianity *self*-destructs in this way, the moral imperative that ruins it cannot, on Nietzsche's view, critically assess itself in the same way that it has as-

---

[19] In this respect, of course, the story Nietzsche tells of the death of God parallels the story he tells of the death of tragedy. In both cases, it is a question of suicide—of an irreconcilable conflict in the values in question. Such a parallel is to be expected for, as Nietzsche says in the *Genealogy*, "All great things bring about their own destruction through an act of self-overcoming" (*GM* III, sec. 27, p. 161). See, in this connection, *The Birth of Tragedy*, sec. 11, p. 76.

[20] By distinguishing 'Christianity as dogma' from 'Christianity as morality', the *Genealogy* suggests that it is Christianity treated *as* a matter of belief that is rendered unbelievable by the demand that one be truthful. But the fact that the beliefs that Nietzsche associates with what he calls Christianity have become unbelievable does not by itself entail that the needs that those beliefs satisfied have been fully understood.

sessed Christian dogma.[21] Therefore, "What is now decisive against Christianity is our taste, no longer our reasons" (*GS*, sec. 132, p. 186). The latter have done all the work it was theirs to do.

But Nietzsche is convinced more specifically that the man of knowledge's commitment to truthfulness will eventually undermine his confidence in the intelligibility of the philosophical preconceptions and prejudices that are expressed in the original Socratic response to the collapse of instinct. For the will to truth questions the intelligibility of these prejudices as much as it does the specific philosophical theories built upon them. And it is, I think, with the confrontation between the will to truth and our philosophical preconceptions that Nietzsche is especially occupied in the opening sections of book III.[22]

In these passages, as in *The Birth of Tragedy*, he is struggling to understand how "knowledge and the striving for the true [eventually] found their place as a need among other needs" (*GS*, sec. 110, p. 170). He wants, that is, to make clear how "knowledge became a piece of life itself, and hence a continually growing power" (ibid., p. 171). To this end, he relates a brief history of the development of what he calls a "subtler honesty and skepticism" (ibid., p. 170). According to *The Gay Science*, the "scrutiny, denial, mistrust, and contradiction" (ibid.) that express themselves in such 'subtler honesty and skepticism' eventually call into question our faith in those "errors" which, he says, have so far proven necessary to the survival of the human species.

In Nietzsche's view, then, for someone committed to truth at any price, the errors that once were necessary to the preservation of his form of life may no longer be so. This is the claim we need most to understand, for it is, as I have suggested, with the friction between the will to knowledge and these errors that Nietzsche is most concerned in the passages at hand. What I want to insist is that the errors in question are not simply the philosophical views that may have developed in response to the specific problems facing human beings, but rather the philosophical interpretations of those problems themselves.

Nietzsche maintains that, in general, "the falseness of a judgment is for us not necessarily an objection to a judgment; in this respect our new language may sound strangest. The question is to what extent

---

[21] This is why he says that 'the problem of science cannot be recognized in the context of science'.

[22] It is extremely important not to underestimate the significance of this second point. Nietzsche maintains not only that a commitment to truthfulness comes into conflict with our specifically philosophical, religious, and moral beliefs, but also—and more basically—that that commitment is at odds with the philosophical, religious, and moral interpretations of the 'needs' those beliefs pretend to satisfy.

it is life-promoting, life-preserving, perhaps even species-cultivating" (*BGE*, sec. 4, p. 11). But this remark suggests that, on Nietzsche's account, until we are clear about the needs that lie behind someone's holding such and such a view to be true, we will not understand what work the believer's beliefs do for him. Nor will the falsity of those beliefs truly matter to the believer until *he* is clear about the use to which he puts them.[23] Thus, because Nietzsche seeks in this way a diagnosis of the impulse to philosophy, he is much less interested in the content of specific philosophical claims than in what he thinks our tendency to make such claims shows about us.

According to *The Birth of Tragedy*, the principal error necessary to the survival of the posttragic Greeks is to be found in a certain understanding of the role reason plays in human life. But this error, we saw, involves a misinterpretation of the problem that reason—in the form of theoretical optimism—had to solve. As we saw, Nietzsche's claim against Socratism was not that we must learn to live without reasons, but rather that we must come to see where it no longer makes sense to *ask* for reasons. And, for Nietzsche, where it makes no sense to ask for a justification, it makes no sense to say that we must learn to do without one. Thus, as theoretical optimism begins to recognize what it wants to call the 'limits' of human cognition, it must learn to distinguish between truth and its commitment to truth, or it must perish. As we saw, drawing the distinction between truth and the commitment to truth does not mean giving up the life of reason altogether, but rather reconceiving—or as Nietzsche says elsewhere, 'revaluing'—its character.

I think, then, that if we follow Nietzsche's lead in *The Birth of Tragedy*, we will see that in general the errors under examination in the opening sections of the third book of *The Gay Science* give voice to similar philosophical worries about the nature of the relationship between the ways in which we experience the world and the way the world is 'in itself'. They are a reaction, in other words, to a particular misunderstanding of our place in the world. Most generally, I think, what Nietzsche considers to be erroneous here is thinking that good sense can be made of

---

[23] Nietzsche allows, therefore, for a fairly remarkable degree of self-deception on the part of the philosopher. On his account, it is as though, in the present age, the philosopher said to himself, 'I know that such and such is false, but I don't believe that it is'. What, according to Nietzsche, brings knowledge and belief together here is an accurate understanding of the use to which the philosopher's theories have so far been put. Thus (and to anticipate), only once he understands that the thing-in-itself is a obstacle that he erects between himself and the world will the philosopher be able to avoid drawing skeptical conclusions, having understood that he is not entitled to speak of a thing-in-itself.

philosophical talk of a *relationship* in this context. Indeed, it is precisely such talk that has become unbelievable to the men of knowledge. Those whose survival is in question in these same sections, then, are those who suffer in one way or another from the fact of obedience, but who misinterpret the object of their suffering as the groundlessness of their culture.[24]

[24] In this context, it is worth reflecting for a moment on the difference between the sort of philosophical errors at stake in the opening sections of this part of *The Gay Science* and the more specifically religious errors Nietzsche discusses elsewhere. It is not always clear what, in his view, distinguishes Christianity from Platonism. Both are condemned for denying life. That is to say, Nietzsche attacks both Christianity and philosophy on the grounds that they turn us away from the world. By the same token, they both involve harmful falsehoods and are to be, on this ground, rejected by the man of knowledge. But if indeed Christianity and Platonism turn us away from the world, they obviously do so in very different—though related—ways: Platonism, on the one hand, is motivated by worries about groundlessness, whereas Christianity is concerned with sinfulness. But what, for Nietzsche, is the difference between rational foundations, on the one hand, and redemption on the other?

Both the Platonist and the Christian suffer from what, for these purposes, we can call 'human finitude'. But a philosophical search for rational foundations for judgment is different from a religious drive for redemption. In the case of the former, Nietzsche criticizes the Platonist for having erected a particular picture of our relationship to the world on the basis of the errors that gave rise to Socratism. In the case of the latter, he provides an elaborate psychological account of the origin of the very idea of sinfulness, and, as in philosophy, many errors are also involved in this particular understanding of human finitude. But the peculiarly religious interpretation of human suffering provided by the experience of sinfulness involves—both to a greater degree and in a different way from philosophy—a particular range of attitudes toward the human body. The idea, very roughly, is that, for the Christian, the body is the source of *evil*, whereas for the philosopher, it is the source of *error*. Moreover, the notion of ressentiment plays a much more prominent role in Nietzsche's psychology of the Christian than it does in his psychology of the philosopher.

Nietzsche means, however, to underscore the fact that a commitment to truthfulness is incompatible both with the errors on which Platonism rests and with the mendacity of Christianity. In the case of the former, the will to truth advocates the caution and care necessary for seeing that, as *The Gay Science* (sec. 111) puts the point, similarity does not imply identity. In the case of the latter, the will to truth advocates a psychological explanation of what were once supposed to be religious features of our experience of the world.

In the end, then, both sinfulness and groundlessness represent interpretations of human life that, in Nietzsche's view, have the effect of alienating us from the world, and they are both condemned *as such*. What is *false*, in Nietzsche's view, is this turning away from the world. That Christianity and Platonism do this in different ways does not seem to affect Nietzsche's judgment that they are false. In general, Nietzsche treats the form of Christianity to which he most objects as something achieved by means of (and expressed in terms of) false beliefs, as dogma. There may, even in Nietzsche's view, be interpretations of Christianity not subject to this sort of objection, which do not treat religion as ontotheology. Paul is always the real enemy here, not Jesus, and it remains an interesting question to ask what Nietzsche might have made of Kierkegaard's work.

The use to which Nietzsche puts the notions of survival and preservation in this context is, therefore, not at all straightforward.[25] To say that something contributes to someone's survival seems at first blush to mean only that it helps to make possible his continued existence. And we might think that Nietzsche meant in the passages at hand to say only that holding certain things to be true—whether or not they really are true—permits certain sorts of human beings to prolong their lives. But if, as I have argued, life is, for Nietzsche, a matter of making sense, then to say that something contributes to the preservation of someone's life is to say that it contributes to the sense he or she makes. On this reading, then, holding certain things to be true (specifically, that 'reasons' are needed) allowed those who became the men of knowledge to make sense of the situation in which they found themselves. Thus, when Nietzsche claims that the problem facing the posttragic Greeks was the collapse of their instincts, he means that their lives had become unintelligible to them. They failed, in particular, to see how they could make sense of their environment without having reasons for making the judgments they made. And although he believes that the Socratic demand for reasons in fact reflects a misunderstanding of the nature of human intelligibility, the philosophical search for grounding nonetheless functions as a way of responding to the world's perceived unintelligibility *precisely by construing the latter in such a fashion that the philosophical life of reason makes sense as a response to it.* Philosophy, in short, is a spectator's way of making sense of life.

Thus, the errors that *The Gay Science* says were once necessary to our survival are rooted in the kind of misunderstanding of and resistance to the world's intelligibility that fueled the original Socratic demand for reasons. The specific philosophical theses that conflict with the will to knowledge are, so to speak, the outcome of the original Socratic response to the collapse of instinct: those who try to live the Socratic life of reason will, in Nietzsche's view, eventually arrive at the sorts of specifically philosophical theses that the will to knowledge now finds unbelievable.[26] Such theses, however, should be assessed in terms of the errors that give rise to them, not primarily in terms of their intrinsic merit as philosophical theories. Once again, Nietzsche means most basi-

---

[25] See, in particular, secs. 110 and 111 of *The Gay Science.*

[26] I do not mean to suggest that Nietzsche believes that every philosophical position is a direct descendant of Socratism itself. The claim is, rather, that the kinds of needs Nietzsche diagnoses beneath the sorts of belief that constitute Christianity as dogma are importantly similar to the ones that drive the original demand for reasons. In each case, it is a need that tends to misconstrue and to disguise itself as a need for grounding, though the picture of grounding will differ from case to case.

cally to ask to what use we put these sorts of belief.[27] This is why I have insisted that his work is most illuminatingly mined for *diagnoses* of philosophical views rather than for arguments against them.

Nietzsche concludes the line of thought we have been examining with the following remark: "We have arranged for ourselves a world in which we can live—by positing bodies, lines, planes, causes and effects, motion and rest, form and content; without these articles of faith nobody now could endure life. But that does not prove them. Life is no argument. The conditions of life might include error" (*GS*, sec. 121, p. 177). Such errors, in other words, can be part of the sense one makes, part of the way in which one makes oneself intelligible. To find them unbelievable is to be unable any longer to make them function as such.

I have been arguing that Nietzsche considers the modern will to knowledge a refinement of the original Socratic demand for reasons. The latter plays a crucial role in Nietzsche's genealogy of what we have become in the present age. But this reading implies that, in his view, the Socratic demand eventually turns on itself; no external criticism of it was needed. This development, however, took time. "It was only very late," Nietzsche says, "that such propositions [as that there are things, substances, bodies; that the will is free, and so on] were denied and doubted; it was only very late that truth emerged—as the weakest form of knowledge" (*GS*, sec. 110, p. 169). It is only now, that is, that men of knowledge have the intellectual leisure—provided by 2,500 years of philosophical and, more lately, scientific reflection—to question the original Socratic failure to understand tragedy.

Locating the errors Nietzsche mentions in the opening sections of the third book of *The Gay Science* only 2,500 years in the past may seem not to place them at a great enough historical distance from the present.[28] Indeed, Nietzsche at least appears to be speaking, in these first

---

[27] If there is a pragmatism to be found in Nietzsche's work, I think it lies somewhere in this direction. But he has no more a pragmatic view of the nature of truth than he does any other view about it. What is pragmatic is the suggestion that we should understand philosophical, religious, and moral beliefs in terms of the use to which they are put. Psychoanalysis may also be said to be pragmatic in this sense.

[28] Readers who are tempted to treat Nietzsche as a phenomenalist may be inclined to think of him as imagining (say, as a matter of historical reconstruction) the errors in question as occurring very far in the past. Alternately, such readers may feel that these errors—like Kantian synthesis—occur all the time, whether we are aware of them or not. If we think of the notions of life, survival, and preservation in evolutionary terms, we are likely to be partial to the former reading. I want to suggest, however, that to treat Nietzsche as a phenomenalist in this sense is to miss the deeper significance of his talk of errors in this context. A flat-footed evolutionary reading of his talk of 'life-preserving errors' does not afford us a clear of view of the sense in which 'positing bodies, lines, planes' and so forth permits us to endure life. We

few aphorisms at least, of more remote reaches of the past. He writes for example that "over immense periods of time [*ungeheure Zeitstrecken hindurch*] the intellect produced nothing but errors. A few of these proved to be useful and helped to preserve the species: those who hit upon or inherited these had better luck in their struggle for themselves and their progeny" (ibid.). We should remember, however, that here, as elsewhere, Nietzsche is trying to account for what we have become in the present age. Thus, to take the phrase *ungeheure Zeitstrecken* to refer to some very far removed region of our prehistorical past makes it difficult to understand the sorts of errors Nietzsche thinks are at stake here and consequently very difficult to understand what he might have intended by trying to call them into question.

In short, I think, Nietzsche took the tragic Greeks as the starting place for his attempt to understand the modern will to knowledge. They are remote enough for genealogical work. And because he starts here, he has some idea of the kind of errors that once 'proved useful and helped to preserve the species', as well as of what it might be like now to live without them. In any event, as I have claimed, the sorts of errors with which Nietzsche credits Socratism are those which have become decisive for us in the present age; it with these that he is most concerned. Let us turn now to the opening sections of book III of *The Gay Science*.[29]

Section 108 opens the third book of *The Gay Science* by turning what is probably Plato's most famous image on its head: "God is dead," Nietzsche writes, "but given the way of men, there may still be caves for thousands of years in which his shadow will be shown." As we will see, what this remark implies is that, though the death of God may have rendered unbelievable our attempts to view either the world or ourselves as in any way fashioned by a divine being, we may still wish to view the world as made, so to speak, in *our* own image—still be tempted, that is, to think that we need a philosophically informative account of why the world appears to answer to our descriptions of it. Section 108 suggests that this wish remains live even in the face of our initial recognition of the unbelievability of the belief in God.

There are, according to Nietzsche, a variety of ways of giving in to this wish—various forms of this fantasy—not the least of which is theo-

---

have good reason not to be confident that we possess at the outset an adequate understanding of Nietzsche's usage of the word 'life' in these contexts.

[29] I do not pretend to have presented an incontrovertible argument against an evolutionary reading of Nietzsche. It should be clear, however, that any such reading must be able to show how the errors once necessary to our survival give rise to what Nietzsche considers the moral imperative that calls those same errors into question.

retical optimism.[30] In section 109, however, he sketches a more general picture of what we must struggle against if the shadow of God is not to obscure our vision: we must, he urges, avoid 'anthropomorphizing' [*Vermenschlichung*] the universe. We must not succumb to our wish to pass from claims about how things appear to us to philosophical claims about the relationship between how they appear and how they are 'in themselves'. Far, however, from encouraging us to remain agnostic about the character of the so-called real world, Nietzsche wants us rather to disavow such talk altogether.

The Gay Science recommends 'caution and care' against the philosophical distinction between appearance and reality, and, if we keep *The Birth of Tragedy* in mind, it is fairly clear on which sort of caution Nietzsche in fact insists. As we have seen, he wants in general to check our tendency to treat what I have called 'obedience' as an interpretation of the world. Once we succumb to this temptation, the question of what justifies that interpretation immediately arises. Nietzsche claims in section 109 that when we think about the total character of the universe in terms of our conceptions of organic life or mechanism, or in terms of the world's perceivable order, we are in effect drawing conclusions about the way things are in themselves from a particular description of the way they seem to us to be. That the universe itself answers to our notions of life, purpose, or order is precisely the sort of philosophical claim Nietzsche believes stands in need of justification. And although he believes we lack any such justification, his call in section 109 to avoid anthropomorphizing the universe is a call to avoid making the sorts of claims that give rise to the demand for justification in the first place.[31]

[30] Though Nietzsche considers Socrates to be the "type of the *theoretical man*" (*BT*, sec. 15, p. 94), he is the "prototype" [*Urbild*] (ibid., p. 97) of the theoretical *optimist* as well. That is to say, not only does Socrates find existence wanting, but he proposes a solution to this problem as well.

[31] Nietzsche writes, "Let us beware of thinking that the world is a living being. Where should it expand? On what should it feed? How could it grow and multiply? We have some notion of the nature of the organic; and we should not reinterpret the exceedingly derivative, late, rare, accidental that we perceive only on the crust of the earth and make of it something essential, universal, and eternal, which is what those people do who call the universe an organism. This nauseates me. Let us even beware of believing that the universe is a machine: it is certainly not constructed for one purpose, and calling it a 'machine' does it far too much honor" (*GS*, sec. 109, p. 167). Nietzsche is here trying to undermine two ways in which we may be tempted to think of the 'world itself' as answering to our categories: the world can, in his view, be said to be neither an organism nor a machine—neither something living nor something mechanical. Nietzsche's argument has the following form: we are entitled to apply the notions of organicity or of mechanism only where they are applicable: only where we can say in what sense something is organic or mechanical. And from Nietzsche's point of view, it is a sign of confusion and foggy thinking to suppose that

According to Nietzsche, when we anthropomorphize the universe we forget that, from the point of view of the economy of the universe as a whole, we are merely what he calls 'exceptions'. "The type of the living," he says, "is merely a type of what is dead, and a very rare type" (*GS*, sec. 109, p. 168). That is to say, our grip on the difference between life and death is not firm enough to justify a philosophical inflation of notions applicable to the former into a picture of the state of things in general. Once again, Nietzsche is insisting that we have no good grounds for taking ourselves to be the measure of the universe itself. Thus, the 'total character of the universe' cannot be said to be, for example, that of a machine, if we cannot (as Nietzsche suggests we cannot) make sense of the idea that the universe was made for some purpose. But we need to understand whether this claim amounts to a recommendation of modesty or whether the latter would not itself be a form of precisely the sort of anthropomorphism Nietzsche wants to discourage.

What, then, does Nietzsche think *can* safely be said about the universe if our notions of life, purpose, and order have no application to it? How shall we understand what he appears to think of as limits to the employment of these notions? The 'total character of the universe', he says, is "in all eternity chaos—in the sense not of a lack of necessity but of a lack of order, arrangement, form, beauty, wisdom, and whatever other names there are for our aesthetic anthropomorphisms" (ibid.). But what does 'chaos' mean here? Does Nietzsche believe that anthropomorphizing the universe is unjustified because the world's true nature is in some way fundamentally at *odds* with our notions of life, purpose, and order? Is he claiming, for example, to know that this is so?

It is tempting to suppose that chaos refers to what Nietzsche might have thought of as something like the ultimate object of all our interpre-

---

the world itself is in any interesting sense either organic or mechanical. Such an argument has the form of a challenge. Nietzsche is demanding that his interlocutor explain in what sense the universe can be said to be organic or mechanical. It may, of course, be possible to answer this challenge, but it is at least fairly clear what sort of consideration Nietzsche would find relevant here: it will not do, he implies, to say that the universe is an immense machine that is constructed to no purpose. The anthropomorphizing philosopher cannot simply say, 'You know, like a building, but no builder'. For the idea of purpose is built into the ideas of construction and of mechanism. It is difficult to know how far to push this sort of reading, because it is, of course, possible to resist the last suggestion and to ask how Nietzsche knows that this is so. His response, I think, would be to ask once again how these notions might be pried apart.

tations, that upon which, as he says, we 'press the stamp' of being.[32] On this reading, 'chaos' would be another name for what he sometimes calls 'becoming'. This thought underwrites the impression that, in saying that we posit bodies, lines, planes, and so on, Nietzsche wishes us to recognize that the order we seem to find in the world is, in reality, only imposed upon it by us. On this reading, the world's true character is not that of being but rather of flux or becoming.[33] Because, however, we cannot live except in terms of the categories of being—of substance, attribute, and so on—we must, if we are to survive, somehow force the world to answer to those categories. This at least appears to be a compelling reading of a remark like the following: "To impose upon becoming the character of being—that is the supreme will to power" (*WP*, sec. 617, p. 330).

According to this interpretation, Nietzsche is supposed to have believed that, in the wake of the death of God, we should take responsibility for the meanings we impose upon the world rather than try to foist that responsibility onto the world itself. This reading lets the notion of 'imposition' guide our interpretation of the concept of responsibility.[34] Understood in this way, the caution and care Nietzsche urges in section 109 should be taken as a warning not to think that we register our having understood the significance of the death of God simply by acknowledging that the order of things is found in the world rather than being imposed upon it by God. Such an acknowledgment would stop short of recognizing our responsibility for the order the world appears to have. Let me try to say why such an interpretation fails as a reading of section 109.

---

[32] See *The Will to Power*, sec. 617. The term Nietzsche uses here is *aufprägen*. Heidegger makes much of the word *Prägung*. Talk of impressing or stamping the character of being upon the 'flux' of becoming is one way to convey the idea that the meaning of events is not simply found or discovered in them, but rather imposed upon them, *created*. I will argue, however, that this relatively straightforward reading of Nietzsche's talk of imposing meaning upon the world is hopelessly at odds with the main thrust of his thought. As in the case of his early Schopenhauerian descriptions of tragedy, the interpretative choice we face here is either to acknowledge a deep tension in his thinking or to find an interpretation of the notions that appear to betoken deep confusion. I recommend the latter approach.

[33] Barry Allen briefly discusses the remarks that most naturally invite this sort of reading in "Nietzsche's Question, 'What Good is Truth?'" See, for example, secs. 517, 715, and 584 of *The Will to Power*. Allen, however, is understandably skeptical about whether Nietzsche ever intended such remarks to provide fuel for a properly metaphysical view of the world's nature.

[34] I want to argue that such an approach gets Nietzsche's meaning backward: we should let the concept of responsibility guide our interpretation of the notion of imposition.

The concept of chaos, I suggest, must be on the same conceptual register as the notions of life, purpose, and order: either we know what we are talking about here or we do not. If we do, then, in the present context at least, chaos is a notion of which we have neither more nor less of a conceptual grasp than we do of life, purpose, and order. And if we do not, then 'chaos' can only be another name for the Kantian thing-in-itself, a notion that, as we shall see, Nietzsche rejects as nonsensical.

It is therefore difficult to see why Nietzsche would use the term 'chaos' as a name for the supposedly real character of the universe—as a name, that is, for something that our notions of life, purpose, and order would fail to capture. His talk of chaos, I think, is better read as warning us away from trying to entertain thoughts about the total character of the universe at all. Indeed, from Nietzsche's point of view, if such thoughts were not in some way harmful, they would simply be idle.

How, then, should we understand his talk of chaos in section 109? It is helpful to bear in mind the fact that the remarks at the beginning of book III are genealogical in nature: Nietzsche is trying in these passages to offer his readers a description of how they—the men of knowledge—got to where they are. Viewed in this light, his talk of chaos here is best understood as a way of drawing our attention to the character of the world prior to our philosophizing about it. *That*, however, is not a brute unconceptualized one-knows-not-what, but rather the intelligible space in which we all live day to day. This is what Nietzsche thinks we try to resist by means of philosophical anthropomorphism. Such a reading, I now want to argue, is the most natural way to take Nietzsche's remarks about chaos once we have gotten over the idea that he means thereby to characterize the world as it is in itself.

To begin, we should note that *The Gay Science* does not offer a *positive* characterization of the total character of the universe as chaos. The intelligibility of this sort of description was ruled out by his warning us away from the application of our notion of purpose to the universe: we can speak neither of the purpose of the universe as a whole nor of its lack of purpose. According to section 109, the total character of the universe cannot be characterized except as an absence of *every* way in which we might try to construe it in our image. But this restriction should include Nietzsche's own talk of the total character of the universe as well. The question, then, is whether his remarks about chaos and the total character of the universe represent an attempt to speak in a way that the present passage suggests we cannot speak.

Section 109's discussion of anthropomorphism should, I suggest, be read dialectically. To speak of limiting the application of our fundamental categories of reason only tends to cloud the issues here. Though on the surface Nietzsche appears concerned to warn us not to think that the intelligible order of things is found simply written into nature, behind this warning lies the further suggestion that we cannot meaningfully speak of the order of things as simply *imposed* upon nature either.

To see this, notice that Nietzsche is speaking from what might be called the point of view of reason itself. As we might expect, this is not a point of view that he believes we can do without. Thus, in *The Will to Power*, he writes, *"we cease to think when we refuse to do so under the constraint of language; we barely reach the doubt that sees this limitation [Grenze] as a limitation"* (*WP*, sec. 522, p. 283). As we will see, because we cannot think except under the constraint of language and because *"rational thought is interpretation according to a scheme that we cannot throw off"* (ibid.), the doubt that he says we barely reach here tends to misconstrue itself as an experience of limits or boundaries, of *Grenzen*. Indeed, the point of insisting that rational thought is interpretation according to a scheme that we cannot throw off is precisely to remind us that good sense cannot be made of philosophical talk of limitations and boundaries in this context. It is, in short, only from the standpoint of *philosophy*—the standpoint Nietzsche is attacking here—that language and reason seem like limitations. Such doubts as we might have about our lives in language are, therefore, badly expressed in these terms. Appearances notwithstanding, then, in *The Will to Power*, section 522, as in *The Gay Science*, Nietzsche is not stressing the difficulty of recognizing that rationality imposes limitations upon our thinking.[35] Rather, his point is to show that we can, as he says, only barely make sense of the talk of limitations in this context at all. We must, therefore, learn to resist the idea that Nietzsche meant somehow to encourage us to accept responsibility for the order we find in the world. For there is nothing in this sense to accept responsibility for, and no one in this sense to do the accepting. We will have to make sense of Nietzschean talk of responsibility in substantially different terms.

It is important to recall that *The Gay Science* warns us not to conclude from the universe's apparent lack of life, purpose, and order that it is more correctly thought of in terms of "heartlessness and unreason" (*GS*, sec. 109, p. 168). The universe, he says, is "neither perfect nor

---

[35] Nietzsche insists, in fact, that it is a "higher triumph" of the ascetic ideal to make us think that there is a realm beyond reason. He speaks here of the "voluptuous pleasure that reaches its height when the ascetic self-contempt and self-mockery of reason declares: *'there is* a realm of truth and being, but reason is *excluded* from it!'" (*GM* III, sec. 12, p. 118).

beautiful, nor noble, nor does it wish to become any of these things; it does not by any means strive to imitate man. None of our aesthetic and moral judgments apply to it"[36] (ibid.). This last thought, however, is deceptive.

As we have seen, an ostensibly natural way to take the claim that none of our aesthetic and moral judgments apply to the universe itself is to understand Nietzsche as insisting that we have no justification for the claim that those judgments do indeed apply to it. On this reading, Nietzsche would, in these passages, be endorsing a kind of epistemological modesty—indeed, a kind of skepticism—on the supposed basis of our inability to achieve a standpoint independent enough of our most basic concepts and categories to assess the adequacy of those categories to the world as it is in itself. This account of Nietzsche's claim thus goes hand in glove with the interpretation of the notion of chaos I rejected above.

Though Nietzsche's remarks seem to invite this reading, it is nevertheless fundamentally at odds both with his denial of the thing-in-itself and with his claim that we cease to think when we try to do so outside the boundaries—*Grenzen*—of rationality. The latter claim denies us the conceptual distance from those boundaries necessary even to begin to see them *as* boundaries. As we have seen, however, this does not mean that Nietzsche believes there is something that we inevitably fail to recognize here. His point is rather that there are no grounds for speaking of boundaries in this context at all.

In urging caution and care, then, Nietzsche is not suggesting that we should acknowledge the limits of human cognition. Section 109 is meant, rather, to tell us something about the very notion of the total character of the universe. It is not to *that*, he insists, that our aesthetic and moral judgments apply; they apply instead to the world. And, as I have said, that they *do* apply to the world is, in the end, what Nietzsche believes we are trying to deny when we anthropomorphize the universe in the ways section 109 sketches for us. According to section 109, then, talk of acknowledging the limits of human cognition could only be another version of the same anthropomorphism Nietzsche would have us avoid. Let us see what light these considerations shed on the nature of the errors that *The Gay Science* suggests are uncovered by the modern will to knowledge.

Nietzsche mentions various "primeval basic errors" [*uralten Grundirr-thuemer*] (*GS*, sec. 110, p. 171) that he insists are typical of a traditionally

---

[36] The German reads, "Es wird durchaus durch keines unserer aesthetischen und moralischen Urtheile getroffen!"

philosophical conception of life. These are the sorts of belief that the imperative to truthfulness eventually calls into question, and, as such, they may be compared with those that constitute Christianity as dogma.[37] "Such erroneous articles of faith, which were continually inherited, until they became almost part of the basic endowment of the species, include the following: that there are enduring things; that there are equal things; that there are things, substances, bodies; that a thing is what it appears to be; that our will is free; that what is good for me is also good in itself" (GS, sec. 110, p. 169). These sorts of views, I have suggested, express what Nietzsche takes to be the subsequent development of the original Socratic quest for justification, and I do not see any truly compelling reason to take his description of these errors here to be more fine grained than that.[38] These are, in other words, examples of a certain kind of thinking. Such articles of faith represent the fruits of our attempts to provide ourselves with a justification for the ways in which we experience the world. On the reading I am proposing, then, the anthropomorphic-philosophical construal of the claim that, for example, there are enduring things constitutes the kind of error without which the non-Socratic Greeks were able to live.[39]

[37] We may also compare Nietzsche's list of errors here to the articles of faith that he mentions in section 121, as well as to the four errors of section 115.

[38] Nietzsche, I suspect, draws up such lists for more than one reason, and we may, if we like, try to distinguish the different needs satisfied by different philosophical views. For example, the use to which belief in free will is put is not necessarily the same as that to which belief in enduring things is put. This fact suggests we may have reason to suppose that Nietzsche would have us distinguish religious, philosophical, and perhaps more specifically moral needs from one another. However significant in themselves, however, such refinements of his particular psychological views are not my main concern here. I mean, rather, to discuss the way in which the will to knowledge comes to question the specifically Socratic presuppositions of such views and, in the process, comes to question its own origins. Showing how this happens is Nietzsche's goal in section 111.

[39] It is difficult to know how best to put this point. From one point of view, it seems simply redundant to speak of a specifically *metaphysical* construal of the claim that there are enduring things—as though we knew what a *non*metaphysical construal of such a claim might mean. From another point of view, however, Nietzsche, as I read him, would hardly wish to *deny* that there are enduring things, if that meant committing himself to the view that there is something else instead. The situation seems more complicated in the case of religious belief. In this context, I take it, Nietzsche denies, first, that we have any reason to hold, for example, that the soul is immortal and, second, that there is indeed anything properly called the soul in a specifically Christian sense. In this particular case, Nietzsche does not suggest that there is a harmless—nonmetaphysical—version of the religious view of the soul that he might be willing to countenance. On the other hand, as we will see in Chapter 3, he does recognize a nonphilosophical usage of the idea of freedom of will. And he says, moreover, that we are permitted to develop nonphilosophical and nonreligious versions of the soul-hypothesis (see *Beyond Good and Evil*, sec. 12).

Our consideration of Nietzsche's use of the notion of chaos suggests that the reason he rejects a claim such as that 'there are enduring things' is not because it is at odds with the true character of the universe,[40] but rather simply because it pretends to be a claim about the true character of the universe at all. In calling such a claim an error, then, Nietzsche is not saying that people not inclined to formulate such views were able to live without enduring things—what, after all, could *that* mean?—but rather that they were able to live without entertaining either this sort of proposition or its denial in the first place. They were, in short, able not to anthropomorphize the universe, because they were immune to the philosophical devaluation of facts about the world in which they live into mere facts about the way in which they happen to view or, as I have put it, to interpret the world.

Belief in such erroneous articles of faith as Nietzsche mentions in section 110 and elsewhere thus turns on the *need* for such beliefs; these are life-preserving errors. Nietzsche's initial diagnostic claim is that one is susceptible to such errors only if one has need of them. But we need to know more about the nature of this need if we are to understand the meaning of this diagnosis. How, then, does Nietzsche conceive the need that issues in philosophical claims about the nature of the universe? What lies behind our anthropomorphizing?

Nietzsche believes that our anthropomorphisms represent life-preserving errors in the sense that they represent a response to—a way of living with—the collapse of instinct.[41] To understand the claim that it is life-preserving to entertain philosophical claims about the nature of the universe, it will help to go back to our earlier consideration of Socratism. It is in this context that we can most clearly see both what kind of error Nietzsche has in mind as well as the sense of preservation he intends.

In a passage I discussed in Chapter 1, Nietzsche makes it clear that when the Greeks' instincts collapsed, "rationality was . . . divined as a *saviour*; neither Socrates nor his 'invalids' were free to be rational or not, as they wished—it was *de rigueur*, it was their *last* expedient. The fanaticism with which the whole of Greek thought throws itself at rationality betrays a state of emergency: one was in peril, one had only *one* choice: either to perish or—be *absurdly rational*" (*TI*, "The Problem of Socrates," sec. 10, p. 33). Quite generally, Nietzsche believes that a philosophical solution can function successfully only by virtue of the

---

[40] Where it might be supposed, for example, that there *are* no enduring things.

[41] In this respect, belief in such errors resembles the ascetic ideals of the *Genealogy:* they permit us to survive for a time, but are eventually undermined.

way in which it construes the problem to which it proposes itself as a solution. In the case of the Socratic life of reason, the problem was understood to be one of justification or grounding: one's application of concepts to the world seemed arbitrary without an appeal to something lying wholly outside the actual use one made of them. Socratism offered the search for the required reasons as a solution to *that* problem. The reasons Socrates sought were supposed to provide the independent standpoint from which to guarantee the legitimacy of one's application of concepts.

Nietzsche suggests, however, that more cautious responses to this problem did not work. He says, "innumerable beings who made inferences in a way different from ours perished" (*GS*, sec. 111, p. 171). As in section 121, what Nietzsche wishes especially to stress here is that the success of the Socratic solution is not in itself a sign of its truth. But the point, again, is not just that these articles of faith are false. Rather, Nietzsche insists that there is no real philosophical problem to which such beliefs could conceivably function as a solution. There is, however, a *psychological* problem that can be construed as a philosophical difficulty in such a way that the Socratic solution makes good sense as a response.[42] It is in this sense that, as he says, life is no argument.

It is along these lines, then, that I want to read Nietzsche's talk in the initial aphorisms of the third book of *The Gay Science* of the errors that are necessary for life. In these same passages, however, he also wants to remind us that what distinguishes the men of knowledge from their Socratic ancestors is that, in the present age, they may no longer have to draw the conclusions that their predecessors drew. In other words, because the man of knowledge is clearer about—or at least because Nietzsche himself is clearer about—the nature of his psychological needs than were his Socratic ancestors, he can be more cautious now than they could then afford to be.

But Nietzsche insists that this state of affairs represents a *development*. "It is something new in history that knowledge wants to be more than a mere means" (*GS*, sec. 123, p. 180). "It was only *very late* that such propositions [that, for example, there are enduring things] were denied and doubted; it was only very late that truth emerged—as the weakest form of knowledge" (*GS*, sec. 110, p. 169, my emphasis). As we have seen, Nietzsche conceives of the doubt and denial to which such philosophical views can be subjected to be a matter of providing a diagnosis

[42] The point here is analogous to Stanley Cavell's suggestion that skepticism converts the human condition into an intellectual difficulty. See Stanley Cavell, *The Claim of Reason* (Oxford: Oxford University Press, 1979), p. 493.

of the philosophical errors without which the Socratic ancestors of the man of knowledge could not live. It is the modern will to knowledge itself that is expressed by such doubt and denial, and that provides Nietzsche with the diagnosis he seeks.

We want to know in what sense Nietzsche believes it is life-preserving to entertain philosophical views about the nature of the universe. In section 111, he asks,

> How did logic come into existence in man's head? Certainly out of illogic, whose realm originally must have been immense. Innumerable beings who made inferences in a way different [*anders schlossen*] from ours perished; for all that, their ways might have been truer. Those, for example, who did not know how to find often enough what is "equal" as regards both nourishment and hostile animals—those, in other words, who subsumed things too slowly and cautiously—were favored with a lesser probability of survival than those who guessed immediately upon encountering similar instances that they must be equal. The dominant tendency, however, to treat as equal what is merely similar—an illogical tendency, for nothing is really equal—is what first created any basis for logic. (*GS*, sec. 111, p. 171)

We should not let the ostensibly Darwinian overtones of these remarks mislead us. Nietzsche says that, because they understood things too slowly and cautiously, those who perished drew different conclusions from those who survived, or perhaps that they failed to draw certain conclusions where a less cautious intellect would not have hesitated.

To say that those who perished made inferences differently from those who survived, however, is not to suggest that—in the sense of obeying different laws of thought—they somehow *reasoned* differently from them. Such a claim would clearly court the incoherence we noted in our discussion of the notion of chaos. In that sense, we simply have no notion of different forms of inference. I think, therefore, that the inference that those who perished failed to make must have been what Nietzsche considers to be the life-preserving (but erroneous) one that what seems to be merely similar is in fact equal. In other words, on Nietzsche's view, those who perished did so *because* they were unable to treat as equal what is merely similar. But what does it mean not to treat as equal what is merely similar? What, that is, does it mean not to find mere similarity good enough? And what, finally, does it mean to perish of this inability?

Some, I suppose, may find it attractive to take literally the ostensibly evolutionary vocabulary Nietzsche employs in this passage. One might be tempted, for example, simply to stop short with the thought that Nietzsche is insisting here that those forms of life that were unable to connect a given experience of (say) being attacked by tigers or of being poisoned by such and such a plant with other 'similar' experiences eventually died out, and to conclude that, in Nietzsche's view, nature somehow selects for those forms of life that, on the contrary, are able to perform the falsifying feat of identification. I have been recommending, however, that we not assume at the outset that we know in what life— and hence survival—consists in this context. In any event, as far as the survival of the species is concerned, it is difficult to see why mere similarity would not be sufficient. For one need not posit equalities to call out 'There's another tiger!' or 'Don't eat that!'. Mere similarity would seem to be perfectly adequate for survival in this sense of the word.

To what, then, do Nietzsche's overtly biological metaphors here point? What does he mean by 'life' here? We should not ignore the hint that talk of similarity and equality offers us: for it is Socrates who demands that we substitute equalities for mere similarities. It is, in other words, Socratism that is unable to survive on mere similarities. As Nietzsche says, Socrates' Greeks had only one choice: either to perish or to become 'absurdly rational'.[43] It is they who, without the cure and expedient of Socrates, would perish in the absence of equalities. It is, in short, a certain *way* of life that dies out in the absence of reasons.

This reading suggests that to treat as equal what is merely similar is, for Nietzsche, to be disinclined to insist on there being something that all items of a given kind have in common that explains why they are items of that kind. To do without this insistence, however, is to be unable to respond to the Socratic demand for reasons. Ceasing to find philosophically problematic the ability to identify items of a given kind without appeal to reasons is what Nietzsche calls 'tragic insight'. However, to find that ability mysterious and yet *not* seek reasons to explain it is to feel oneself threatened by what Socratism calls 'contingency', but to lack a response to that threat. It is, we might say, to be anxious but to lack a way of dissolving one's anxiety. As we have seen, Nietzsche's suggestion in section 109 is that the real solution to such anxiety—one that is available to the men of knowledge—consists not in the search for reasons nor even in resolutely foregoing that search, but rather in the exercise of such caution and care as is necessary to uncover its true sources. Such circumspection, however, no more involves one in an alternative form of rationality than did the tentativeness of those who perished.

[43] See sec. 10 of "The Problem of Socrates," in *Twilight of the Idols*, p. 33.

In section 111, therefore, as in *The Birth of Tragedy*, Socratism seems to be the object of Nietzsche's diagnosis. For it is, of course, Socrates who treats as equal what is merely similar, in the sense that he insists that there must be something that, for example, all courageous actions have in common in virtue of which they are courageous, and Socrates who claims that an inability to specify—in the form of a definition— that common feature signals one's ignorance of the nature of courage. Nietzsche maintains, however, that nothing is really equal; there are nothing but similarities in life. There is, for example, no single respect or set of respects in which all courageous actions are similar to one another. The fact of their similarity does not, he insists, justify Socrates' insistence that we can recognize that similarity only on the basis of an underlying equality. To deny that anything is really equal means, therefore, to deny that there is such unity to our life with concepts as Socrates presupposes there must be. It is to claim that philosophical prejudice—and not reason—motivates the demand for more than mere similarity. To claim that treating as equal what is merely similar is what first creates the basis for logic, therefore, is Nietzsche's way of saying that it is this 'dominant tendency' that lies at the root of Platonism.

Our second question was what does it mean to perish of an inability to treat as equal what is merely similar? On the reading we are considering, Nietzsche maintains that those who failed to draw the peculiarly Socratic conclusion from their experience of similarities did not survive. If we avoid the evolutionary muddle discussed above and recall that, on Nietzsche's view, the Socratic Greeks had only one choice available to them—either to perish or to be absurdly rational—then the following interpretation suggests itself. To say that those who were unwilling or unable to treat as equal what is only similar perished is to say that one cannot avoid the search for reasons once the need for them has been felt and articulated as such. Socratism, in other words, was the only way to make sense of a life that otherwise failed to make sense. This is why Nietzsche says that the Greeks had need of Socrates as an expedient and a cure.

Thus, when in section 121 Nietzsche says that life is no argument in favor of the truth of philosophical claims about the nature of the world, he means that the fact that philosophical thinking in terms of 'causes and effects, motion and rest, form and content' allows certain forms of life to make sense of themselves does not prove that belief in such things is in principle necessary to all forms of life. Someone who was not prey to the philosophical demand for justification would simply have no need for such beliefs in their philosophical form, and therefore could make only psychological sense of someone who insisted that he did have need of them. As in *The Birth of Tragedy*, then, Nietzsche means to argue here that a willingness to entertain beliefs of this sort is a sign that something has gone wrong at the outset. The 'primeval basic errors' that he catalogues in the passage at hand—the belief in enduring things, substances, bodies, free will, cause and effect, and so forth—are the means whereby philosophers have sought to provide grounds where they mistakenly thought grounds were lacking.

This reading suggests, I think, that Nietzsche had no real interest in the nature of knowledge per se. For, as we have seen, on his view, the will to knowledge calls into question the point of view from which such interests are usually expressed. The undoing of epistemology, I suggest, is the ultimate consequence of the modern commitment to truthfulness. Thus, in a passage to which I have already referred, Nietzsche says that "in antiquity the dignity and recognition of science were diminished by the fact that even her most zealous disciples placed the striving for *virtue* first, and one felt that knowledge had received the highest praise when one celebrated it as the best means to virtue. It is something new in history that knowledge wants to be more than a mere means" (*GS*, sec. 123, p. 180). In the present age, in other words, the will to knowledge becomes a power in its own right. Thus, whereas Socratic dialectics functioned initially as a reactive means of coping with what presented itself as a fear of groundlessness or contingency—when knowledge, in other words, was thought to be a means to virtue—it eventually takes on a life of its own. As an *end*, however, the will to knowledge comes eventually to conflict with the errors involved in the pursuit of happiness by means of knowledge, that is, with what Nietzsche calls Socratism.

In the present passages, moreover, Nietzsche is *enacting* this conflict. That is to say, he is trying in these very passages to account for the necessity of what he himself is doing in these same passages. He himself is the "thinker . . . in whom the impulse for truth and those life-preserving errors clash for their first fight, after the impulse for truth has proved to be also a life-preserving power" (*GS*, sec. 110, p. 171). It is *as such* that he recounts the development of the will to knowledge—a development that he describes in the following terms:

> This subtler honesty and skepticism came into being wherever two contradictory sentences appeared to be *applicable* to life because both were compatible with the basic errors, and it was therefore possible to argue about the higher or lower degree of *utility* for life; also wherever new propositions, though not useful for life, were also evidently not harmful to life: in such cases there was room for the expression

of an intellectual play impulse, and honesty and skepticism were inno-
cent and happy like all play. Gradually, the human brain became full
of such judgments and convictions, and a ferment, struggle, and lust
for power developed in this tangle. Not only utility and delight but
every kind of impulse took sides in this fight about "truths." The
intellectual fight became an occupation, an attraction, a profession, a
duty, something dignified—and eventually knowledge and striving
for the true found their place as a need among other needs. (Ibid.,
p. 170)

Our reading of *The Birth of Tragedy* suggests a fairly natural interpretation of Nietzsche's remarks here about the 'two contradictory sentences
which appear applicable to life because they are both compatible with
the basic errors'. The basic errors Nietzsche has in mind are, I think,
those that motivate the Socratic life of reason, those that fuel the view
that knowledge is necessary to happiness. As we have seen, there are
indeed two contradictory claims that appear compatible with the fundamental features of the Greeks' experience of the world after the death
of tragedy: one is that such features are written into the nature of
things, and the other that such features are 'merely cultural'. Not being
tempted by this dichotomy characterizes tragic insight. If, however, one
has made the initial Socratic error of treating obedience as interpretation, then one may well find oneself pulled by either of the poles of
this dichotomy. Nietzsche's remarks in section 110 should be read along
the same lines. Seeing through this dichotomy would permit us to avoid
anthropomorphism, and this seems like a fair description of what
Nietzsche himself is trying to do in the passages at hand.

Nietzsche's Denial of the Thing-in-Itself

A principal implication of *The Birth of Tragedy's* attack on Socratism
is, I think, that Nietzsche had no real interest in articulating a properly
philosophical account of our relationship to the world. His lack of interest in the nature of knowledge is borne out in the passages from
The Gay Science that we have been exploring. We concluded that, on
Nietzsche's view, a commitment to truthfulness should undermine our
confidence that good sense can be made of the philosopher's assurance
that epistemological theories answer real questions. As I intimated at
the outset, then, the effect of the modern will to knowledge should
ultimately be to bring us to ask whether epistemological questions are
not really symptomatic of a kind of dissatisfaction with our lives that

tends in general to mischaracterize itself as a fear of being cut off from the world, confined to appearances.

I would like now to take up this last suggestion by means of an examination of Nietzsche's famous denial of the thing-in-itself. I aim to show that, for him, the thing-in-itself should be understood ultimately as an obstacle the philosopher erects between himself and the world. For Nietzsche, what the philosopher takes to be a bridge *to* the world— namely, the philosophical idea of the way the world truly is as an anchor for the ways in which we take it to be—really functions to keep the world at bay. As we will see, making sense of this claim involves appreciating the way in which the idea of a thing-in-itself represents a particular fantasy of mind-independence that can best be expressed in terms of a certain conception of interpretation. The idea that it is a fantasy that is involved here helps to flesh out the claim that Nietzsche's philosophical investigations are fundamentally psychological in character.

In a number of passages—primarily in his notebooks—Nietzsche ridicules the idea of a thing-in-itself.[44] I would like in this section to articulate my sense of what motivates him to heap scorn upon what in one form or another can appear to be a notion that it is very difficult to do without. To this end, I will make use of a concept that is often used to come to terms with Nietzsche's thinking: that of *interpretation*. I want to argue that, properly understood, his denial of the notion of a thing-in-itself places important constraints upon the work we—and he—can ask that concept to do. As I will try to make clear, though an interpretation must be *of* something, it can only be of something that the interpreter in some way *understands*. Someone inclined to resist Nietzsche's denial of the thing-in-itself may feel that the notion of understanding itself stands in need of explanation, and may well wish to appeal to the concept of interpretation to provide the desired account. As I understand him, however, Nietzsche denies that such an account is forthcoming because the notions of interpretation and understanding are inextricably intertwined.

In Nietzsche's view, the idea of a thing-in-itself expresses a fantasy of access to the world—to the object of our interpretations—by means of something wholly independent of what we in fact understand. It is this picture of independence he wishes to undermine. But this picture commonly fuels readings of Nietzsche that insist in one way or another that, according to him, the character—and even existence—of the inter*preted* depends upon that of the interpre*ter* (who, in turn, is somehow constituted by his interpretations). I want to argue, then, that it is pre-

---

[44] See, for example, *The Will to Power*, secs. 553, 556, and 557.

cisely this sort of reading that is undermined by Nietzsche's attack on the thing-in-itself.

Many readers have found it tempting to suppose either that Nietzsche had a substantive account of truth or that such an account can be reconstructed from his ostensibly epistemological remarks. But our reading of *The Birth of Tragedy* and of the foregoing passages from *The Gay Science* suggests that, in Nietzsche's view, there is nothing for such theories to be *of*. For him, a theory of truth would have to incorporate some account of the relationship of what we say to the things about which we speak. As a theory of anything else, it would be difficult for him to see of what interest a theory of truth could conceivably be. He would in any case find that philosophical talk of theories of truth rests on confusions and errors, and that the question 'what makes our judgments true?' is not one for which we need to provide a philosophical answer.

Keeping in mind the principle upshot of his first major work, then, I would like in what remains of this chapter and in the bulk of the next to consider in a more general way a pair of claims that are commonly associated with Nietzsche's work, but which, I believe, are rarely understood. On the one hand, he denounces the notion of a thing-in-itself as contradictory. On the other hand, he sometimes suggests that we ourselves make some sort of contribution to the character of our experience of the world, and therefore bear a kind of responsibility for it. The question we need to ask about both claims is, roughly, what the point for Nietzsche in making them might be if, as I have been insisting, he had no use for epistemology.

In one form or another, both ideas will be familiar to most of Nietzsche's readers. Indeed, they often seem to be two sides of a single thought. For to say that truths are created rather than discovered can seem to be simply another way of claiming that every view is an interpretation. This is the doctrine commonly known as perspectivism.[45] On this view, interpretations, as such, do not reflect the real nature of the world, but represent rather the result of an imposition of order and meaning upon what does not in and of itself really possess them. Thus, Nietzsche is often thought to have endorsed at least some version of the claim that the truth is made rather than found. He is also thought

[45] As I noted in the Introduction, this formulation of the doctrine of perspectivism is due to Alexander Nehamas. I want to ask in what follows just how *informative* such a doctrine can be meant to be. To anticipate, I think that *The Birth of Tragedy* casts serious doubt on any reading of Nietzsche's later work that relies heavily upon the notion of interpretation. This notion does not seem conceptually rich enough to do the work such readings appear to require of it. Or so I mean to argue.

to have believed that while some revel in their responsibility for the createdness of truth, others revile it.

If it is put as crudely as this, of course, few are likely to think it worthwhile to bother either to praise or to condemn such a view, and so most commentators devote significant effort to formulating versions of both points which are subtle enough that Nietzsche might plausibly be construed as endorsing them. I have, nonetheless, stated both claims in this bald form in order not to lose sight of the main issue at hand: that it is not clear what the *point* would be in denying that any of our views capture the world's real nature, if one believed that the philosophical request for justification rests on the sorts of confusions and misunderstandings articulated first in *The Birth of Tragedy*.

Our reading of *The Gay Science* suggests that Nietzsche's denial of the thing-in-itself is intended to convey in different terms the same conception of our life in language for which he argues in *The Birth of Tragedy*. That is, the claim that the notion of a thing-in-itself is contradictory is meant to show that philosophical talk of justifying claims about the correspondence of our judgments to the world as it is in itself rests upon a misunderstanding of our practices of judgment, a misunderstanding that expresses itself in terms of a certain philosophical conception of the world's independence of those practices. The philosopher, on Nietzsche's view, fears that if he is denied access to something wholly independent of the ways in which he happens to view things, he will remain confined to a merely subjective grasp of the world, cut off from its real nature. It is this fantasy of confinement Nietzsche wishes most to understand. As elsewhere, however, his aim is to *expose* it, not to erect another philosophical structure on its basis.

My suggestion that the denial of the thing-in-itself is, in effect, something for which Nietzsche already argues in *The Birth of Tragedy* is likely to meet with resistance by readers who assume that in his earliest work he maintains the possibility of a kind of noncognitive awareness of the world's true—that is, Dionysian—nature. This view leads some readers to conclude that when, in his later work, Nietzsche explicitly denies the thing-in-itself he is rejecting some part of his early doctrine.[46] But while

[46] See, for example, Maudemarie Clark, *Nietzsche on Truth and Philosophy* (Cambridge: Cambridge University Press, 1990). Clark argues at length that Nietzsche's views on the nature of truth evolve over the course of his career. On her reading, Nietzsche's early claim that truth is an illusion rests upon a 'metaphysical correspondence theory of truth' that he later rejects in favor of a 'minimal correspondence theory'. Nietzsche is therefore obliged to forfeit the right to condemn human knowledge as illusory, and his mature view has it that we can know what we, as knowers, are so to speak fitted to know. Clark admits that this last view is extremely thin— almost a truism—but I am more skeptical than she appears to be about whether it

the denial of the thing-in-itself is clearly incompatible with this Schopenhauerian interpretation of the idea of Dionysian nature, we have
seen that Nietzsche's primary goal in *The Birth of Tragedy* was effectively
to reject that interpretation and hence, I suggest, already to deny the
thing-in-itself. Let us examine, therefore, his later—ostensibly more explicit—rejection of that notion.

There seem primarily to be two different—and perhaps competing—
ways in which Nietzsche denies the thing-in-itself. On the one hand,
he sometimes appears to deny that we have any *right* to talk about the
nature of the world as it is in itself. At times, he takes this to imply
that we should remain agnostic about the thing-in-itself, uncommitted
as to whether something really answers to that notion. Elsewhere, however, he seems to reject the idea of a thing-in-itself outright on something like this same basis. For example, he writes about Kant:

> The sore spot of Kant's critical philosophy has gradually become vis-
> ible even to dull eyes: Kant no longer has a right to his distinction
> "appearance" and "thing-in-itself"—he had deprived himself of the
> right to go on distinguishing in the old familiar way, in so far as he
> rejected as impermissible making inferences from phenomena to a
> cause of phenomena—in accordance with his conception of causality
> and its purely intra-phenomenal validity—which conception, on the
> other hand, already anticipates this distinction, as if the "thing-in-
> itself" were not only inferred but *given*. (WP, sec. 553, p. 300)

But in published remarks that antedate this passage Nietzsche seems
to shy away from an unqualified denial of the existence of a thing-in-
itself. "It is true, there could be a metaphysical world; the absolute
possibility of it is hardly to be disputed. We behold all things through
the human head and cannot cut off this head; while the question nonetheless remains what of the world would still be there if one had cut it
off" (*HAH*, sec. 9, p. 15).[47] In contrast to section 109 of *The Gay Science*,
Nietzsche appears here to be making an epistemological claim about

---

counts as a view at all (see *Nietzsche on Truth and Philosophy*, p. 40). Although I agree
that Nietzsche had no interest in working out a substantive theory of truth, I am not
convinced that Clark has fully appreciated the spirit of this claim. The view she
attributes to Nietzsche is so thin—roughly that we can know what we can know—
as to gain what content it may have wholly from the view it pretends to deny. But
the rejected view seems so incoherent that it is difficult to see how anyone—even
Schopenhauer—could be tempted to endorse it in the first place.

[47] Clark cites this passage in support of her claim that Nietzsche's so-called middle-
period position on the nature of truth commits him to a philosophically flawed
metaphysical correspondence theory.

what we can know. Indeed, it looks as though he is placing—in a roughly Kantian fashion he would appear later to reject—limits on the powers of human cognition. When read in context, however, it is unclear whether he means to claim that there might be some real nature of the world as it is in itself to which we will never have access, or whether he considers it just as dogmatic to claim that there is not such a metaphysical world as to claim that there is. The line of thought that we have followed from *The Birth of Tragedy* suggests the latter reading, but the question is not settled by the letter of the text.

Nietzsche's denial of the thing-in-itself, however, also takes the more fundamental form of a claim that the notion of a thing-in-itself is nonsensical or paradoxical, *widersinnig*. In his notebooks, for example, we find passages like the following:

A "thing-in-itself" just as perverse as a "sense-in-itself," a "meaning-in-itself." There are no "facts-in-themselves," for a sense must always be projected into them before there can be facts. (*WP*, sec. 556, p. 301)

The "thing-in-itself" nonsensical. If I remove all the relationships, all the "properties," all the "activities" of a thing, the thing does not remain over; because thingness has only been invented by us owing to the requirements of logic, thus with the aim of defining, communication (to bind together the multiplicity of relationships, properties, activities). (*WP*, sec. 558, p. 302)

"Things that have a constitution in themselves"—a dogmatic idea with which one must break absolutely. (*WP*, sec. 559, p. 302)

Ostensibly, the point here is that to have determined all the properties of a given thing, all its relationships with the properties of every other thing, is to have given a complete description of that thing's nature.[48] There is nothing else—no thing as it is in itself independent of those properties and relationships—left over. These remarks appear, moreover, to support a common reading of Nietzsche according to which he would supposedly treat talk of a thing-in-itself as a way of trying to avoid responsibility for the sense we project into the world. I will discuss both what is right and what is wrong about this reading in the next chapter. For the moment, however, we should merely note that such a

---

[48] For an eloquent interpretation of this idea, see chapter 3 of Alexander Nehamas, *Nietzsche: Life as Literature* (Cambridge: Harvard University Press, 1985).

reading does not explain what Nietzsche might mean in saying that the notion of a thing-in-itself is in some way *widersinnig*.

I want to suggest that, as in the case of other philosophical fantasies, Nietzsche's denial of the thing-in-itself is meant primarily to question the *value* of that notion. That is to say, he means to ask what it is *for*. What work, in other words, does belief in a thing-in-itself do for us? What does the philosopher's insistence on a thing-in-itself show the psychologist about the former's understanding of our relationship to the world? In calling the thing-in-itself nonsensical, Nietzsche suggests that there is something incoherent in thinking that our grasp of the world—of, so to speak, the object of our interpretations—somehow reaches out to a thing-in-itself. He wants, however, to know why anyone might be inclined to think the contrary. A natural suggestion to make here might be that the philosopher thinks that, unless our interpretations reach in some sense beyond themselves, we will be restricted or *confined* to them, cut off from the world itself. It is not clear, however, how we should understand this idea of confinement. On Nietzsche's view, it is very difficult to specify just what it is to which the philosopher fears we will be confined without the thing-in-itself. We might be tempted to say 'to our interpretations', but, as we will see shortly, precisely that way of speaking is ruled out by Nietzsche's rejection of the thing-in-itself. How, then, would he have us understand the philosopher's fear of confinement?

As we have seen, Nietzsche holds that philosophical gestures toward the so-called bounds of language are empty. The claim that the notion of the thing-in-itself is nonsensical similarly functions as part of his larger diagnosis of our tendency toward anthropomorphism. We should, therefore, be careful not to treat his denial of the thing-in-itself as a claim about the limits of human cognition. For as we should by now expect, if the thing-in-itself is thought of as an absolutely un-interpreted one-knows-not-what lying wholly outside the bounds of language, Nietzsche considers the notion to be nonsensical or contradictory in the sense that to give it content we would have to try to imagine something that, he holds, we *cannot* imagine. Thus, the philosopher's putative worry about confinement cannot be understood in properly psychological terms as confinement to language.

I said above that the idea of a thing-in-itself represents a particular fantasy of mind-independence that can best be expressed in terms of a certain conception of interpretation. It is in these terms, I think, that we can begin to make something of the philosopher's worries about confinement. As I said, Nietzsche's denial of the thing-in-itself appears to be one aspect of a larger perspectivist thesis about the status of what we say about the world: namely, that our claims that this or that is the case can be no more than interpretations. But without also insisting on the other aspect of that thesis—namely, that we make some sort of contribution to the character of our experience and so bear responsibility for it—the claim that every view is an interpretation is nothing more than another way of expressing the idea that our judgments do not grasp the character of the world as it is in itself. That is to say, Nietzsche's views about interpretation seem, at first glance, to be largely negative or critical.

I do not think, however, that good sense can be made of the idea of what I have called our contribution to experience until we understand what Nietzsche's denial of the thing-in-itself indicates about his use of the notion of interpretation in general. To put the point in what is perhaps more popular terminology, we cannot understand the function of the idea that truth is *created* until we understand the function of Nietzsche's denial that it is *discovered*. I want to argue that for Nietzsche an interpretation is not something for which we are responsible, but rather something to which we can fail to be responsive. And I would like to put this last point by saying that, in Nietzsche's view, interpretation comes to an end in understanding.[49] Expressing the idea in this fashion helps to dissolve the sense that the notion of interpretation can be used to articulate an alternative to traditional epistemology. Following the lead of *The Birth of Tragedy*, we might also say that interpretation comes to an end in *obedience*. For our interpretations—our perceptions, beliefs, judgments, and so on—must always be of something that in some way we understand. To go back to the case of Socratism, if we say that in claiming that someone is courageous we are interpreting the concept of courage, then, on Nietzsche's account, the object of that interpretation is a courageous person—not, say, an organism onto which we somehow project that concept. Understanding (obedience), however, is not guaranteed by anything other than our willingness to go on with the concepts in question. This last claim forms the heart of Nietzsche's so-called perspectivism, and it is the subject of the next

[49] This, of course, is how Heidegger would like to put the point as well. See, in particular, sec. 32 of his *Being and Time*, trans. John Macquarrie and Edward Robinson (New York: Harper and Row, 1962). For a related discussion in a different context, see James Tully, "Wittgenstein and Political Philosophy, Understanding Practices of Critical Reflection," *Political Theory* 17 (May 1989): 172–204. I am not sure Tully sees how similar Heidegger's position is to the one he attributes to Wittgenstein. I am indebted to Edward Minar for the phrase 'interpretation comes to an end in understanding'. See his "Paradox and Privacy," *Philosophy and Phenomenological Research* 54 (March 1994) and "Wittgenstein and the 'Contingency' of Community," *Pacific Philosophical Quarterly* 72 (1991): 203–34.

chapter. Would Nietzsche, then, recognize an acceptable and informative usage of the notion of interpretation in this context? What, if anything, does that idea convey for him?

There is, of course, *one* use of the term that we can rule out from the outset. Nietzsche argues in effect that treating obedience to the authority of one's culture as an interpretation is the error at the root of Socratism. The intelligibility of the request for a justification of one's culture depends upon one's being able to make sense of the idea of culture *as* an interpretation. The primary effect of tragedy, however, is the dissolution of the philosophical outlook according to which it makes sense to speak of culture as an interpretation. We might say, then, that the tragedies showed their audiences what a culture could *not* be—namely, an interpretation somehow projected onto the world.

From Nietzsche's point of view, then, the consequence of thinking of culture in terms of interpretation is that doing so inevitably invites the demand for justification. But he would also have us recognize that, in this context, the notion of interpretation simply idles. If, however, there were a use of the notion of interpretation that did not invite that demand, then, I think, Nietzsche should not find the concept objectionable. We may indeed speak of our judgments about the world as interpretations in such a fashion so as not to conjure Socratism, but only in a *trivial* sense. For, in this sense, interpretation neither represents an arbitrary imposition on the world, nor somehow reaches out to a brute and uninterpreted thing-in-itself. Interpretation must, rather, be of something that is itself neither a further interpretation nor something wholly uninterpreted. It must, that is, be of something that is understood.

While Nietzsche's own use of the term is hardly unequivocal, I think that it is in something like this trivial sense that he sometimes speaks of our grip on the world as one of interpretation. In this sense, the claim that our relationship to the world around us is one of interpretation is not a claim whose denial he finds wholly intelligible. It is, for example, in this sense that we might read his claim that none of our aesthetic and moral judgments apply to the universe itself as a claim about interpretation. For those judgments are about—that is, are interpretations of—the world we understand: section 109 means in effect to challenge us to say of what *else* our interpretations could be. This same sense of interpretation is also in play in Nietzsche's insistence that 'rational thought is interpretation according to a scheme we cannot throw off'. His diagnostic claim in general is that a confused conception of interpretation leads one to suspect that one's judgments somehow fall short of the world itself, that the world one understands is something other than the world as it is in itself.

Inasmuch as Nietzsche denies any philosophical problem of how interpretation as it were succeeds in being about what is understood, I think that, in his view, the idea that interpretation is of what is understood must be the trivial one we discussed above. It is a claim intended to forestall a problem, not to solve one. On the other hand, he believes that the very problem that philosophers call upon the idea of interpretation to solve arises only on the basis, in effect, of a misunderstanding of—or, as he would put it, a 'devaluation' of—the claim that interpretation comes to an end in understanding. In other words, the perspectivist thesis that our judgments are interpretations gets what content it has only from philosophical attempts to dispute it. In this sense, I think, Nietzsche's denial of the thing-in-itself does not involve a particularly negative claim at all, for it is not clear that he believes that we can get so far as even to question it.

On the reading I am proposing, then, Nietzsche's rejection of the thing-in-itself indicates that what is at stake in the claim that our judgments are mere interpretations is not a substantive picture of something that should take the place of cognition, but rather a claim about the kind of thing a judgment—and hence knowledge—can be. It is, therefore, difficult to believe that he intended his denial of the thing-in-itself to underpin the suggestion that our relationship to the world may be construed on the model of interpretation in anything other than the trivial sense we have most recently been considering. Though interpretation, in one sense of the term, is indeed an activity in which human beings do occasionally engage, the idea that such an activity somehow characterizes our relationship to the world in general expresses exactly the picture of our situation as human beings for which Nietzsche has no use. The point of the claim that interpretations are of something understood is, thus, precisely to *deny* that interpretation is a relationship between the interpreter and the world.

Nevertheless, as long as we do not attribute to him the very picture of interpretation that, from the beginning, he denounces as unintelligible, we can, if we like, say that Nietzsche thinks every view is an interpretation. But this version of the perspectivist thesis neither has nor is meant to have any real philosophical content. It is not meant to explain something about our relationship to the world for which traditional epistemology failed to account. Once again, Nietzsche's diagnostic concern is with the human, all too human insistence on a thing-in-itself—with what he understands to be our attempt to deny his claim about interpretation.

I have argued that, for Nietzsche, at its most general level the idea of a thing-in-itself expresses the philosophical prejudice that interpretation must be of something completely independent of that interpretation. In other words, the thing-in-itself expresses the fantasy of an ultimate object of interpretation. On this reading, to say that the notion of the thing-in-itself is paradoxical or nonsensical is to accuse of incoherence the picture of interpretation that it expresses. The philosophical insistence that for interpretation to be more than merely a fact about us it must be of a world that is wholly independent of us is rooted in the idea that an interpretation that succeeds in being about the 'mind-independent' world does so *because* it is more than a fact about us.[50] But, according to Nietzsche, what the philosopher does in effect is to treat our understanding of the world as a mere—perhaps as an anthropological—fact about how we happen to view it.

Nietzsche's picture of the philosopher, then, is roughly of someone in the grip of the familiar skeptical doubt that any fact about how we view the world could guarantee that that view is faithful to the world's nature. He insists, however, only a confused idea of what it means to 'have a view of the world' leads one to this sort of impasse. Thus, in saying that there is something incoherent or nonsensical—something *widersinnig*—in the very idea of a thing-in-itself, Nietzsche is suggesting that we are importantly at odds with ourselves when we try to deny that interpretation comes to an end in understanding. And he aims to bring home to us the fact that this particular fantasy of the world's independence of our beliefs and judgments about it tends to undermine itself. Indeed, as I suggested, the thing-in-itself is, for Nietzsche, an obstacle—a barrier—that the philosopher places between himself and the world—perhaps as a way of finding his desire for it tolerable.[51]

To see how a conception of the thing-in-itself might in this way serve to obscure the fact that, as I put it, interpretations come to an end in

[50] We must bear in mind that it is a certain *picture* of the world's independence of our judgments—or interpretations—that is under attack here. I do not mean to construe Nietzsche as denying that, for example, believing something to be the case and its really being the case are two different things. What he balks at, rather, is the particular inflation of that difference that gives rise to philosophical questions about how beliefs actually succeed in being *about* anything. From the point of view I am trying to articulate here, the philosophical attractiveness of the idea of a thing-in-itself is simply the insistence that, because there is undeniably a difference between beliefs and their 'objects', there must be room to seek an *account* of that difference and hence of their relationship to one another. We miss this important point if we read Nietzsche's denials of the thing-in-itself as simply a quasi-Hegelian insistence on the uselessness of a certain notion. Moreover, this latter reading threatens to impute a quasi-Hegelian idealism to Nietzsche—a view he would surely reject.

[51] For a pertinent psychoanalytic discussion of the idea of an obstacle, see Adam Phillips, "Looking at Obstacles," in *On Kissing, Tickling, and Being Bored* (Cambridge: Harvard University Press, 1993).

understanding, recall our earlier discussion of the Socratic error. That error consists in treating obedience as an activity of interpretation, as the application of standards. Socrates rightly sees that an application of standards stands in intelligible need of justification. And he reasons that if the application of a concept to the world is not ultimately to be *arbitrary*, that application must rest upon something other than our ordinary ways of going on with the concept. From Socrates' point of view, if such instincts are all that we have to go on, then nothing ties our interpretation of our concepts to the world. This implies that, for him, something other than the mere interpretation of our concepts must ground that interpretation, because no interpretation, he insists, can justify itself. He concludes, therefore, that something that is *not* an interpretation—something, in other words, wholly other than our practice with the concept in question—must provide the requisite justification. This, I think, is the fantasy expressed by the idea of a thing-in-itself. As Nietzsche construes him, what Socrates believes he needs is something utterly independent of our practices of judgment that would serve to bind those practices to the world.

Though we seem to have strayed far from specifically Kantian territory, I think it is the complete independence of the desired justification for our practices of judgment from those same practices that, for Nietzsche, makes the Socratic fantasy a fantasy of a thing-in-itself. Because Socrates insists that nothing about our lives can justify the sense we make of the world, he believes that if what pretends to provide the desired justification is not truly independent of the practices whose justification we seek, then those practices rest on nothing significant at all. They—and our lives with them—are, in this sense, groundless or contingent, and we are, in this same sense, confined to them.

Nietzsche believed that tragedy once functioned as a response to the Socratic demand for reasons. As we have seen, his denial of the thing-in-itself points in the same direction. He means to deny that we attach any sense to the idea of something completely independent of our practices of judgment that might serve to provide foundations for the latter. And to claim that we fail to attach sense to this idea is to claim that the picture of judgment upon which the request for justification depends is not intelligible. On the other hand, we have also seen how—once that demand is taken to heart—the fantasy of a thing-in-itself nevertheless serves to make life intelligible to someone puzzled in the way in which Nietzsche believes Socrates' interlocutors were puzzled. The notion of a thing-in-itself serves to express a picture of interpretation as a relation between the interpreter and the interpreted, a relationship that needs to be secured by rational justification. Nietzsche believes that to construe interpretation in this manner is in effect to deny that interpretation comes to an end in understanding. But this denial, he contends, leaves us without a serviceable idea of interpretation in the first place.

Because it treats understanding as itself a further interpretation, the fantasy of a thing-in-itself expresses the philosopher's desire that interpretations be of something other than what is understood. But no such thing as the philosopher takes interpretation to be really could be an interpretation at all. As I suggested, then, although the thing-in-itself seems to the philosopher to be a bridge *to* the world, from Nietzsche's point of view, it is rather something that the philosopher places *between* himself and the world. It is, as I said, something the philosopher puts in the way of his desire, a way in which, as Nietzsche has it, he tries to deny his will to power.

What I understand Nietzsche to be arguing here is relatively straightforward. If our relationship to the world is construed as a matter of interpretation, then it is natural to ask what our interpretations are interpretations of. And if, as some suggest, the object of our interpretations is itself a further interpretation, then it seems reasonable to ask of what *that* interpretation is an interpretation. The upshot, for Nietzsche, is that the philosopher cannot appeal to the notion of interpretation to motivate his concern to providing philosophical grounding for interpretation. It makes sense to call the object of interpretation an interpretation only *because* interpretations come to an end somewhere. But this implies that no properly philosophical point is expressed by treating the object of our interpretations as itself an interpretation. Thus, by saying that the notion of the thing-in-itself is incoherent, Nietzsche means to show that the philosopher's worry about a putative lack of grounding for our aesthetic and moral judgments cannot be understood on its own terms. This is what it means to say that the fantasy of a thing-in-itself undermines itself. What the philosopher *is* worried about, Nietzsche is saying, cannot be expressed in terms of a demand for justification any more than the tragic Greek's suffering can be expressed in terms of contingency.

Understanding and Resistance

To know what Nietzsche might mean in suggesting that the object of our judgments is in some way colored by those very judgments, we need to understand what he means in denying that we have access to the world as it is, wholly independent of those judgments. To this end, we have in the preceding section explored the nature of his denial of the thing-in-itself. Access to something completely independent of our judgments appears to the philosopher to be the only way to guarantee their objectivity, to guarantee our confidence that, in making judgments about the world, we reach beyond ourselves in a substantive sense. The philosopher fears that, without access to the world as it is in itself, we remain confined to the circle of our judgments, to our interpretations. Nietzsche asks what *value* the notion of a thing-in-itself—of a world wholly independent of our practices of judgment—has for the philosopher, to what *use* he puts that notion. Why, he asks, does the philosopher *need* to believe that our interpretations are of something completely independent of them?

According to Nietzsche, the very idea of a thing-in-itself is paradoxical or nonsensical, *widersinnig*. A straightforward diagnosis of the philosophical insistence on the thing-in-itself is therefore not, strictly speaking, possible. We cannot, in Nietzsche's view, make any obvious sense of the object of the philosopher's insistence. We cannot say, for example, that the philosopher flees an experience of the groundlessness of appearance. But Nietzsche seeks to remind us that the philosopher nevertheless uses this sort of nonsense to obscure the sense that he in fact makes of the world. Just *this* is the kind of sense that can be made of the notion of the thing-in-itself. To put the point in the terms I introduced in the last chapter, on Nietzsche's view, belief in the thing-in-itself presents itself as a piece of philosophical resistance to the intelligibility of the world. It is in these terms that we should understand Nietzsche's claim at the end of the *Genealogy* that 'man would rather will nothingness than *not* will'. This suggests that belief in a thing-in-itself is a barrier—a hindrance—the philosopher places between himself and the world. But the mere fact that the psychologist can make this kind of diagnostic sense of such an apparently nonsensical notion shows, in Nietzsche's view, that the philosopher's resistance to the world is a *this*-worldly phenomenon, a piece of human psychology. Not willing is never an option for a living being.[52] Like the Socratic life of reason, then, belief in the thing-in-itself has—for certain forms of life anyway—survival value. It is a way of making sense of life.

I have argued that Nietzsche's claim that the notion of a thing-in-itself is nonsensical is meant as a reminder that interpretation comes to an end in understanding. Belief in a thing-in-itself functions as a

---

[52] "It will be immediately obvious that such a self-contradiction as the ascetic idea appears to represent, 'life *against* life,' is physiologically considered and not merely psychologically, a simple absurdity [*einfach Unsinn*]. It can only be *apparent*" (GM III, sec. 13, p. 120).

means of forgetting that this is so. This claim must, however, be understood diagnostically. Nietzsche does not suppose that the philosopher would think of himself as denying the claim that interpretation comes to an end in understanding. In fact, the philosopher pretends to grant this point, but then goes on to ask in what such understanding consists. Nietzsche insists, however, that the philosopher imagines that there is a problem here only because he treats understanding itself as one more interpretation, and then asks what is special about it.

On this account, the notion of the thing-in-itself cannot express the idea of something lying completely outside the bounds of sense, for we simply have no such idea. Rather, it expresses a philosophical fantasy that gives rise to the epistemological problem about our so-called relationship to the world. Though the idea of something that is in this way independent of our practices has no more philosophical content than a more properly Kantian notion of a thing-in-itself, Nietzsche does think it makes sense *as* a fantasy. And he concludes that the philosopher's desire for access to something completely independent of interpretation conceals a wish that our interpretations not be of the world that they are of: this world. In short, that desire expresses philosophical resistance. As such, the philosopher's wish to be unintelligible is itself a form of intelligibility.

The point here, as elsewhere, is that something that, in Nietzsche's view, makes no sense on its own terms is shown nevertheless to make sense as a symptom of resistance to the world's intelligibility. I closed Chapter 1 with the suggestion that the philosopher's apparent desire for something more to go on than our ordinary practices with a concept conceals a wish that those practices be *less* than they are. If we appreciate how the insistence on a thing-in-itself functions as a tool of the philosopher's resistance, the content of this suggestion becomes clearer.

The philosophical insistence on a thing-in-itself gives voice to a fear of confinement—confinement to the circle of our representations, to our opinions, our judgments, our interpretations. But the notion of confinement makes good philosophical sense on its own terms only if we can make sense of something lying outside that to which one fantasizes one may be confined. And because, in Nietzsche's view, no philosophical sense can be made of the idea of something lying outside the bounds of language, he concludes that no such sense can be made of the notion of confinement here. His diagnosis of the thing-in-itself is meant, however, to remind us what kind of sense *can* be made of the philosopher's fear. According to that diagnosis, it is not the world itself that the philosopher says must be conceived as—or concealing—a thing-in-itself, but rather our *access* to the world must be thought of as somehow mediated by something completely independent of us. Neither we nor the world in which we live are good enough for the philosopher.

Thus, we are not far at all from the conclusions we drew from our reading of *The Birth of Tragedy*. The philosopher's insistence on a thing-in-itself is a form of life-denial, a way of resisting the sense the world makes. The present formulations of those conclusions may help us better understand those passages that lead readers to speak of Nietzsche's sense of our contribution to the character of the world, for, as I now want to argue, that contribution should be understood as a matter of *overcoming* resistance to the world and of our responsibility for failing to do so.

CHAPTER 3

THE KNOWER'S CONTRIBUTION
TO THE KNOWN

Responsibility and Responsiveness

We have been concerned so far to understand one of the ideas that fuels Nietzsche's so-called perspectivism: his denial of the thing-in-itself. That denial, I argued, is meant as a reminder that interpretation comes to an end in understanding; we have explored the function of that reminder in the context of Nietzsche's conception of knowledge. Following the lead of *The Birth of Tragedy*, however, I have been careful to avoid the suggestion that Nietzsche might have intended this reminder to make a positive contribution to our philosophical understanding of the world's intelligibility. What content it does have comes, I said, solely from appreciating the sort of nonsense involved in trying to deny it. This is one way of understanding the idea that Nietzsche repudiates any clear-cut opposition between a tragic affirmation of life and a moral repudiation of it.

This reading, I now want to argue, places important constraints on any interpretation of the other idea that fuels the doctrine of perspectivism: the idea, that is, that we somehow impose interpretations on the world, and that we are therefore responsible for the sense we make of life. Because Nietzsche rejects the idea of a thing-in-itself as nonsensical, I will argue, we cannot understand what I have called our contribution to the intelligible character of our experience to be a straightforward matter of imposition. Meaning is not, in this sense, something we impose on the world, because we simply have no idea what the object of such an imposition could be. The most straightforward reading of the notion of responsibility for meaning is therefore ruled out.

It should by now be clear that Nietzsche's interest in knowledge does

not lie in trying to provide answers to specifically philosophical questions about its *nature*. From his point of view, there simply are no such
questions. He is interested rather to understand the character of our
commitment to knowledge—the value he understands us to place upon
it. My aim in this chapter and the next is to make clear in what
Nietzsche thinks that commitment consists, and to explain in what
sense, in his view, it remains a moral one.

In the remainder of this introductory section, I want to lay out as
succinctly as I can the basic interpretative question confronting the reading I have developed so far: namely, what sense are we to make of the
idea, commonly attributed to Nietzsche, that, in knowing the world,
the knower contributes something to the known? Nietzsche's apparent
denial that knowledge represents a discovery suggests to many readers
that he must believe that it represents a creation instead. Making clear
in what sense, if any, Nietzsche believes that our ways of viewing the
world represent an imposition upon the world will involve us in a discussion of the idea of will to power. 'Power,' as I will argue in the
following section, in a significant number of contexts is simply
Nietzsche's name for the constraints that making sense exercise upon
us. Such constraints are, in Nietzsche's view, psychological in nature. If
this reading is right, then we have further reason to suppose that
Nietzsche believes there is something seriously amiss with the idea that
knowledge involves the imposition—in a philosophical sense of the
word—of an interpretation upon the world.

On this reading, then, our contribution to the known simply cannot
be a matter of an imposition upon it. This, as we will see in the concluding section of this chapter, is not what Nietzsche means by 'will.' As I
suggested in the Introduction, 'will' is Nietzsche's name for commitment. Accordingly, talking about will to power is, for him, one (very
schematic) way of talking about the fact that we make sense. Thus, the
expression 'will to knowledge' refers to our commitment to truthfulness. It is Nietzsche's name, in other words, for the fact of our obedience
to the authority of the imperative to tell the truth.

As we have noted, such obedience can fail. There is room, in other
words, to talk about strength or weakness of will in this context. The
aim of the next chapter is to make clear in what weakness of the will
(to truth) consists. This project will involve us in a lengthy discussion
of section 344 of *The Gay Science*. In this long aphorism, Nietzsche argues
that the man of knowledge's commitment to truthfulness is, as he puts
the point, pious. To the extent that it is, Nietzsche condemns that commitment as nihilistic. I want to understand in what sense we may speak
of morality in this context. I will argue that the morality of the man of

knowledge's commitment to truthfulness consists in the latter's unwillingness to acknowledge the historical character of that commitment. As we will see, however, overcoming his resistance here does not commit the man of knowledge to the view that the modern will to knowledge is a historical contingency. On the contrary, the point is, rather, to acknowledge that commitment's necessity for us. We do so, Nietzsche maintains, by understanding in what sense it represents an *achievement*. It is along these lines, I will argue, that we should understand the *Genealogy's* talk of a growing self-consciousness of the will to truth.

Nietzsche suggests that we may distinguish a conditional from an unconditional (or pious) commitment to truthfulness, and in the next chapter I try to make clear what such conditionality involves. We will want to know what Nietzschean self-consciousness amounts to here. In Chapter 5, we will explore the way in which morality—specifically, the morality of pity—is an obstacle to such self-consciousness.

Now, as I have suggested, the idea that—the considerations of the preceding chapter notwithstanding—we are indeed in some way responsible for the meaning we impose upon the world appears to be a quite natural consequence of denying that such meaning is simply found. If meaning is not discovered—not somehow written into the very nature of things—then, it seems, it must in some way be created, and we, as creators, must accordingly bear responsibility for our creation. Because, however, we have no idea of how the world might be fitted for interpretations, it seems that the latter cannot simply be imposed upon the world. A good interpretation *reveals* something about what it interprets, and in the absence of a concrete alternative it expresses nothing to say of such an interpretation that it is only an interpretation.

I think that this familiar friction between creation and discovery tends to support our attributing to Nietzsche only a trivial usage of the notion of interpretation, according to which he does not employ it in place of that of cognition. Certainly, nothing is gained by treating knowledge as a matter of interpretation, if we cannot say how something can be both a creation *and* a discovery. Nevertheless, Nietzsche does speak—again, especially in his notebooks—in ways that ostensibly invite talk of imposing meaning on the world, and we need to know what to make of these sorts of claims. He writes, for example, "We can comprehend only a world that we ourselves have made [*gemacht*]" (*WP*, sec. 495, p. 272). Elsewhere, he says, "Not 'to know' but to schematize—to impose upon [*auferlegen*] chaos as much regularity and form as our practical needs require" (*WP*, sec. 515, p. 278). He also says that "to impose upon [aufzuprägen] becoming the character of being . . . is the supreme will to power" (*WP*, sec. 617, p. 330), a claim that guides Heidegger's reading of Nietzsche.

These sorts of remarks also seem to support the idea that Nietzsche thought that we bear some sort of responsibility for the world we 'make'. Indeed, as I suggested in the Introduction, he appears to many to believe that nihilism is the result of an inability to recognize one's right to posit or impose new meanings in the wake of the demise of 'our highest values'. In many respects, however, the passages from *The Will to Power* usually cited in support of such a reading are not really representative of Nietzsche's published reflections.[1] Nevertheless, in one form or another, these are exactly the sorts of views often associated with Nietzsche's mature thought, and even his published writing often appears to invite this sort of reading. This is why I have spoken of our contribution to the intelligible character of our experience. The idea is simply that because good philosophical sense cannot be made of the idea that the sense we make of the world is somehow already written into the nature of things, the sense we make therefore represents something we bring to our experience. Talk of a contribution, of course, is vague enough to cover a variety of more specific philosophical proposals, but, as in Chapter 2, we are here concerned with a diagnosis of the confusions that motivate such proposals, and not with those proposals themselves. We need, therefore, to know what to make of a claim such as 'we can only understand a world we have made' in the light of our understanding of Nietzsche's denial of the thing-in-itself.

In its most straightforward form, I have argued, the denial of the thing-in-itself is meant to show that no good sense can be made of the idea of some brute, uninterpreted stuff as the purported object of interpretation. Accordingly, I suggested that this claim be read as a reminder about the notion of interpretation—as telling us, in effect, what an interpretation of the world can be. But that same reminder also suggests that we do not have a ready model for understanding the imposition of meaning of which Nietzsche speaks, and thus no obviously serviceable understanding of the apparently concomitant idea of our responsibility for that imposition. Let us be clear about this last point.

I argued that by rejecting the idea of the thing-in-itself as nonsensical, Nietzsche wishes to remind us that the world is an intelligible place— to recall us to what, in a philosophical mood, we have forgotten. Thus,

---

[1] This is one reason many commentators insist that no compelling interpretation of Nietzsche's thought should defer to the specious authority of *The Will to Power* and his notebooks generally.

the point—if not quite the force—of this reminder is the same for us as that of the ancient tragedies was for their audiences. The tragedies, remember, presented the fact of their audiences' obedience to the authority of their culture, the fact, in other words, that membership in their culture is possible only on the condition that they let these things—heroes and so forth—be the things they are. The threat of contingency is dissolved by appreciation of the fact that obedience does not provide a standpoint from which to raise doubts about the authority of culture. As we have seen, such doubts arise only when obedience is treated as interpretation, as a relationship adopted toward the conventions of that culture. In Chapter 2, we saw how Nietzsche tries to show that the picture of interpretation expressed by the philosophical insistence on an ultimate object of interpretation gives voice to a similarly distorted understanding of our place in the world. To appreciate this insight properly is to acknowledge something like the *world's* authority for the knower.

But these considerations suggest that meaning is something to which Nietzsche believes that we are—or fail to be—*responsive*, not something for which we can be said, in a Socratic sense, to be responsible. The notion of responsiveness here suggests something passive, something that one is called upon to let happen, rather than to *do*. This is what our reading of *The Birth of Tragedy* prepared us for: the tragic Greeks expressed their obedience to the authority of their culture by letting things be what they were. But when Nietzsche says, for example, that 'we can only understand a world we have made', the idea of making appears here to indicate something more active than a mere willingness to let things be the things they are.[2] If letting things be the things they are is not exactly something it makes sense to say that we do, then how shall we understand Nietzsche's talk of imposition, positing, importation, and so forth? How, generally, shall we understand the idea of what I have called the knower's contribution to the known? Consider again Nietzsche's claim that, 'to impose upon becoming the character of being is the supreme will to power'. We have been exploring what Nietzsche means by becoming, or as he also calls it, 'chaos'. Our considerations so far suggest that whatever Nietzsche means by 'the character of being', it

[2] The locution 'letting things be the things they are' slightly modifies the phrase Heidegger uses in "On the Essence of Truth" to describe a certain form of human freedom: 'letting beings be'. See "On the Essence of Truth," in Martin Heidegger, *Basic Writings*, ed. David Farrell Krell (New York: Harper and Row, 1977).

cannot be a matter of seeing becoming *as* something. Is there something more substantial to be said?

The Will to Power

Any adequate treatment of Nietzsche's conception of the knower's contribution to the known should involve some discussion of his notion of will to power. It is the will to power that is often credited with—indeed as—the imposition of form or structure upon what, in itself, lacks it. In a word, we might say that the will to power *interprets*. As elsewhere, my strategy in coming to terms with these ideas is to try to show what is right and what is wrong with what I take to be an apparently straightforward reading of Nietzsche's usage.[3]

'Will to power' is commonly understood to be Nietzsche's name for what organizes or structures our experience of the world. Very roughly, 'power' is taken to mean something like 'control' or 'domination', and the latter, in turn, is then taken to be what is achieved by the imposition of a given interpretation upon something that in itself in some way underdetermines it. The expression 'will to power' is, in this way, thought to designate the interpretative character of all experience.[4]

Nietzsche does indeed express himself in ways that appear to support this sort of reading. For example, in the *Genealogy* he says that "whatever exists, having somehow come into being, is again and again reinter-

[3] I do not suppose that what I will have to say here about the will to power amounts to an adequate interpretation of every aspect of Nietzsche's usage. I am interested only to articulate my sense of the way in which Nietzsche speaks specifically of knowledge as 'a power', and of the will to truth as a form of will to power.

[4] Actually, a whole range of different interpretations take this form, depending upon how the notion of control is understood. Thus, we can speak of a political will to power in the crude sense of one group controlling—that is, dominating—the actions of another by means of force. We can speak of another form of will to power, also political, where one group controls the actions and choices of another by means of influencing its conception of the options available to it, say, by means of propaganda. Finally, we can talk, in a more Foucaultian vein, of will to power in the sense that a given range of cultural institutions and practices (Foucault calls them 'technologies')—say, of self-examination—determine which courses of actions some segment of the population will find intelligible. We can speak of each of these forms of will to power as an interpretation in the sense that, in one way or another, they allow both the subjugated and the subjugators to make sense of themselves. The important thing to notice is that, on this sort of reading, power is not anything like the 'essential nature of reality'; it is not a metaphysical notion. This is, of course, only one reading—indeed, a relatively contemporary one—of a remarkably complex notion, and it is a reading that can be resisted on a variety of grounds.

preted to new ends, taken over, transformed, and redirected by some power superior to it; all events in the organic world are a subduing, a becoming master, and all subduing and becoming master involves a fresh interpretation, an adaptation through which any previous 'meaning' and 'purpose' are necessarily obscured or even obliterated" (*GM* II, sec. 12, p. 77).

Here is another representative passage:

> Life is essentially appropriation, injury, overpowering of what is alien and weaker; suppression, hardness, imposition of one's own forms, incorporation and at least, at its mildest, exploitation. . . . Even the body within which individuals treat each other as equals . . . if it is a living and not a dying body, has to do to other bodies what the individuals within it refrain from doing to each other: it will have to be an incarnate will to power, it will strive to grow, spread, seize, become predominant—not from any morality or immorality but because it is living and because life simply is will to power. . . . "Exploitation" does not belong to a corrupt or imperfect and primitive society: it belongs to the essence of what lives, as a basic organic function; it is a consequence of the will to power, which is after all the will of life. (*BGE*, sec. 259, p. 203)

It is common enough to want to treat the sort of interpretation mentioned in the passage from the *Genealogy* quoted above as one form—perhaps a milder one—of the exploitation Nietzsche mentions in the second passage. But I think it would be more appropriate to try to think of exploitation as itself a form of interpretation.[5]

In any event, while there is much disagreement about the kinds of considerations that may have led Nietzsche to the notion of will to power—as well as about how widely he meant to apply it[6]—it may be

[5] This appears to be how Foucault sometimes understood Nietzsche. It might be objected, however, that doing so blinds us to the distinction between exploitation and other forms of power, thus committing one, as Jürgen Habermas puts it, to an "uncircumspect levelling of culture and politics to immediate substrates of the application of violence" (*Philosophical Discourse of Modernity* [Cambridge: M.I.T. Press, 1987], p. 290; quoted in Barry Allen, "Government in Foucault," *Canadian Journal of Philosophy* 21, 4 [December 1991]: 421–40). Such a reading is based on a confusion, however. Power, as Foucault and Nietzsche think of it, is not always a matter of violence. In any case, we can certainly distinguish between different interpretations and between different kinds of interpretation. It makes sense to treat political or economic exploitation as a kind of interpretation where it determines which choices someone finds intelligible. This need not be all that such exploitation does.

[6] One may wonder whether Nietzsche began—as Kaufmann, for example, contends he did—from psychological considerations about our motivations to action and

tempting to suppose that the model of organizing and structuring life with which Nietzsche can usefully be understood to have operated, at least at times, is that of a reader interpreting a text.[7] Such readings stress Nietzsche's rejection of the idea that it is in any way possible or desirable to live a life without structure or meaning.[8] They also rightly point out that Nietzsche was concerned to understand the human needs that express themselves in various misconceptions of what makes life meaningful, and not to encourage us to live without meaning. These readings then endeavor to develop a workable understanding of his conception of what a structured—that is to say, meaningful—life amounts to. The model of interpreting a text is often appealed to in this context because a successful reading is thought to have the virtue not merely of coherently organizing the otherwise disparate features of a given work, but also, as I said above, of revealing something in the text that we must in some way recognize as already there—that is, as something we have, so to speak, found.

If the idea of a reader interpreting a text seems a compelling model of what Nietzsche believes it is like to find meaning in the world and to live, in this sense, a life with structure, this is because it is after all natural to think of a successful interpretation as a combination of invention and discovery.[9] That is, insofar as we cannot properly account for the success of an interpretation—for what makes it, as we might wish to say, binding upon what it interprets—solely in terms of its character as an artifact of the interpreter, it seems we must also speak of discovery. At the same time, however, interpretations are underdetermined by what they interpret. Because they are after all human inventions, the

sought in some way to generalize his conclusions to a more abstract, metaphysical view.

[7] Alexander Nehamas makes frequent appeal to such a model in *Nietzsche: Life as Literature* (Cambridge: Harvard University Press, 1988). Once again, my point is that such readings are symptomatic of a certain sort of confusion Nietzsche diagnoses in his readers. I want to suggest that, as it is usually understood, the model of a reader interpreting a text is not a useful way of approaching Nietzsche's idea that we can understand the phenomena I have been referring to as authority and obedience in terms of a notion of power. If, however, one does not feel the pull of the interpretation I am rejecting, then, from Nietzsche's point of view, so much the better.

[8] Richard Rorty advances just the view of Nietzsche these readings rightly reject when he speaks of "Nietzsche's charge that the philosophical tradition which stems from Plato is an attempt to avoid facing up to contingency . . . Nietzsche thought that the test of human character was the ability to live with the thought that there was no convergence" (Rorty, *Philosophical Papers*, Vol. 1 [Cambridge: Cambridge University Press, 1991], p. 32).

[9] In sec. 12 of *Beyond Good and Evil*, for example, Nietzsche himself characterizes the psychological reinterpretation of the notion of the soul as invention and discovery [*erfinden* and *finden*].

notion of interpretation can seem to promise insight into what it means to acknowledge or otherwise 'to take responsibility for'—our contribution to the character of our experience.

We want to understand Nietzsche's claim that we can only understand a world that we have made. Let me sketch a reading of Nietzsche's usage of the notion of will to power that gives some content to the idea of 'making' here. We want to know what, if anything, he believes the knower 'does' to the known in the process of knowing it. I have claimed so far that Nietzsche's rejection of the thing-in-itself places restrictions upon the ways in which we understand in what sense one might speak of a contribution the knower makes to what he knows. But I think that Nietzsche's denial of this paradoxical notion permits us to articulate a more positive reading as well. The idea that interpretation must come to an end in something understood—in the practices that let these things count as the things they are—implies that we might intelligibly speak of a form of constraint in this context. We are, that is to say, constrained by what we understand. I want now to take up the suggestion I made in Chapter 1 that this notion of constraint allows us to make some sense of Nietzsche's talk of power. Once it is clearer what 'power' means in this context, we can begin to make sense of at least one way in which Nietzsche employs the notion of will.

Nietzsche is, I think, interested quite generally in the phenomenon of what I have called constraint. As I claimed in the Introduction, he is most specifically concerned to understand the sort of constraint that the virtue of honesty exercises on the men of knowledge. He is troubled above all by the failure of their obedience to the authority of that which conditions them in the present age: the imperative to be truthful. I have been arguing, furthermore, that he does not want his readers to reject that authority or in any way to transcend it, but rather to understand the character of their resistance to it. This reading has quite general implications for our understanding of Nietzsche's conception of his own relationship to the present age. It suggests, for example, that we can understand the Overman of *Thus Spoke Zarathustra* not as a hope for the future of humanity, but rather as an obstacle that Zarathustra tries to erect between himself and the last man of the present age, a way in which he tries to *foreclose* his future. That is to say, we should understand the doctrine of the Overman as a piece of Zarathustra's resistance to the constraint the present age exercises on him.[10]

[10] I believe I am, in this interpretation, substantially in agreement with Robert Pippin. See his "Irony and Affirmation in Nietzsche's *Thus Spoke Sarathustra*," in *Nietzsche's New Seas*, ed. Michael Allen Gillespie and Tracy B. Strong (Chicago: University of Chicago Press, 1988), pp. 45–71.

More broadly, however, what Nietzsche objects to in morality generally—as in the philosophical search for objective grounds for judgment
more specifically—are precisely these attempts to speak in ways that
do not rely upon our letting things count as what they are. Our attempts
to speak and to act outside these constraints manifest what he calls
"the worst of tastes, the taste for the unconditional" (*BGE,* sec. 31,
p. 43). Someone with a taste for the unconditional cannot understand
how meaning anything could depend upon our willingness to engage
in the human, all too human practices that make our interpretations
what they are. This outlook holds that anything that depends upon
nothing more than our willingness to engage in such practices can never
amount to more than mere opinion. Indeed, this 'worst of tastes' refuses
to allow even this much, because, unless there is some way to ensure
that we are all speaking about the same things at least some of the time,
even mere opinion becomes impossible. Without such guarantees, the
expression of opinion seems reduced to the level of inarticulate
grunting.

Such bad taste is expressed by philosophers' "lack of historical sense,
their hatred of even the idea of becoming, their Egyptianism" (*TI,* "Reason in Philosophy," sec. 1, p. 35). This is why "they think they are
doing a thing honour when they dehistoricize it, *sub specie aeterni—*
when they make a mummy of it" (ibid.). Nietzsche goes on: "All that
philosophers have handled for millennia has been conceptual mum-
mies; nothing actual has escaped from their hands alive. They kill, they
stuff, when they worship, these conceptual idolaters—they become a
mortal danger to everything they worship. Death, change, age, as well
as procreation and growth, are for them objections—refutations even.
What is, does not become; what becomes, is not. . . . Now they all
believe, even to the point of despair, in that which is. But since they
cannot get hold of it, they look for reasons why it is being withheld
from them" (ibid.). 'Becoming' here refers to all that philosophy, as
Nietzsche sees it, has tried to devalue by treating as nothing more than
features of human psychology and convention. The point of opposing
becoming as a category to being is simply to get at the idea that the
philosophical opposition between logic and psychology has itself—in
the sense we are exploring here—a history. That opposition is itself
something that 'becomes'. In this sense, the philosophical opposition
between being and becoming is a feature, in *Nietzsche*'s sense, of our
psychology. By calling this opposition into question, he means to reject
the philosophical devaluation of the latter. And if we can make no philosophical sense of the opposition between logic and psychology, then, in

Nietzsche's view, we can make only psychological sense of philosophy's devaluation of psychology.

However, as we should by now expect, though Nietzsche is in a quite general way interested in the fact of constraint, he is not committed to trying to produce a theoretical account of it. On the contrary, what concerns him is the fact of our resistance to constraint—our unwillingness to let things count as the things they are. It is this unwillingness that is under investigation in his various inquiries into the origins of morality. In short, Nietzsche proposes only a psychology of resistance. Such a psychology, I suggest, is what is at stake in the doctrine of will to power.

Our reading of *The Birth of Tragedy* has already confronted us with the idea of constraint. Tragic obedience to the authority of culture is achieved by overcoming what is, in effect, a failure to let things count as the things they are. I have argued that the only content to be given to this talk of letting things count as the things they are is that of a description of human practices. There is, in other words, no magical action or event that binds interpretations to their objects—nothing that in this sense might justify our interpretation of the world. We might call the sorts of constraints in question here 'the constraints of intelligibility.'[11] Obedience to such constraint is what I have called 'making sense'. To treat obedience as interpretation is, as Nietzsche explains, to fail to make sense—it is to find the world unintelligible in the way he claims only a spectator can. This is why Nietzsche believes that the Socratic demand for reasons makes sense only to a spectator.

That the Socratic demand can, nevertheless, come to make sense is what suggests that there is conceptual room to speak meaningfully of constraint in this context. Our responsiveness to constraint can fail, and it is such failure that gives content to the idea of constraint. Where we

[11] As we will see later, 'constraints of intelligibility' is really much too fancy a way of putting what should be a perfectly pedestrian point. All I have in mind in speaking of constraint here is that Nietzsche believes that, as we stand, we tend to resist (this, again, is a psychological claim, but as opposed to what?) taking responsibility for what we say. What does it mean to take responsibility? Again, Nietzsche's is a pedestrian notion of responsibility. It means, in *his* sense, to 'give reasons', that is, to back up what one says with evidence, to know what one is talking about, to be prepared to retract claims that one no longer believes, to tell the truth—in short, to do what one has to do to make oneself understood. Nietzsche's complaint about us is that, by and large, we resist doing this, that we would rather foist the responsibility off onto someone else, or even to talk in such a way that the issue of responsibility can be avoided altogether. There are both philosophical and more ordinary, 'man in the street', ways of avoidance. Nietzsche would have us recognize that, in each case, it is a matter of avoiding the fact of history: avoiding the fact that speech has consequences.

can make no sense of the idea of failure, I think, both the ideas of constraint and responsiveness begin to idle. But though the possibility of such failure leads the philosopher to ask in what success consists, it is precisely of the demand for such a positive account of intelligibility that Nietzsche wants a diagnosis.

As I mentioned in Chapter 1, Nietzsche himself does occasionally speak of terms of constraint in this connection. But his most famous name for this idea is 'power'. For example, in a passage I quoted in Chapter 1 he clearly uses 'power' in this sense. He claims that 'knowledge became a piece of life itself, and hence a continually growing power—until eventually knowledge collided with those primeval basic errors: two lives, two powers both in the same human being'. It is the growth of this power—that is, the way in which the Socratic will to truth has become fateful for us—that we have been trying to understand. In another passage with which we have been concerned, Nietzsche speaks quite explicitly of constraint. He insists, as we saw, that 'we cease to think when we refuse to do so under the constraint [Zwange] of language; we barely reach the doubt that sees this limitation as a limitation'. He might as well have spoken here of the authority (or power) of language.[12]

'Will', on the other hand, is Nietzsche's name for our contribution to intelligibility. As with power and the idea of constraint, there are a number of more or less equivalent terms that might be used to designate the same idea. Thus, in the context of my reading of *The Birth of Tragedy*, I have spoken of obedience as the properly tragic response to the authority of culture. I have spoken more generally of obedience as letting something count as the thing it is. The will, then, is the speaker's responsiveness to the constraints of intelligibility. On this reading, the expression 'will to power' refers, then, to the fact of the world's intelligibility. This suggests that, for Nietzsche, morality in the sense that concerns us here represents a form of weakness of will, and hence a kind of unintelligibility. Strength of will, on the other hand, is the perfection of responsiveness. As we will see presently, Nietzsche conceives of such perfection as a form of freedom.[13]

Nietzsche says that 'to impose upon becoming the character of being is the supreme will to power'. But it should be clear that something's

---

[12] For an intriguing discussion of the idea of authority in this context, see James C. Edwards, *The Authority of Language: Heidegger, Wittgenstein, and the Threat of Philosophical Nihilism* (Tampa: University of South Florida Press, 1990).

[13] My usage of the idea of perfection in this context owes much to Stanley Cavell's discussion of Emerson's influence on Nietzsche. See his *Conditions Handsome and Unhandsome* (Chicago: University of Chicago Press, 1990).

having the 'character of being' in this sense cannot be construed merely as a matter of the application of human conventions. It cannot be construed, that is, as some merely anthropological fact about us, as a fact, in other words, about the way we happen to employ our concepts. Nietzsche's point is precisely that no such fact about us could conceivably be made into something's 'character of being'. There is no brute something that, to pick some pedestrian examples, we see as a table, no mere movement that we see as aggressive or courageous, no mere shape of the mouth that we see as a smile. Things like this simply count as tables, as aggression or courage, as smiles. It is to these and similar things, he insists, that we must be—and for the most part are—responsive, but their being these things cannot exactly represent something for which we may be held responsible.

I am suggesting, in other words, that we use the idea of the character of being to help illuminate that of imposition. In particular, I think we should treat the locution 'character of being' as shorthand for 'character of being _____', where the blank may be filled in with whatever we like—an outrage, help, a fact, pretense, a question, an answer, and so on—and try to see what light such a reading sheds upon Nietzsche's usage of the notion of imposition. We may find it tempting, however, to proceed in the opposite direction, trying, in effect, to determine what Nietzsche meant by 'character of being' by simply taking for granted that we understand the sense of imposition. Yet, in one way or another, such a reading construes Nietzsche as encouraging us to recognize our confinement to the circle of our interpretations. And as I have argued, the aim of his attack on the notion of the thing-in-itself is precisely to denounce this sort of epistemological modesty as philosophically unmotivated and, at least on its own terms, incoherent.[14]

Treating the ideas of character of being and imposition in the way I suggest we should is likely to create in some readers what is, from Nietzsche's point of view, an all-too-familiar resistance. From a philosophical perspective, it may not seem immediately obvious what he might mean in speaking of the character of being, or at least that the sense of that notion is not as transparent as that of imposition. But I think many of our interpretative difficulties are resolved by realizing that, of the two notions, that of the character of being is surely the more transparent. What our discussion of Nietzsche's rejection of the thing-in-itself should have brought home to us is that by 'character of

---

[14] Remember, however, that Nietzsche believes that there is psychological sense to be made of this idea: it is an obstacle the philosopher erects between himself and the world.

being' Nietzsche means more or less just what he says, whereas by 'imposition', it seems, he cannot mean—at least in a philosophical tone of voice—what he says. Being, for Nietzsche, is not something to be explained by the notion of imposition, because there is, in this sense anyway, nothing to be explained. Thus, the character of being, for example, a table is just that: being a table. In other words, the expression 'character of being' refers to the place where interpretations come to an end: the world itself. Something has the character of being, in other words, if it exercises constraint or power over us. But if this is indeed how we should understand Nietzsche's locution, then, as I have suggested, we simply cannot take straightforwardly his talk of imposition. The only thing we 'do' when we make sense is to let our interpretations come to an end in understanding. And although we do precisely this whenever we make sense, making sense is not something we do in any way other than is expressed by the common locution, 'that makes sense'. We 'make' sense—we are intelligible—but we do not (in a philosophical sense) *create* it. We talk about the world, but no gap between us and the world is bridged in doing so.

As I said, resistance to this reading stems, in large part, from the fact that it so naturally seems to some readers that Nietzsche meant to use the notion of imposition to explain what the character of [something's] being (say) courageous or a table comes to. The claim that talking about the character of being is in effect just another way of reminding us that interpretations come to an end in understanding will seem, from this point of view, simply to beg the philosophical question Nietzsche should be trying to answer: namely, what justifies us in calling this act courageous? According to the crudest example of this sort of reading, Nietzsche is supposed to believe that the fact that this stuff—sense data, say, or whatever else one feels is meant by 'becoming' in the passage at hand—counts as a table is to be explained by an appeal to the fact that in some way we make it so count. And because we impose this interpretation upon such stuff, we bear responsibility for the fact that it counts as the thing it seems to be. On such a reading, what justifies our calling this stuff a table is only our willingness to do so.

By now, however, this picture should seem quite implausible. This is because, from Nietzsche's point of view, the proposed application of the idea of imposition is incoherent. Our discussion of his denial of the thing-in-itself should have convinced us that we have no handle on the notion of the object of an interpretation, unless that object is something we already in some way understand. But this implies that there is no obvious content to assign to the notion of interpretation as imposition.

Let us try to see, then, where taking Nietzsche at his word about the character of being gets us.

To stick with our example, the character of being a table is, on the reading I am proposing, only that something be a table. I said that the fact that this thing counts as a table is not something for which Nietzsche thinks we can intelligibly be held responsible. It is rather something to which we must be—and, once again, are by and large—responsive. From a properly philosophical point of view, I think, this is all that Nietzsche's talk of imposition can come to. Talk of responsiveness solves no standing philosophical problem about our relationship to the world. Thus, taking the idea of character of being at face value suggests that there is nothing special we are doing when we are so responsive. But if there is nothing special we do in being responsive to the character of something's being a table, then what are we to make of Nietzsche's talk of imposition? Why does he speak of responsiveness in terms that suggest activity rather than passivity? How, in other words, does he employ the concept of will? And what does it mean to claim that morality (in the specifically Socratic sense at stake in this discussion) represents a form of weakness of will?

'Will', I said, is Nietzsche's name for a speaker's responsiveness to the constraints of intelligibility. (As we will see in Chapter 5, 'will' is also a name for what the Genealogy calls 'responsibility'.) By speaking of the will in terms that suggest activity, he suggests that something is achieved in making sense, that responsiveness to constraint represents some sort of accomplishment. I think that he speaks of imposition, positing, imprinting, schematizing, and so on, by way of getting at the idea that making sense involves overcoming our resistance to doing so.[15] As he sees it, being human at all is a matter of overcoming such resistance. This, I suggest, is why he thinks he can meaningfully say that "the world viewed from inside, the world defined and determined according to its 'intelligible character' . . . would be 'will to power' and nothing else" (BGE, sec. 36, p. 48). Such a remark does not seek to

---

[15] We might say that talking about imposition, schematizing, and so on, is corrective of a certain philosophical picture of what the world's intelligibility must consist in, namely, that it must be something that human reason somehow finds written into the order of things. But only if we read Nietzsche along something like the lines I have suggested here can we really see what it might mean to speak of correction in this context. Nietzsche's point is, not that it is just false that the world's intelligibility is discovered or found, but that the very idea that it is is a piece of philosophical resistance—something that he does desire to correct. But the correction here can only be psychological in nature; it is not something achieved by means of an alternative philosophical picture. Imposition is not a philosophical metaphor.

articulate what Socratism would consider an ontological point, but rather what Nietzsche thinks of as a psychological one.[16]

Nevertheless, because the Socratic philosopher refuses to allow that intelligibility could depend upon facts about us, he finds the idea of an achievement involved in making sense to be deeply objectionable. 'Such sense as depends upon us,' the philosopher thinks, 'is not worth making!' This is the conclusion Nietzsche's diagnosis of the thing-in-itself should have led us to expect, for the philosopher cannot bear the idea that we do indeed make sense and seeks to foist responsibility for doing so onto a fantasy of something completely independent of us.

In Nietzsche's view, then, we can speak of making sense as something that we do—of meaning as something that we impose—only in a psychological sense. In other words, talk of imposing being upon becoming is not best read as a *philosophical* claim at all. In a philosophical sense, there simply is nothing that we do to make sense. There is no philosophical difficulty here to be overcome, no gap to be bridged between the sense we make and the world itself. Psychologically speaking, however, our moral needs introduce a gap between ourselves and the sense that we make.

As I claimed in Chapter 1, Nietzsche believes that our resistance to being intelligible is fundamental to the kind of creatures we have become. We find the necessity of responsiveness profoundly offensive. Responsiveness itself, however, is fundamental to any form of human life. Without it, there simply *is* no life in the sense that interests Nietzsche. This he holds to be true even if, as in the present case, our responsiveness is distorted by resistance. He most often speaks of responsiveness as a form of suffering, and suggests that not to suffer in this way would be, in effect, to cease to be human. But he also holds that Socratism has been our most successful philosophical response to—that is, interpretation of—our suffering. Thus, in this second sense as well, to suffer is, in Nietzsche's view, to be human, and the cessation of suffering would spell the end of humanity as we have known it. This is why Nietzsche writes in the preface to *The Birth of Tragedy* that "the question of the Greek's relation to pain, his degree of sensibility, is basic: did this relation remain constant? or did it change radically?" (*BT*, sec. 4, p. 21).[17]

[16] From Nietzsche's point of view, of course, such psychological points may be said to be ontological just because he is concerned to undermine the standpoint from which we usually draw that distinction. There 'is' anything—the world has the character of being—only on the condition that we let it be what it is. And we 'do' *that* only on the condition that we overcome our resistance to doing so.

[17] More generally, Nietzsche holds that "the problem [of life] is that of the meaning of suffering: whether a Christian meaning or a tragic meaning" (*WP*, sec. 1052, p. 543).

In our discussion of *The Birth of Tragedy*, we explored in some detail the nature of the tragic understanding of suffering. I claimed there that the Christian-moral interpretation—namely, that we suffer from the meaninglessness of life—involves a misunderstanding of the nature of the suffering in question. Ultimately, it is the meaningfulness of life that, in Nietzsche's view, philosophy finds most objectionable. As we have seen, to suffer from the meaningfulness of life is to find the necessity of responsiveness offensive. It is to feel that, insofar as human intelligibility depends upon such responsiveness, we proceed in the dark, without grounds. But, as we have also seen, the intelligibility of the Socratic philosopher's objection to responsiveness depends on treating it as interpretation—as the application of concepts. And this implies, I argued, that the philosopher's concerns about the apparent groundlessness of this interpretation depend upon his having already distorted the phenomena at hand. In Nietzsche's terms, the philosopher treats the will as something independent of the action of judgment, and then asks what guides it. But from Nietzsche's point of view, this last question only betrays the fact that he has failed properly to understand the nature of responsiveness, the real character of human will.

While this interpretation is still quite abstract, it should nevertheless be clear why Nietzsche would consider Socratism to be a form of weakness of will. Finding philosophical concerns about groundlessness intelligible depends upon a failure of responsiveness. This failure is signaled by a philosophical conception of the will: the philosopher conceives of responsiveness or obedience as the application of concepts to the world. But the diagnosis that Nietzsche proposes of this failure is not simply that the philosopher or moralist operates with a mistaken *conception* of will. Rather, as in the case of the philosophical insistence on the thing-in-itself, Nietzsche wants to show how the philosopher's conception of the will is symptomatic of his resistance to the necessity of responsiveness. Indeed, the philosopher's will may be said to be weak in the sense that responsiveness itself has become unintelligible to him.

In speaking of weakness of will, I have, of course, not meant to suggest that the philosopher lacks what might be thought of as the intellectual or spiritual fortitude to face up to the groundlessness or contingency of the practices in terms of which he makes sense of his life. The philosopher himself might describe his situation in precisely these terms, and he will point to the need for such grounding as a justification for his search for something more secure than our willingness to let things count as the things they are. But from Nietzsche's point of view, the philosopher cannot be taken at his word, because his description of his problem amounts to a misinterpretation of his real needs, a misunderstanding of the true nature of his particular form of human suffering.

To summarize the argument so far, Nietzsche's talk of imposition, positing, schematizing, and so forth, suggests that constraint—or power—only is what it is insofar as we are responsive to it, only insofar as we learn to submit ourselves to it. Power must, as it were, be met halfway. And although Nietzsche can make no good *philosophical* sense of the idea that we can do otherwise than to make sense, nothing forces our obedience to constraint—nothing external to our lives *compels* our responsiveness. Finally, it is the idea of overcoming resistance to such responsiveness that gives content to the suggestion that the will is, for Nietzsche, in some way active—that making sense represents an achievement.

In the present age, Nietzsche insists, the way in which we make sense of ourselves is as knowers. In other words, the value we place upon knowledge itself has come, in his view, to represent a human achievement. But knowledge, he says, is always a matter of "placing oneself in a conditional relation to [what we know]" (*WP*, sec. 555, p. 301). Nietzsche's conception of knowledge, then, turns on a picture of being conditioned by what one knows. The idea of being conditioned suggests that our relationship to the world is one of passivity, and I have argued that Nietzsche's use of the notion of the will may be interpreted accordingly. By way of conclusion, I would now like to try to say a bit more about this idea of will as obedience or responsiveness to constraint, because, at least in what he thinks of as its properly philosophical form, Nietzsche quite clearly rejects the concept of will.

Nietzsche's Conception of the Will

Where Nietzsche speaks of will in connection with the value he understands us to place upon knowledge, I have spoken, instead, of commitment. Thus, when he talks about the modern will to knowledge, I have suggested that we may understand him to be talking about our present commitment to truthfulness. Talking about the *will* to knowledge, then, is his way of trying to explore the virtue of honesty in the present age. In this section, I want to see what can be said about the idea of will so understood. For while Nietzsche is sharply critical of what he thinks of as the philosophical notion of will, I will argue that he retains a nonphilosophical—or, as I have put it, psychological—conception of it.

Nietzsche articulates his most famous criticism of the philosophical

conception of the will in section 19 of *Beyond Good and Evil*. As elsewhere, so in the case of the will, philosophers have, he says, "adopted
a popular prejudice and exaggerated it" (*BGE*, sec. 19, p. 25). The particular prejudice at stake here is that willing is something simple, something to which we have more or less direct intuitive or introspective
access, something, in short, that may be understood independently of
its surroundings. Both the view that a free agent is the wholly undeter-
mined cause of its actions and the view that we can specify the cause
of someone's actions independently of those actions depend, according
to section 19, upon a distorted conception of the will:

> Philosophers are accustomed to speak of the will as if it were the best-
> known thing in the world; indeed, Schopenhauer has given us to
> understand that the will alone is really known to us. . . . But again
> and again it seems to me that in this case too, Schopenhauer only did
> what philosophers are in the habit of doing—he adopted a popular
> prejudice and exaggerated it. Willing seems to me to be above all
> something complicated, something that is a unit only as a word—
> and it is precisely in this one word that the popular prejudice lurks,
> which has defeated the always inadequate caution of philosophers.
> So let us for once be more cautious, let us be "unphilosophical": let
> us say that in all willing there is, first, a plurality of sensations. . . .
> Therefore, just as sensations . . . are to be recognized as ingredients
> of the will, so, secondly, should thinking also: in every act of will
> there is a ruling thought—let us not imagine it possible to sever this
> thought from the "willing," as if any will would then remain over!
> Third, the will is not only a complex of sensation and thinking, but
> it is above all an affect, and specifically the affect of command. (*BGE*,
> sec. 19, p. 25)

Though Nietzsche's immediate target in this passage appears to be
Schopenhauer, we can nevertheless recognize more recent philosophical accounts of agency as versions of the sort of view he rejects. In
rehearsing arguments for and against such views, one is sometimes
asked to account for the difference between someone's raising her arm
and her arm merely rising. It is natural to answer that in the former
case, the agent intends or 'wills' her arm to rise, whereas in the latter,
her intentions play no—or at least not the proper sort of—role. Granting this point, one is then supposed to reflect upon the special internal
connection between an intention and the movement in question. The
philosophical puzzle is, roughly, to say what in the case of an action

makes the connection between an intention and a movement more than merely accidental.[18]

Nietzsche would insist that this whole picture of actions, as composed of discrete intentions (or acts of will) lying behind movements whose character is specifiable independently of the intention in question, is based on confusions and oversimplifications that he considers quite typical of our usual philosophical lack of caution and care. Willing, he says, is 'something complicated, something that is a unit only as a word'. Ignorance of this fact is responsible for the mistaken philosophical picture of action as composed of an act of will in the appropriate causal relationship to a movement. Consequently, Nietzsche tries to be, as he says, unphilosophical enough to offer a more plausible description of the phenomena in question.

According to section 19, willing is not a simple, brute psychological phenomenon that functions as the driving force of action; it is something intelligible, something that has a recognizable content and structure. Though the will is composed of various sorts of sensations, thoughts, and affects, the crucial affect is that of commanding. An adequate grasp of the nature of the affect of the command is essential for understanding Nietzsche's conception of freedom of the will. And a proper understanding of this last notion is crucial for understanding the contribution Nietzsche suggests that we make to the intelligibility of the world.[19] Let us see, then, how he conceives of freedom of the will.

He writes, "That which is termed 'freedom of the will' is essentially the affect of superiority in relation to him who must obey: 'I am free, "he" must obey'—this consciousness is inherent in every will. . . . A man who wills commands something within himself that renders obedience, or that he believes renders obedience" (ibid.). An action must have both of these components—commanding and obeying—and cannot properly be understood in terms of just one of them. We are, however, misled into attributing to the will a kind of causal efficacy behind the ostensibly physical aspect of actions because we misinterpret what

[18] There are, of course, many problems with this way of posing questions about the nature of action. In particular, we do not have to start with the idea that the agent somehow *directs* her movements via her intentions. But I have not meant to suggest that Nietzsche's discussion of will might make some contribution to the philosophy of action per se, but only to illustrate a particular misunderstanding to which Nietzsche finds philosophers prone. For a related discussion of Nietzsche's treatment of the philosophical concept of will, see Bernard Williams, "Nietzsche's Minimalist Moral Psychology," *European Journal of Philosophy* 1, 1 (1993): 4–14.

[19] Here again, however, Nietzsche does not intend what he has to say about willing to contribute to the solution of a philosophical puzzle. On the contrary, the use to which he puts that notion is, in his special sense of the term, 'psychological'.

Nietzsche calls the 'delight of the person exercising volition'. The sense of overcoming resistance gives rise to the feeling of power that we mistake as causal efficacy; it is this feeling that produces the popular prejudice that the will is a unified and simple event that lies at the *source* of actions rather than is an integral component of them.[20]

In one sense, then, the idea of freedom of the will represents an illusion that results from failing to realize that obedience is as much a part of action as is commanding. A person's identification of himself with the affect of command—an identification that Nietzsche seems to think is encouraged by an associated sensation of power—gives rise to the mistaken view that the will suffices for action in the sense of being the cause of it. This illusion is a crucial part of the specifically moral picture that Nietzsche condemns of what he calls 'the doer behind the deed'. The view that freedom of will—and hence moral responsibility—depends upon the idea of being able to do otherwise requires the illusion he claims to uncover in section 19.

Nietzsche therefore rejects what he thinks of as the specifically philosophical interpretation of the idea of free will, not because he believes determinism to be true, but rather on the grounds that there is nothing of which determinism could be true—or, for that matter, false. He concludes: "Suppose someone were . . . to see through the boorish simplicity of this celebrated concept of 'free will' and put it out of his head altogether, I beg of him to carry his 'enlightenment' a step further, and also put out of his head the contrary of this monstrous conception of 'free will': I mean 'unfree will'. . . . The 'unfree will' is mythology; in real life it is only a matter of strong and weak wills" (*BGE*, sec. 21, p. 29). Thus, it is only by mistake that we speak in philosophical tones of freedom and unfreedom of the will. But to what, then, do Nietzsche's 'strength' and 'weakness' of will refer? An answer to this last question should shed light on the sense in which he is nevertheless willing to speak of freedom of will. As I have said, he does wish to retain the right to use *some* version of that notion.

---

[20] One way to think about Nietzsche's remarks here is that he is trying to understand, among other things, how philosophers pass from a psychological phenomenon to a philosophical problem. How—to stick with the example at hand—do we come to construe the 'delight of the person exercising volition' as (or as evidence of) a causal power behind his movements. There is, indeed, room to make psychological sense of the idea of freedom of will. As we will see at some length in Chapter 4, Nietzsche wishes to retain and rehabilitate a nonphilosophical use of this same idea. There is, in his view, all the difference in the world between a person whose will is free and one whose will is not. But there is, for him, no properly philosophical problem about the relation between, as we now might put it, intention and action to which the phenomena point. Thus, the philosophical inflation of the popular

According to section 19, the affects of command and obedience are united in anything that can be counted as an action. Unless we take account of both of these features, Nietzsche claims, actions will be unintelligible to us: mere movement somehow coupled to an independent act of will. He argues that we cannot make sense of the notion of the will as the cause of action in this sense. The will is rather an aspect of actions that makes them what they are, but it is not specifiable independent of the action it conditions as the particular will that it is. As Nietzsche says, "'will' can affect only 'will'—and not 'matter' (not 'nerves,' for example)" (*BGE*, sec. 36, p. 48). This suggests that, in his view, strength of will is a form of self-mastery.

Nietzsche claims that the affect we associate with freedom stems from the will's tendency to identify with its successes. The presence of this affect signals strength of will.

"Freedom of the will"—that is the expression for the complex state of delight of the person exercising volition, who commands and who at the same time identifies himself with the executor of the order—who, as such, enjoys also the triumph over obstacles, but thinks within himself that it was really his will itself that overcame them. In this way the person exercising volition adds the feelings of delight of his successful executive instruments, the useful "under-wills" or under-souls—indeed, our body is but a social structure composed of many souls—to his feelings of delight as commander. *L'effect c'est moi:* what happens here is what happens in every well-constructed and happy commonwealth; namely, the governing class identifies itself with the successes of the commonwealth. In all willing it is absolutely a question of commanding and obeying. (*BGE*, sec. 19, pp. 26–27)

The inability to identify with one's successes, on the other hand, is a symptom of weakness of will. A will can be said to be weak in this sense if it is incapable of recognizing its effects as its own.

The illusion, however, that it makes sense to speak of the will as freely exercising causal powers upon bodily movements stems from the illegitimate philosophical attempt to separate from one another the affects of commanding and obedience. If we do so, then obedience appears to be something external to the will, and what feels to us to be freedom will in fact be its opposite. Thus, Nietzsche says:

---

prejudice lying behind theories of free will consists not simply in bad phenomenology, but also—and more important—in seeing problems where in fact there are none.

inasmuch as in the given circumstances we are at the same time the commanding and the obeying parties, and as the obeying party we know the sensations of constraint, impulsion, pressure, resistance, and motion, which usually begin immediately after the act of will; inasmuch as, on the other hand, we are accustomed to disregard this duality, and to deceive ourselves about it by means of the synthetic concept "I," a whole series of erroneous conclusions, and consequently of false evaluations of the will itself, has become attached to the action of willing—to such a degree that he who wills believes sincerely that willing suffices for action. . . . In short, he who wills believes with a fair amount of certainty that will and action are somehow one; he ascribes the success, the carrying out of the willing, to the will itself, and thereby enjoys an increase of the sensation of power which accompanies all success. (Ibid., p. 26)

This discussion of the will remains quite abstract until we have a better idea what Nietzsche might count as action in the relevant sense. For the reasons I have suggested, it seems unlikely that he is talking about actions such as raising one's arm. Indeed, one suspects that, from Nietzsche's point of view, such actions are at best only philosophical artifacts. What, then, does he count as action?

In Chapter 5 we will see that, in a very general way, Nietzsche considers *speaking* to be action in the sense that is occupying us here. For the moment, however, I want to suggest only that overcoming resistance to the world's intelligibility might be said to be part of what he believes acting to be.[21] Remember that we are trying to understand in what sense, if any, meaning might be said to be imposed on or projected into the world. I argued that, from Nietzsche's point of view, the only sense such talk of imposition or projection could have is psychological sense. For the sort of meaning whose presence in the world Nietzsche is trying to account for cannot be the result of something we impose upon the world. It is rather something to which we are—and can, in a variety of ways, fail to be—responsive. My point here is that, as long as we feel that the constraints of intelligibility are external to us, our wills may be said, in Nietzsche's sense of the term, to be weak. On the other hand,

---

[21] Activity, in the specifically Nietzschean sense, is a psychological term, and should be contrasted with reactivity. I will take up this distinction again in Chapter 4. For the moment, we should remember only that when Nietzsche is trying to say what action is, he is not answering a philosophical puzzle about relation between, for example, intentions and movements. He denies that there is such a puzzle, and the questions he asks about activity and reactivity operate at a wholly different level.

the ability to identify with those constraints—to make them our own—can, I think, be called 'strength of will'.

The Birth of Tragedy provides clear examples of both strength and weakness of will in this sense. To have a strong will is to be able to resist the Socratic demand for reasons; it is to have one's instincts intact. To give in to that demand, however, is a sign of weakness of will. Being a spectator of one's community signals the decay of instinct and the collapse of authority. *Beyond Good and Evil* describes weakness of will in the following terms: "It is almost always a symptom of what is lacking in himself when a thinker senses in every 'causal connection' and 'psychological necessity' something of constraint, need, compulsion to obey, pressure, and unfreedom; it is suspicious to have such feelings—the person betrays himself" (*BGE*, sec. 21, p. 29). In this passage, Nietzsche is clearly employing the notion of constraint in a sense different from that in which I have used it so far.[22] As I have claimed, the Socratic spectator considers the constraints of intelligibility to be external to himself in this way. They constrain him in the sense of confining him, and he feels himself to be in a position to ask what makes their authority binding on him. He stands, in other words, over against them and asks about their justification. But this is constraint in the sense of compulsion. Strength of will, on the other hand, is a matter of responsiveness or obedience, of 'constraint' in the sense in which I have been using that term here. Obedience, however, is not a special internal relationship that one bears to one's language or culture. It is a spectator's error to think that it is, and it is a spectator's error to think that freedom of will in Nietzsche's sense is freedom *from* those constraints.

In other passages, however, Nietzsche indeed refers to obedience as freedom of will, and even goes so far as to represent it as self-determination. "Once a human being reaches the fundamental conviction that he must be commanded, he becomes 'a believer'. Conversely, one could conceive of such a pleasure and power of self-determination, such a freedom of the will that the spirit would take leave of all faith and every wish for certainty" (*GS*, sec. 347, pp. 289–90). Faith, he says,

---

[22] But this is simply a different sense of 'constraint'. The aim of the passage at hand, it seems to me, is precisely to drive home the need to distinguish between these two different senses of 'constraint' or 'will': that of compulsion and that of authority. "Most thinkers and scholars," Nietzsche writes, "picture every necessity as a kind of need, as a painstaking having-to-follow and being-compelled." Whereas "artists seem to have more sensitive noses in these matters, knowing only too well that precisely when they no longer do anything 'voluntarily' but do everything of necessity, their feeling of freedom, subtlety, full power, of creative placing, disposing, and forming reaches its peak—in short, that necessity and 'freedom of will' then become one in them" (*BGE*, sec. 213, pp. 139–40).

"is always coveted most and needed most urgently where will is lacking; for will, as the affect of command, is the decisive sign of sovereignty and strength" (ibid. p. 289). To be self-determining, in this sense of the term, is to have what might be called 'the courage of one's obedience'. Contrariwise, to be a believer is to feel that the only authority worthy of one's obedience is one that compels with, so to speak, logical neces- sity and, hence, with absolute certainty. Nietzsche insists, however, that our obedience is no more than a fact about us. The only necessity he is willing to speak of in this context is that of instinct. Such necessity is psychological in nature; it is only a fact about us. To be a believer, on the other hand, is to think of oneself as standing in need of something stronger than the necessity of one's instincts. Weakness of will, then, is a matter of thinking that the world's authority must be external to oneself, because one cannot see—and in fact resists seeing—how it could de- pend on nothing more than the fact of our obedience to it.

'Will to power', I suggest, is a name for the fact that we make sense. It is in this spirit that Nietzsche writes in a note from 1885, "This world is *The Will to Power*—and nothing besides! And you yourselves are also this will to power—and nothing besides! (*WP*, sec. 1067, p. 550).[23] As Heidegger likes to say (though with a different point), the will to power is a 'unitary phenomenon'.[24] Power in this sense requires will (con- straint requires responsiveness); the latter is not an incidental feature of intelligibility. This is why Nietzsche generally distinguishes what he calls 'power' from logical, psychological, and mechanical forms of compulsion. In any linguistic community Nietzsche would be willing to count as a culture, nothing forces one to speak in the way one speaks. Authority that *coerces* speech remains external to the speaker. Socrates' error is to suspect that all authority is coercive in this fashion. In Nietzsche's sense, however, authority depends upon obedience, and Socrates' suspicions are the sign of a slavish inability to distinguish authority from compulsion.

[23] These are, in other words, psychological claims. In trying to make sense of such remarks, however, we may be tempted to append to it a 'from our point of view'. But Nietzsche insists that there is nothing to be made of the point of contrast such a qualification suggests. For it is nothing less than the world itself—the world in which we live—that may be said to be will to power.

[24] To put the point in other words, we might say that the conventions in terms of which we understand ourselves and the world *must* be applied. Otherwise the notion of convention idles. But if we can only speak helpfully of conventions as applied, then the notion of convention seems to do no philosophical work on its own, and we now want to know in what their application consists. It is here, I think, that Nietzsche fails to see any general philosophical problem about either action or intelligibility.

Let us consider these points in summary fashion. I said at the outset that Nietzsche's doctrine of perspectivism is fueled by two intimately related views and could not properly be appreciated independently of them. First, Nietzsche denies the thing-in-itself. Second, he suggests that we bear responsibility for the contribution we make to the intelligible character of the world. Properly construed, however, the first—apparently negative—view reflects the principal conclusion of *The Birth of Tragedy* that, as I put it, interpretation comes to an end in understanding. This reading suggests, however, that the second—and ostensibly more positive—view should be understood as claiming that the responsibility in question is a matter of responsiveness to the constraints of intelligibility, rather than of responsibility for something we do. In this sense, responsibility is, for Nietzsche, a psychological not a philosophical notion.

I have also tried to show how the two views that fuel the doctrine of perspectivism are summed up in the claim that the intelligible character of the world is will to power. More specifically, I suggested that we understand 'power' as Nietzsche's name for the constraints that making sense exercises on us. Power is where interpretations come to an end: those institutions and practices in terms of which we make sense of our lives. Nietzsche's talk of power, then, is another way of getting at the upshot of his denial of the thing-in-itself.

'Will', on the other hand, is his name for our contribution to the fact of the world's intelligibility. It refers to our responsiveness to what constrains us. It is what the philosopher mistakenly believes we must add to our interpretations to bind them to the world. On this reading, to claim that the world is will to power is to claim that the world is fundamentally intelligible—'fundamentally' in the sense that Nietzsche's diagnoses of philosophical errors always return us to what he thinks of as the philosopher's attempts to deny the undeniable. Finally, I claimed that this interpretation of the notion of will to power implies that Nietzsche considers the resistance to intelligibility he diagnoses at the root of philosophy to be evidence of a kind of weakness of will expressed by an unwillingness to let things count as the things they are. Thus, instead of offering us an epistemology, the two views that fuel Nietzsche's perspectivism provide a highly abstract articulation of the sort of tragic insight we explored in our reading of *The Birth of Tragedy.*

When properly understood, the views on the basis of which one might be tempted to attribute to Nietzsche a doctrine of perspectivism tell us only that (to keep to our pedestrian example) this thing's being a table is something to which we are responsive, not something for which we are responsible. This last claim says no more than that, for example, we sit at such things on chairs in order, for instance, to write letters, eat meals, converse, negotiate contracts, and so on. The temptation to take Nietzsche to be claiming that, in some substantive philosophical sense, it is in virtue of our conventions and practices that it counts as a table is a temptation he would have us resist. Thus, the positive content to be gleaned from perspectivism can only be psychological in character. However, it cannot be said, in a philosophical tone of voice, to be 'merely' psychological, because 'responsiveness' refers to our situatedness in what we might, following Wittgenstein, call 'our form of life'. From Nietzsche's point of view, to insist that it is solely from the 'perspective' of our conventions and practices that this is a table is, in effect, to indicate that, by and large, we do not make such claims. On the reading I have proposed here, 'weakness of will' is the perspectivist's expression for the philosophical tendency to forget this fact.

I have tried, by means of the very pedestrian example of something's being a table, to articulate my sense of what, in view of his attack on Socratism, the so-called doctrine of perspectivism might mean for Nietzsche. But the application of this interpretation of Nietzsche's doctrine to claims about things like tables and chairs may seem to stretch credibility as a reading of *Nietzsche*'s interests in particular. In other words, someone might complain that, while such an interpretation of perspectivism might be made to work as a reading of Heidegger or even of the later Wittgenstein, Nietzsche himself was simply not concerned with examples of this sort. As it is, it may, in any case, be difficult to see what could possibly be meant by claiming that, by and large, we let such things count as tables. For it is not clear that, outside the classroom, the perspectivist—as I have interpreted his view—ever has any concrete occasion to entertain such claims. Indeed, the apparent triviality of the doctrine suggests an objection to our reading of the notion of will to power that we should now address. As far as things like tables and chairs are concerned, one might protest that there is simply no content at all to the notion of letting things count as the things they are. That is, while it might be granted that some sense can be made of Nietzsche's notion of power if we agree something's being a table cannot be in any substantial sense a matter of interpretation, there appears—in the present context anyway—to be nothing for Nietzsche's talk of will to be about. We can speak of responsiveness or will if we like, but it is hard to see how such talk adds anything to the reminder that interpretation comes to an end in understanding. Thus, to insist on talk of responsiveness in the context of our dealings with

THE KNOWER'S CONTRIBUTION TO THE KNOWN   149

tables and chairs can seem to exchange a philosophical confusion about imposition for what will strike some as a form of animism.

If we are to get any further with our notion of responsiveness as it applies to Nietzsche's work in particular, we will have to find a more compelling example of resistance than what a more or less parochial philosophical interest in grounding our claims about things such as tables and chairs will allow us to uncover. We need, in other words, an example of something Nietzsche considers to be fundamental to who we are, the authority of which he thinks we are inclined to resist, if we are adequately to understand the character of the resistance in question.

But we have such an example at our fingertips: the will to knowledge itself, the man of knowledge's Socratic inheritance. In the relevant sense, the will to knowledge is itself a form of power, one that Nietzsche believes we tend to resist. Thus, if there is a failure of obedience that is especially of concern to Nietzsche, it is connected with what he thinks we—that is, we men of knowledge—have become.

I am recommending a sharp shift of focus here. In this chapter, we have largely been concerned with Nietzsche's conception of knowledge itself. On the reading I have proposed, that conception is psychological in character. His views about knowledge are of a piece with his attack on Socratism in *The Birth of Tragedy*. The latter suggests that, in a philosophical frame of mind, we give voice to a particular kind of dissatisfaction with the ordinary conditions of intelligible speech—a dissatisfaction that leads us to look for something better than what we ordinarily go on in applying our words to the world. Nietzsche tends, as I suggested in Chapter 1, to treat such dissatisfaction as a symptom of our hatred of history—our ill will against time. In his view, we quite generally find offensive the idea that speaking intelligibly demands something of us, that speech, in short, has consequences. This is an idea we will explore at greater length in Chapter 5. At present, however, I am suggesting that we take a look at another form of resistance manifested by what Nietzsche calls 'the spirit of revenge': namely, the man of knowledge's hatred of his history *as* a man of knowledge.

As we have seen, the notions of history and responsibility are, for Nietzsche, intimately related. Indeed, it is to Socratism's attempt to drive a wedge between them that he most objects. In Nietzsche's view, an understanding of the kind of responsibility we bear for the meaning of our words cannot be divorced from a recognition of the historical character of human speech in general. In this chapter, we have been concerned to understand the nature of our Socratic inheritance: the modern will to knowledge. We have asked, in other words, what it means to say 'God is dead'. As I remarked in the Preface, saying that

God is dead is Nietzsche's way of reminding us that we must now take responsibility for what we say about the world, rather than trying as we have in the past to foist such responsibility onto a fantasy of the way the world is in itself. We have seen how that fantasy distorts our conception of the nature of the responsibility Nietzsche believes we can be said to bear for the sense we make. Finally, I have argued that it is our commitment to truthfulness itself—the will to knowledge—that brings these points home to us. It is, in short, what Socratism has become that, in Nietzsche's view, renders Socratism itself unbelievable.

Now I also said in the Preface that Nietzsche holds that the death of God is an *event* as a way of making clear that he believes we bear responsibility for, roughly, the fact that we now have to take responsibility for what we say about the world. In other words, to treat the death of God as an event is to acknowledge that who we are—our modern commitment to truthfulness—represents an *achievement*. As he says in *The Gay Science*, the death of God is something that we ourselves have brought about, something we have *done*. "There has never been a greater deed; and whoever is born after us—for the sake of this deed he will belong to a higher history than all history hitherto" (*GS*, sec. 125, p. 181). It is in this context that we must now try to see what the Nietzschean notion of responsibility comes to.

Nietzsche is convinced that, as we stand, we fail to take responsibility for our commitment to truthfulness—we are not properly responsive to it. We fail, in short, to understand the death of God *as* an event. Our will to truth, he says, is not self-conscious. It remains moral or pious in character, and is, to that extent, life-denying. If we are to understand what 'resistance' and 'responsiveness' mean for Nietzsche, we will have to come to terms with this last claim.

As I have argued, the question of our Socratic inheritance troubles Nietzsche from the time of *The Birth of Tragedy*. But the idea of a Socratic inheritance can be understood in two ways. On the one hand, we can speak of a Socratic inheritance in the sense of a certain conception of the nature of knowledge. From this point of view, what we inherit from Socratism is, in effect, as understanding of what is wrong with Socratism. On the other hand, we can also speak of a Socratic inheritance in the sense that our current understanding of the errors involved in Socratism is itself an inheritance that can, in Nietzsche's opinion, be questioned. It is with this latter sense of the idea of our Socratic inheritance that I take Nietzsche himself to have been most concerned. For even in *The Birth of Tragedy* "it was the problem of science itself, science considered for the first time as problematic, as questionable" (*BT*, "Attempt at a Self-Criticism," sec. 2, p. 18) that troubled him. And as we have seen, it is with the problem of science that he begins to articulate his principal question about the present age. He is expressly concerned to understand the character of the man of knowledge's commitment to science, his scientism. It is that commitment that Nietzsche thinks the man of knowledge misunderstands, and it is that misunderstanding that embodies his resistance to what he has become in the present age. This same question of science occupies Nietzsche in the opening sections of the fifth book of *The Gay Science* in particular, and most specifically in section 344, and to that long aphorism I now turn.

CHAPTER 4

THE WILL TO KNOWLEDGE

*The Gay Science, Section 344: The Character of
Our Commitment to Truthfulness*

> In us there is accomplished—supposing you want a formula—
> the self-sublimation of morality.
>
> *Daybreak,* preface, sec. 4, p. 4

> *New Struggles.*—After Buddha was dead, his shadow was still
> shown for centuries in a cave—a tremendous, gruesome
> shadow. God is.dead; but given the way of men, there may still
> be caves for thousands of years in which his shadow will be
> shown.—And we—we still have to vanquish his shadow too.
>
> *The Gay Science,* sec. 108, p. 167

It is almost always in connection with the men of knowledge that
Nietzsche uses the first person plural. If they understood themselves
aright, they would be among those he calls his rightful readers, his
"unknown friends" (*GM* III, sec. 27, p. 161). In *The Gay Science,* section
344, however, he argues that the attitude of these individuals toward
truthfulness—the value they place upon knowledge—remains pious,
their will to knowledge moral. And their piety, he says, stands in the
way of self-knowledge. It is what prevents them from becoming what
they are.

As we will see, however, it is not at all obvious what might be meant
by saying that the modern will to knowledge represents a *moral* commitment. This much is clear: Nietzsche considers the high esteem in which
the men of knowledge hold honesty generally—and intellectual honesty, in particular—to represent a specifically moral evaluation of that

virtue. But he does not seem to mean by this that the demand that one be truthful expresses a recognizably moral requirement simply because it purports to tell one what one ought to do. Nor, I think, does he mean to argue that it is somehow because the men of knowledge are honest for the sake of no other end they happen to have that that imperative is a moral one.[1] As we will see, this is not—anyway not exactly—what he means in saying that their will to truth is unconditional.[2] But there is indeed something about the attitude they adopt toward the demand to be truthful—something, that is, about the character of their honesty—that Nietzsche condemns as moral, and that he seeks to undermine. This attitude constitutes the man of knowledge's special brand of nihilism: his indifference to what he has become in the present age. And it is the nihilism Nietzsche seeks to combat in those he considers his rightful readers.

To see what it might mean to speak of the piety of the modern will to truth, we must bear in mind that Nietzsche often uses the notion of morality to designate *any* way of living that, in his view, seeks to deny life.[3] Though hardly informative about what we ordinary think of as morality, I think it is this usage that is at stake in section 344. I will argue in this chapter that our commitment to truth may, according to Nietzsche, be said to be life-denying in the sense that it is rooted in an unwillingness to acknowledge its own *historical* character—what we might think of as the *fact* of its history.[4] Although it is not altogether

[1] Remember that *The Gay Science* claims that it is characteristic of the present age that, as Nietzsche puts it, knowledge wants to be more than a mere means. See, again, sec. 123.

[2] For an example of Nietzsche's usage of the term 'unconditional' in this context, see sec. 27 of the third essay of the *Genealogy*, where Nietzsche speaks of "unconditional honest atheism (and *its* is the only air we breathe, we more spiritual men of this age!)" (p. 160).

[3] Nietzsche often says that morality is life-denying. (See, for example, *The Antichrist*, sec. 7.) But at least in some contexts, to say that morality is life-denying is to speak tautologously. 'Morality', in Nietzsche's usage, seems to *mean* little more than 'that which is life-denying'. And though I think I can see why, for example, the Socratic demand for reasons counts as moral in this sense, I do not understand as well as I would like to why Nietzsche calls any such attitude 'moral'. In any event, it is something else to claim that those attitudes and practices that we ordinarily recognize as moral—attitudes and practices, for example, that concern our obligations to others—are life-denying—a claim Nietzsche is also notorious for making. The task at hand, however, is to understand in what sense our commitment to truth might be said to be moral in the sense of being life-denying. Later on, I will try to make clear how morality—in a more conventional sense of the word—tends to mask the life-denying character of our will to truth.

[4] The sense in which we may speak of history here is complicated. Nietzsche's point is genealogical, not genetic. Because we find it all too easy to associate the idea of history with that contingency, we must bear in mind here that Nietzsche wants

clear to me why Nietzsche wants to call such unwillingness 'moral', I think I can show in what sense an unwillingness to acknowledge history may be said to be life-denying, and I think I can make clear the way in which Nietzsche thinks this form of life-denial is at work in the modern will to knowledge.[5]

To acknowledge the historical character of the will to knowledge is, for Nietzsche, not merely to recognize the historical antecedents of that commitment, not merely to see that this or that political, intellectual, or spiritual struggle in the past has contributed to the value we presently place upon truth telling. Rather, it is properly to appreciate the fact that we are *only now* in a position to care about such facts at all; it is to see that such progress is somehow definitive of who we are. According to Nietzsche, the so-called death of God is fateful for us in the present age. This, I want to argue, is precisely what the piety of the man of knowledge's commitment to truthfulness prevents him from recognizing. He does not see in what the sense of fate consists in this context. From his point of view, the idea of history suggests, if anything, that of contingency—as though he, so to speak, just happens to be committed to being truthful. But just this is the nihilism of indifference I mentioned in the Introduction. I suggested in Chapter 2 that this form of nihilism is the expression of resistance to the authority of the imperative to be truthful, and this is the conclusion for which I wish to argue here. Resisting the authority of the imperative to be truthful is not a matter of being unwilling to face up to the sorts of hard truths uncovered by the will to knowledge. Rather, Nietzsche's point is that the man of knowledge—the truth teller—resists understanding the fact that he has *become* a man of knowledge. It is my aim in Chapter 5 to

---

to drive a wedge between the two. Readers often wish to say that that which has a history—as does the modern will to knowledge—is contingent in the sense that it might as well have been different. But Nietzsche considers, in a way it is a chief burden of this chapter to make clear, that what is historical for us—specifically, the will to knowledge—is *fateful* for us, necessary. The thought that one might have been different from what one is has no more meaning for the man of knowledge than would, for the tragic Greek, the (Socratic) thought that, were one not Greek, one might not interpret one's concepts in the ways one does. It is the aim of a genealogical—as opposed to a genetic—account of our values to show how history and necessity come together in this way.

[5] We have, of course, already seen one sense in which we might think of resistance to the historical character of life as life-denying: the Socratic insistence on reasons amounts to resisting the historical character of life in the sense that one seeks, in a philosophical frame of mind, to avoid taking responsibility for what one says. As the second essay of the *Genealogy* suggests, human speech may be said to be historical in the sense that what we say has consequences. Speech is part of human life; this, indeed, is Socrates' objection to it.

show in what sense morality can be said to stand in the way of the truth teller's recognizing the historical character of his commitment to truthfulness.

It is important to recognize at the outset that Nietzsche understands the piety of the man of knowledge's commitment to truthfulness not in terms of his conception of knowledge itself, but rather in terms of the character of the value he places upon it. More specifically, the man of knowledge is not guilty of holding a metaphysical conception of the nature of truth. Indeed, as we have seen, from Nietzsche's standpoint, he can quite simply deny that there is conceptual room to articulate such views in the first place. Nietzsche holds, however, that the man of knowledge's *commitment* to truth—the way in which he cares about it—remains pious or moral in the sense of being life-denying. And he believes this to be so on the grounds of the man of knowledge's conviction that modern science represents a fundamental alternative—an 'opposing ideal'—to that which anyone committed to knowledge must reject in metaphysics, religion, and moral philosophy. In other words, it is just insofar as the will to truth denies the intimacy of its connection to what Nietzsche elsewhere calls the 'ascetic ideal' that Nietzsche holds it to be in fact the noblest expression of that ideal. This is, as I see it, the main thesis of section 344. The man of knowledge believes, in other words, that his investment in modern science represents a fundamentally nonmoral and life-affirmative perspective. But Nietzsche insists that, just insofar as the man of knowledge believes that this is so, it cannot be so. This reading suggests, however, that Nietzsche understands the piety of the modern will to truth in terms of its attitude toward the past—indeed, toward the fact of having a past at all. From the nihilist's point of view, the modern commitment to truthfulness represents a complete break with the past. But because Nietzsche seeks to strengthen that commitment rather than to reject it, the view that science is a clear-cut alternative to philosophy and religion must function, for him, as a piece of resistance to the authority of knowledge in the present age.

In order to make sense of this last claim, however, we will need to understand in precisely what sense Nietzsche considers the man of knowledge to believe that science represents a nonmoral outlook on life. Because, fairly obviously, if, from Nietzsche's own point of view, the faith in science represents a commitment to truth instead of to the philosophical, religious, and moral falsehoods that formerly governed our lives, then the will to truth is in *that* sense an alternative to the ascetic ideal. Our present commitments represent an alternative to our past commitments in the sense that truth is an alternative to falsity.

In what way, then, does the modern will to truth represent a moral commitment after all? And what, finally, does Nietzsche take to be the effect on the man of knowledge of acknowledging the fact that it does?

According to both the *Genealogy* and *The Gay Science,* men of knowledge treat the value of truthfulness as an alternative to morality in the sense that their commitment to truth appears to them to be clearly opposed to the sort of moral, religious, and philosophical faiths they reject. Thus, Nietzsche writes, "they tell me [that an alternative—an 'opposing will'—to the ascetic ideal] is not lacking, it has not merely waged a long and successful fight against this ideal, it has already conquered this ideal in all important respects: all modern science is supposed to bear witness to that—modern science which, as a genuine philosophy of reality, clearly believes in itself alone, clearly possesses the courage for itself and the will to itself, and has up to now survived well enough without God, the beyond, and the virtues of denial" (*GM* III, sec. 23, p. 146). The point here, however, is not that 'this-worldly' science tells us the truth where 'other-worldly' philosophy sought to deceive us. Nietzsche certainly believes that this is so, and in claiming that, in effect, he denies that science is an alternative to philosophy, I do not mean to suggest that he does not hold truth to be an alternative to falsehood. So far anyway, there could hardly be a greater difference. In the passage at hand, however, Nietzsche is claiming that science appears to the men of knowledge as the alternative to traditional philosophy *considered as a way of life*—as a radically different employment of human reason, affirmative of the actual world in which we live precisely where philosophy sought to deny it. It is an opposing *ideal.* Thus, when I speak here of science, I mean to designate a particular form of life, not a body of theories.[6]

Nietzsche thus rejects the idea that a scientific *outlook* represents an alternative to the philosophical one it supplants: "No! this 'modern science'—let us face this fact!—is the best ally the ascetic ideal has at present, and precisely because it is the most unconscious, involuntary, hidden, and subterranean ally!" (*GM* III, sec. 25, p. 155). The modern will to truth "is this [ascetic] ideal itself in its strictest, most spiritual formulation, esoteric through and through, with all external additions abolished, and thus not so much its remnant as its *kernel*" (*GM* III, sec. 27, p. 160).

As I have claimed, it is precisely the scientific person's conviction that knowledge and faith are starkly *opposed* outlooks that Nietzsche

---

[6] This usage is consistent with Nietzsche's interest in the *will* to knowledge, on the one hand, and his *dis*interest in the *nature* of the knowledge, on the other.

condemns as moral. In his view, not only does the will to knowledge represent a kind of faith in its own right, but it is an essential aspect of the very system of faith that it rejects.[7] In fact, as we will see, because the practice of genealogy is itself motivated by the will to truth, Nietzsche considers *it* to be an aspect of the same form of life that it undermines. For the will to truth to become self-conscious, I suggest, is for someone committed to truthfulness to become aware of this last fact. But to make sense of this last claim, we will need to understand better the relationship Nietzsche finds between the so-called ascetic ideal and the scientific faith that pretends to have thrown it over. It is this relationship that, in his view, the will to truth seeks to deny.

What needs to be made clear in advance, however, is the precise *way* in which the will to knowledge considers itself to be an alternative to what Nietzsche broadly construes as morality. Giving up the view that it is such an alternative is essential to overcoming the form of nihilism that threatens the man of knowledge. But Nietzsche's point is not simply that, insofar as the ascetic ideal has itself told us all along to tell the truth, a specifically scientific obedience to that same imperative cannot constitute an alternative to that ideal. This much, of course, he does indeed believe to be true. In his view, the modern will to knowledge is what morality itself has become.[8] Section 344, however, argues for the more puzzling claim that, because it calls upon us to reject and to deny *ourselves* along with our former philosophical illusions, the will to knowledge conceals what Nietzsche calls a 'will to death'. We deny ourselves, in this sense, when we refuse to recognize the intimate relationship between the needs expressed by the beliefs we reject in the name of knowledge and the commitment to truthfulness that grows out of those beliefs. (Both, Nietzsche argues, express our human, all too human hatred of history.) The denial of this relationship is what makes the man of knowledge's commitment to truthfulness a moral commitment. But this means, I think, that the nihilism concealed in his piety is expressed by his conviction that morality in general can simply be cast away in the name of reason. Nietzsche's point, then, is not so much that the man of knowledge refuses to acknowledge *what* he has become (he knows, in other words, that he is a truth teller), but that he resists

---

[7] This is a consequence of Nietzsche's claim that Christianity as dogma perishes at the hands of its own morality.

[8] In this context, I am using the term 'morality' in its broadest sense to refer to those practices of justification the *Genealogy* condemns as ascetic in general, and to what I have treated as Socratic philosophy in particular. A moral outlook is one that, in one way or another, turns away from this life in favor of another. Disappointment and dissatisfaction with the world in which we live is a mark of morality in this sense.

seeing *that* he has become what he has become. This, in Nietzsche's view, is what the man of knowledge's failure to understand the death of God comes to. We need to know, however, what Nietzsche means in speaking of self-overcoming in this context: why isn't the death of God a matter only of seeing that what we used to believe is false? What room is there for more self-consciousness about one's commitment to truthfulness than that? This is our chief interpretative problem.

My goal in this book has been to understand what Nietzsche conceives as tragic insight into the value of knowledge. This is the so-called problem of science; it is how Nietzsche approaches the question of what it means to be human in the present age. A properly tragic obedience to the imperative to be truthful is expressed, he insists, in a sense of the price one pays for the achievement of that obedience—in an appropriate understanding of the death of God. This is what 'becoming what one is' amounts to for the man of knowledge. On the reading I am proposing, tragic insight into the value of knowledge would express one's sense of the relationship between, as we might put it, faith and reason—between these two powers. The will to truth gains self-consciousness by appreciating the fact of this relationship. But what kind of connection does Nietzsche believe is at stake here? What is it that he thinks the will to knowledge seeks to deny by treating our commitment to truthfulness as a radical alternative to the ascetic ideal?

The Gay Science suggests that we begin to appreciate the connection between reason and faith when we acknowledge the fact of a struggle between the will to knowledge and the errors that will renders unbelievable. It is not obvious, however, what the talk of struggle comes to in this context.[9] Nietzsche grants that Christian dogma is false. This, indeed, is part of his point about the present age. Our reason, he asserts, has in fact *triumphed* over our faith.[10] Whatever struggle there might

---

[9] As the nihilist makes clear, 'struggle' is not the happiest term in this context. That 'God is dead' simply *means* that certain things are unbelievable. There is no friction here in the sense of a live conflict between truth and falsehood; one may of course have difficulty recognizing a falsehood for what it is, but once there is such recognition, there is no room to talk about anything but falsehood. Such is the nature of belief. But Nietzsche talks about a battle in this context, and seems to suggest that there is room to make separate sense of ourselves as, so to speak, *victors* in the fight against falsehood. It is such falsehood that is overcome by Christianity as morality (by the will to truth). But we need to know how he thinks of self-consciousness about such overcoming. Certainly, there *was* a struggle between reason and faith. Nietzsche wants to say that who we are now are those people who *used* to believe those things. But he wants to remind us that those were *our* beliefs—that this was a *self*-overcoming.

[10] The first essay of the *Genealogy* makes a precisely parallel point about so-called master morality. See sec. 9 in particular.

once have been must have taken place between our desire to tell the truth and our desire not to know it. Such a conflict of desires, one suspects, is common enough. In the present case, however, it seems—ideally anyway—to have been decided.[11] How, then, can Nietzsche propose to tell us what it makes sense to believe? We believe what we believe, after all. And it appears that whatever else we may happen to believe *about* what we believe can itself be nothing more than further belief. Where, then, is the self-consciousness the *Genealogy* associates with a nonpious will to truth? What is it to be aware of having overcome oneself?

As I have noted, when confronted with Nietzsche's talk of the growing self-consciousness of the will to truth, it often appears tempting to suppose that he means us to envision a time when we will be able to cast our commitment to knowledge aside, when we can exchange it for a different one. This, however, is a temptation worth resisting, because Nietzsche is asking about our *commitment* to truth, our *will* to knowledge. When he says that "the value of truth must for once be experimentally *called into question*" (GM III, sec. 24, p. 153),[12] he does not mean to reject that value, but rather to ask about the special character of our current commitment to it. And although he is convinced that this is a question that commitment in its present 'pious' form cannot ask of itself, nothing would be further from his intentions than that we should somehow step outside the will to truth in order to question it from some other point of view.[13] This, indeed, is precisely the philosophical move he wishes to block. For we simply have no point of view other than that of knowledge. Nietzsche thus means to shed light on our resistance to the authority of the imperative to be truthful. It is from

[11] Such a claim may seem premature, and Nietzsche certainly leaves plenty of room for backsliding. Section 110 of *The Gay Science* says that what I have called 'reason and faith' are now 'clashing for their *first* fight'. But, as we will see shortly, sec. 125 makes it clear that God *is* dead. In other words, just as Socratism triumphed over tragedy, so the modern will to knowledge has triumphed—in some individuals anway—over Socratism.

[12] The German reads, *"in Frage zu stellen."* The emphasis is Nietzsche's.

[13] Nietzsche's claim that 'the problem of science cannot be recognized in the context of science' suggests, naturally enough, that there is some context *other* than that of science from the point of view of which we can question the character of the value we presently give to science, only if we think of 'the context of science' as an interpretation, perspective, or point of view to which we currently subscribe. But just this is what Nietzsche is at such pains to deny. The will to knowledge is *not* an interpretation in this sense of the word; it is—or anyway should be—a commitment. Nietzsche's criticism of our lives as we stand is that, as long as we do not acknowledge the fact of its history, our commitment to truthfulness is a hollow one.

this (psychological) standpoint alone that his talk of self-consciousness derives its content.

We have not yet seen in any depth how Nietzsche conceives of the relationship between faith and reason—between, that is, our former philosophical errors, on the one hand, and the will to knowledge, on the other. But it should be clear that, from the standpoint of the piety he diagnoses in the modern will to knowledge, talk of struggle, conflict, tension, or even friction in the present context must appear to be the voice of intellectual nostalgia at best, or at worst an expression of a kind of madness.[14] The nihilist insists, in effect, that if, as Nietzsche agrees, God is indeed dead—if, that is, those beliefs really are unbelievable— then the death of God simply cannot matter to us in the way he appears to believe that it should. To see how Nietzsche responds to this claim, let me provide an overview of the main point of section 344.

As I have suggested, Nietzsche means in this aphorism to argue that it is the character of our current commitment to truthfulness and not anything we happen to believe about the nature of truth itself that makes the modern will to knowledge a moral, nihilistic, or life-denying commitment. He realizes, however, that from the nihilist's point of view, it will be nearly impossible to see what, if anything, is amiss with the will to knowledge. The nihilist's devotion to the truth renders unbeliev- able the moral, religious, and philosophical beliefs in terms of which he formerly made sense of life. According to section 343, the so-called death of God simply *is* the unbelievability of these beliefs. Nietzsche himself must acknowledge the fact of their unbelievability. But then it is very difficult to see what else might be required of the man of knowl- edge in order to credit him with self-consciousness about his commit- ment to truthfulness.

We may begin unpacking these claims by reminding ourselves of the chief conclusions we reached regarding Nietzsche's interest in the topic of knowledge in general. In Chapters 2 and 3, we tried to understand in what sense, if any, Nietzsche thinks one can speak of the relationship between the knower and the known as one of interpretation. More specifically, we wanted to know what he means in claiming the following:

The biggest fable of all is the fable of knowledge. One would like to know what things-in-themselves are; but behold, there are no things- in-themselves! But even supposing that there were an in-itself, an unconditioned thing, it would for that very reason be unknowable!

[14] For how can the believer hanker after what he knows to be false?

Something unconditioned cannot be known; otherwise it would not be unconditioned! Coming to know, however, is always "placing oneself in a conditional relation to something"————one who seeks to know the unconditioned desires that it should not concern him, and that this same something should be of no concern to anyone. This involves a contradiction, first, between wanting to know and the desire that it not concern us (but why know at all, then?) and, secondly, because something that is of no concern to anyone is not at all, and thus cannot be known at all.—

Coming to know means "to place oneself in a conditional relation to something"; to feel oneself conditioned by something and oneself to condition it—it is therefore under all circumstances establishing, denoting, and making-conscious of conditions (not forthcoming entities, things, what is "in-itself"). (WP, sec. 555, p. 301)

I have argued that, properly understood, such remarks do not provide the outlines of an epistemology, but rather are intended to indicate the kinds of questions Nietzsche thinks make sense about what he here calls 'conditions'. The idea of conditions suggests that Nietzsche believes there is no specifically philosophical room to raise the usual sorts of epistemological worries about our relationship to the world. What interests him, rather, is our philosophically informed unwillingness to let ourselves be conditioned by what we know. And, as I have explained, he conceives of this difficulty as a psychological problem.

As we have seen, however, Nietzsche is quite interested in the *will* to knowledge—in how knowledge has come to be an end in itself rather than, as he believes formerly was the case, merely a means to further ends. As knowledge becomes in this sense a power, he notes, it comes into conflict with other ends, specifically with those of our philosophical, religious, and moral attempts to make sense of life. As I read it, the point of section 344 is to help us rightly to conceive the special character of that conflict. Specifically, Nietzsche argues that if knowledge is indeed understood as an end only on the condition that we properly acknowledge the fact that our commitment to it has *overcome* our former articles of faith, then it is a sign that we are resisting the constraint that knowledge exercises upon us if we fail to make proper sense of the deeper connection between philosophy, on the one hand, and our faith in science, on the other.

Let us be clear about what needs interpretation here. As we have seen, Nietzsche speaks of the present age as one of transition. At the beginning of the fifth book of The Gay Science, for example, he describes our historical situation in the following terms: "we born guessers of riddles who are, as it were, waiting on the mountains, posted between today and tomorrow, stretched in the contradiction between today and tomorrow, we firstlings and premature births of the coming century, to whom the shadows that must soon envelop Europe really should have appeared by now" (GS, sec. 343, p. 279). At first blush, the most obvious way to understand such talk is to read Nietzsche as thinking of the death of God at once as the end of one way of confronting life and as pointing to the possibility of some new and absolutely other way. It is this idea that fuels the conviction that the present age is, in Nietzsche's view, transitional in the sense of lying between an old and exhausted way of doing things and a newer and possibly more promising one. The question I suggest Nietzsche means us to ask, however, is what precisely this understanding of modernity could really mean to someone committed to truthfulness.[15] It is difficult to see how the man of knowledge could conceivably be in a position seriously to consider adopting any outlook that conflicted with his commitment to truthfulness.[16] This is why I have suggested that the shift of perspectives Nietzsche's talk of transition implies involves the strengthening of a weakened will to truth, not the overcoming of one commitment in favor of another. Thus, although it is often thought that his talk of transition envisions a time when we would no longer live in the grip of morality, I understand section 344 to instruct us to interpret the idea of transition differently. But we still need to know what strengthening our commitment to truthfulness might actually look like. (What, in other words, is the shape of the resistance that has to be overcome here?)

How, then, does Nietzsche conceive of the relationship between faith and the will to knowledge? Initially, he suggests, there is no real struggle at all. People believe what they needed to believe. For "even if a morality is grown out of an error, the realization of this fact would not so much as touch the problem of its value" (GS, sec. 345, p. 285). "For

---

[15] Indeed, the first-blush reading of Nietzsche's remarks about the so-called transitional status of the present age hardly amounts to an interpretation of them. In other words, it is at best only a statement of what needs to be interpreted, not a statement of the desired interpretation itself.

[16] This is partly a point about any form of commitment (as I have used that term here), and partly it is a point about a commitment to truthfulness in particular. Someone really committed to something is not in a position to treat that commitment as optional. The point is not that no commitment can be questioned, but rather that from the point of view of that commitment certain questions are simply not going to be live. On the other hand, because a commitment to truthfulness is a commitment to find out what one *believes*, one is certainly not in a position to consider what one believes to be optional. To believe something is to hold it to be true. What shakes belief is finding out that one is—or might in some particular instance be—wrong.

this," he goes on, "is how man is: An article of faith could be refuted before him a thousand times—if he needed it, he would consider it 'true' again and again, in accordance with that famous 'proof of strength' of which the Bible speaks" (*GS*, sec. 347, p. 287). Nevertheless, Nietzsche is convinced that the struggle between faith and reason has become in some way definitive of the present age, and that it has been (or anyway will be) decided in favor of reason. We—some of us, that is—are now in a position to recognize the falsity of our former beliefs. Though the value of knowledge was not always taken as seriously as it is presently, "the faith in science . . . [now] exists undeniably" (*GS*, sec. 344, p. 281). That faith leads inexorably to the death of God. But section 344 suggests that to say that science has *simply* triumphed over faith is in some way to misconceive the significance of that event and, hence, to misunderstand what it means to be a man of knowledge. The main interest of Nietzsche's investigation into what he thinks of as the moral prejudices embodied in the modern will to knowledge lies, therefore, in the degree to which those investigations can clear up what he takes to be a prevalent misunderstanding of our situation in the present age.

Nietzsche holds that the will to knowledge is the modern individual's Socratic inheritance. The modern will to knowledge, in other words, is what the original Socratic response to the collapse of instinct has become in the present age. We may properly speak of inheritance in this context because Nietzsche believes that how one responds to the authority of the imperative to be truthful expresses the strength or weakness of one's commitment to it.[17] Like most "good things," he writes, the will to knowledge is "costly beyond measure: and the law still holds that he who has [such good things] is different from he who obtains them. Everything good is inheritance: what is not inherited is imperfect, is a beginning" (*TI*, "Expeditions," sec. 47, pp. 100–101). The distinction Nietzsche draws here between having and obtaining a good

[17] Again, it is difficult to suppress the nihilist's question at this juncture: 'What could possibly express a stronger commitment to truthfulness than simply acknowledging the falsity of our former philosophical, religious, and moral beliefs? What more could one intelligibly be required to do?' Nietzsche's response to these questions is quite complicated. For in a sense *nothing* more is required. He thinks, however, that the man of knowledge tends to deny the historical character of his commitment, and in this way to alienate himself from it. But to acknowledge the historical character of the will to knowledge is, as we will see shortly, to affirm its necessity for us. And to do that, paradoxically enough, is to recognize that it is of a piece with what it overcomes. This is what I mean in speaking of acknowledging the errors uncovered by the will to knowledge as our own. Nietzsche's idea is, roughly, that the nihilist's commitment to truthfulness is at odds with itself as a commitment unless he acknowledges its fateful character.

thing echoes the difference he sees between activity and reactivity generally. To 'have' a good thing in this sense is to will it. Thus, to speak of the will to knowledge as an inheritance is to underscore the relationship between it and what preceded it. For the will to knowledge grows precisely out of that which it eventually rejects as unbelievable. This is one reason that Nietzsche speaks of *self*-overcoming in this context.

I have claimed that, in Nietzsche's view, the men of knowledge resist the authority of the imperative to be truthful—they fail, that is, to inherit it properly—if they deny the fact of a struggle between our errors and the will to knowledge that overcomes them. They begin to appreciate *which* power knowledge is only when they acknowledge the deeper connection between it and the errors it uncovers. Overcoming one's resistance to the constraint exercised by the imperative to be truthful is a necessary condition of that inheritance. And that resistance, Nietzsche maintains, is somehow manifested in our wish to see the will to knowledge as a radically alternative outlook to the ascetic perspective it renders unbelievable.

I suggested in the Introduction that Nietzsche considers the death of God to be something inherently difficult to understand. But as we have seen, it is not clear why he believes this to be so. Let us remind ourselves of the difficulty here. According to Nietzsche, whoever is committed to the truth 'at any price'—unconditionally—fails properly to assess his recognition of the falsity of those articles of faith in terms of which he formerly made sense of his life. It is here that Nietzsche locates the man of knowledge's resistance to the authority of the imperative to be truthful. Such resistance, he maintains, is a form of nihilism. But because the most natural thing to say about the death of God appears to be that it is simply the effect of our recognition of the erroneous character of those articles of faith, the only sort of resistance that makes sense in this context is that which is expressed by our reluctance to face up to the facts of the matter: namely, that our philosophical beliefs and moral ideals were invented by human beings in response to human needs. We resist, if anything, only being honest enough with ourselves. From this point of view, then, it appears that nothing could be *easier* to understand than the death of God.

Thus, although section 344 maintains that the nihilist's failure to understand the death of God is a matter not of his unwillingness to let go of his former faiths, but rather of his eagerness to declare them simple falsehoods and of his hope that, in doing so, he may have done with them, if Nietzsche is to argue that such an attitude toward the past is a form of self-blindness, he will have to do so without in any way *denying* that God is dead. The *truth* of this claim is not in question.

As we will see shortly, what section 344 struggles to make clear instead is Nietzsche's contention that that particular truth does not make the right sort of difference to us if we fail to treat our ability to utter it as an accomplishment.

In *The Gay Science*, as in the *Genealogy*, then, Nietzsche rejects the idea that science—once again, considered as a way of life—might be an alternative to what, in the name of knowledge, that very way of life rejects in the ascetic ideal. He writes:

> No doubt, those who are truthful in that audacious and ultimate sense that is presupposed by the faith in science *thus affirm another world* than the world of life, nature, and history; and insofar as they affirm this "other world"—look, must they not by the same token negate its counterpart, this world, *our* world?—But you will have guessed what I am driving at, namely, that it is still a *metaphysical faith* upon which our faith in science rests—that even we seekers after knowledge today, we godless anti-metaphysicians still take our fire, too, from the flame that is thousands of years old, that Christian flame which was also the flame of Plato, that God is the truth, that truth is divine. (*GS*, sec. 344, pp. 282–83)

But, as we have seen, it is the *faith* in our faith in the scientific pursuit of truth that Nietzsche considers to be metaphysical, not any conception we happen to have about the nature of truth itself. The godless and anti-metaphysical men of knowledge do not affirm another world in *this* sense. They know that *this* world—what Nietzsche calls *our* world— is the only world of which it makes sense to speak. Indeed, precisely this realization is what constitutes their knowledge of the death of God. But if they are not burdened by philosophical theories about the nature of truth, then in what sense is their faith in science still metaphysical?

As we will see presently, section 344 begins by ruling out one popular answer to this question: namely, that it is by denying that science is only one perspective among others that the modern will to truth might be accused of retaining a metaphysical faith in truth. Such an account would indeed avoid the problem of saddling the man of knowledge with a philosophical view about the nature of truth. But Nietzsche nevertheless rejects this answer to our question. For, as we will see, in his view, the man of knowledge can be in this sense of the word as 'perspectivist' as he likes, and still stand accused of latent piety. What I am suggesting, in other words, is that Nietzsche appreciates that the nihilist will be anxious to claim to be as thoroughly self-conscious as possible about his commitment to truth. I will argue, however, that though the man of knowledge's commitment to truthfulness brings home to him the fact that intelligible speech is something for which we bear only *human* responsibility (as we have seen, the unconditionally committed man of knowledge will be eager to affirm precisely this claim), in Nietzsche's view, he remains prey to a particular misunderstanding of the fact that only now, in the present age, can he tolerate being reminded of this fact. In other words, being able to understand the fact that Socratism is an error (in the specifically Nietzschean sense) is an *achievement*. This is what section 344 insists the unconditionally committed man of knowledge fails to appreciate. He lacks, as Nietzsche will say, historical sense and has, consequently, no claim to the future. Let us turn now to the details of section 344.

Nietzsche's Conception of Scientific Discipline

Nietzsche begins with a criticism of scientific pretensions to detachment and objectivity. On his account, it is nearly definitive of the scientific way of life that it refuses to adopt any view of the world as more than a provisional hypothesis. This, indeed, is why science tends to think of itself as a 'this-worldly' discipline. The will to truth aims, in other words, at a *disinterested* search for knowledge. "In science conviction has no rights of citizenship, as one says with good reason. Only when they decide to descend to the modesty of hypotheses, of a provisional experimental point of view, of a regulative fiction, may they be granted admission and even a certain value in the realm of knowledge—though always with the restriction that they remain under police supervision, under the police of mistrust" (*GS*, sec. 344, p. 280). This hostility toward convictions, however, is itself more than a mere hypothesis.[18] But then, as a way of life, the scientific rejection of all convictions depends upon something that, by its own lights, is itself a conviction: namely, that truth is, as Nietzsche says, needed more than any other thing. In this sense, then, science's claims to detachment are hollow; like any human activity, it is motivated by a particular set of needs, interests, aims, and values. Nietzsche believes, therefore, that strictly speaking, there is no such thing as science 'without any presuppositions'; this thought does not bear thinking through" (*GM* III, sec. 24, p. 151). "The question whether *truth* is needed must not only have been affirmed in advance, but affirmed to such a degree that the principle, the faith, the conviction finds expression: '*Nothing* is needed *more* than

---

[18] Remember that 'science' here is to be construed broadly enough that Nietzsche's own investigations count as science in the relevant sense.

truth, and in relation to it everything else has only second-rate value'"
(*GS*, sec. 344, p. 281). Nietzsche says that it is 'with good reason' that
science allows itself no convictions. But even though in his view the
scientific discipline of doing so depends upon what is in effect a prior
conviction—indeed, one "that is so commanding and unconditional
that it sacrifices all other convictions to itself" (ibid.)—mere self-
deception about this fact is not sufficient, in his eyes, to motivate the
charge of life-denial. The latent morality of science is not concealed
here. It is, nevertheless, this insistence on the unconditional value of
truth that Nietzsche considers to be moral. Yet, as we will see, it is the
actual *content* of such a conviction, and not merely its presence, that
makes the scientific commitment to truthfulness pious.

Section 344's thesis, then, is not simply that science fails to understand its character as a practice. Such a conclusion would, of course,
imply that, its pretensions notwithstanding, science is after all one faith
(perhaps one 'perspective') among others. Nietzsche does, indeed, believe that this much is true. But the mere fact of science's unacknowl-
edged dependence on conviction does not, in Nietzsche's view, serve
to reveal the piety of its will to truth, for not all convictions are moral
convictions.

It is important to be clear about this last point. The commitment to
truth Nietzsche holds to be characteristic of the scientific attitude is
the expression of a conviction, a 'faith'. This means that science fails
adequately to understand itself if it does not acknowledge the presence
of this faith *as* a faith. But such an elision is not yet—or at least not
directly—a *moral* failure in Nietzsche's sense of the term. In fact, the
man of knowledge could, I take it, simply admit that the scientific will
to truth does after all presuppose such a conviction, and then happily
go about his scientific business until someone shows him a better one.
In sum, I think we should resist concluding that in section 344 Nietzsche
wants to indicate merely that science fails to see that in some sense it
represents just one more way of representing the world—one perspective among others. Nietzsche, I think, believes that this much is true
about science. But simply being willing to acknowledge the fact that
scientific practice depends upon a nonscientific value does not amount
to the desired self-consciousness about one's will to truth.

The Moral Conviction behind the Scientific Attitude

I said that not all convictions are moral convictions. What, in
Nietzsche's view, makes the conviction upon which scientific discipline

depends a moral one? Why does he twice say that 'even we seekers after knowledge today, we godless men and anti-metaphysicians, we, too, still derive *our* flame from the fire ignited by a faith millennia old, that Christian faith . . . that truth is divine'? Once again, his point is not that men of knowledge have a metaphysical conception of the nature of knowledge. They are, in that sense, this-worldly thinkers. Nor, again, is he merely arguing that science, too, rests on a kind of faith. Rather, what makes science pious in Nietzsche's eyes is the particular faith it is: namely, the character of its distinctive commitment to truthfulness, specifically, what Nietzsche calls its *unconditionality*.

Section 344 considers two interpretations of the unconditional nature of the scientific will to truth: first, that it is the will not to allow oneself to be deceived, and second, that it is the will not to deceive, not even oneself.[19] He rejects the first reading because, on this account, "science would be a long-range prudence, a caution, a utility" (ibid., p. 281). He maintains that one would want never to allow oneself to be deceived only if one had found that being deceived was in some way always harmful. He insists, however, that everything tells us that, as we are, we need both truth and untruth, both trust and mistrust.[20] This, in fact, is why both the will to truth and our primeval errors are at war within us. As we have seen, Nietzsche thinks that we needed the errors and illusions that eventually came to conflict with the will to truth. To try to do without them would have been simply impossible for us.[21]

Nietzsche concludes that the conviction on which the metaphysical faith in science rests could "never have come into being if both truth and untruth constantly proved to be useful, which is the case. Thus— the faith in science, which after all exists undeniably, cannot owe its origin to such a calculus of utility; it must have originated in spite of the fact that the disutility and dangerousness of 'the will to truth,' of 'truth at any price' is proved to it constantly. 'At any price': how well we understand these words once we have offered and slaughtered one

---

[19] Nietzsche is having a little fun here: the first interpretation considers the impera- tive 'Be truthful!' to be hypothetical (roughly, 'tell the truth, because it's good for you to do so'), while the second believes it to be categorical (roughly, 'tell the truth, no matter what'). Nevertheless, the second interpretation does not show the will to truth to be moral on the Kantian grounds that it is categorical. On Nietzsche's ac- count, it is moral in the sense that it is life-denying, and its mere categoricality is not enough to demonstrate that this is so.

[20] Indeed the very investigations at hand seem to suggest as much. Once again, I want to resist a phenomenalist reading of such passages. As I see it, Nietzsche believes that his attack on Socratism—as well as his genealogy of the modern will to knowledge more generally—shows in what sense untruth and trust are needed.

[21] Our choice, as we saw, was either to perish or to become absurdly rational.

faith after another on this altar!" (ibid.).[22] In other words, the will to truth itself shows us just how much we have needed (and may continue to need) precisely the beliefs, errors, and articles of faith in terms of which we have so far made sense of life. Indeed, it is precisely the diagnosis of those errors that shows us the *fact* of our needs here. As we have seen, that diagnosis points to our disappointment with the fact of the world's intelligibility—a disappointment that, though it expresses itself in terms of a request for justification, ought nevertheless not, in Nietzsche's view, to be understood as a disappointment with the lack of such a justification.

So Nietzsche opts for his second interpretative hypothesis: namely, that the unconditional will to truth is the expression of an imperative not to deceive anyone, not even oneself. And *"with that,"* he says, *"we stand on moral ground"* (ibid.). The imperative, 'I will not deceive, not even myself', suggests that the unconditional will to truth is a commitment to proceed with the destruction of the errors and illusions in terms of which we made sense of our lives after the demand for reasons had become binding on us, *in spite of the dangers involved.* That is to say, it is because life itself requires these errors and illusions that doing away with them may be said to be dangerous. The danger is in part that, in depriving ourselves of the Socratic solution to the problem of suffering, we will be left with only our old uncomprehending interpretation of it. Thus, the assault waged by the unconditional will to truth against such errors and illusions as have proved crucial to our survival so far is, at least in this way, hostile to life. Such hostility contributes to the piety of the unconditional will to truth, and this is (again in part) why Nietzsche suspects that the will to truth might be 'a concealed will to death': "For you have only to ask yourself carefully, 'Why do you want not to deceive?' especially if it should seem—and it does seem!— as if life aimed at semblance, meaning error, deception, simulation, delusion, self-delusion, and when the great sweep of life has actually always shown itself to be on the side of the most unscrupulous polytropoi" (ibid.). The polytropoi in question are, I submit, precisely those errors and illusions in terms of which we have so far given voice to our disappointment with life. Once again, however, the intended effect of Nietzsche's diagnosis is to drive us to dissatisfaction with those expres-

---

[22] As we saw in Chapter 2, the dangerousness of the will to truth is not a matter of life-threatening effects of, for example, resisting the temptation to equate one experience of a tiger or a poisonous plant with another. Rather Nietzsche's point is that the will to truth threatens to deprive us—in the ways we have been examining— of the faiths in terms of which we have so far made sense of our lives.

sions of our dissatisfaction, not to quell the disappointment at their root. Such suffering is not an inessential feature of human life.

This reading may seem to suggest an important difficulty with our interpretation so far. Section 344 argues that insofar as we have need of the errors that conflict with the value we place on truthfulness, the unconditional will to truth is a principle that is hostile to life, and it is, for that reason, a moral principle. But because I have construed the errors by means of which we have been able to endure life as being themselves the means whereby we have so far responded to our suffering from the constraints of intelligibility, it can seem difficult to make sense of the claim that the demand that one deceive no one, not even oneself, is a life-denying maxim. For how, we might wonder, can something that is inimical to the hostilities that we direct toward life (toward the fact of intelligibility) itself be hostile to life? Our understanding of how Nietzsche means us to grasp the significance of the death of God hinges upon how we respond to this question. Only when we confront it do we begin to understand what the piety of the will to truth really amounts to.

On the reading I have proposed, to say that one merely 'endures life' is to say that one finds the ability to make sense puzzling or mysterious. Such a one does not see how meaning could depend upon facts about him—upon, as I put it, his obedience to authority—and, therefore, seeks something radically independent of that obedience in terms of which to justify it. Seen in this light, the various metaphysical, religious, and moral means of enduring life are ways of trying to find more secure grounds for interpretation than the simple fact of obedience. We express our resistance to the fact that interpretations come to an end in understanding by treating understanding as itself a further interpretation—one that we then find to stand in need of justification. Thus, to someone who merely endures life, the very fact of the world's intelligibility appears to give rise to those forms of philosophical, religious, and moral inquiry that seek in one way or another to provide what Nietzsche calls 'reasons'.

But by construing morality in terms of resistance to intelligibility, I seem to have withdrawn Nietzsche's grounds for accusing the will to truth of life-denying piety. Insofar as the will to knowledge calls upon us to reject ascetic morality to the extent that it is rooted in errors and illusions, our commitment to truthfulness appears to be perfectly life-*affirming*. Once again, the point is simply that if life-denial is understood to be a matter of affirming another world than the natural and historical one in which we live day to day, then, in the absence of a philosophical view about the nature of truth itself, nothing seems *less* life-denying

THE WILL TO KNOWLEDGE   171

than the imperative to tell the truth. In a way, then, by suggesting that the will to knowledge undermines Socratism by questioning its interpretation of the human, all too human needs that give rise to it, we have been driven back to the nihilist's insistence that the most reasonable response to our recognition of the falsity of all that Nietzsche considers to be Christian dogma is to say, 'Well, if it's false, then it's false, and so much the worse for us if we needed—or even continue to need—such falsehoods. We simply are not entitled to them!'.

I think that we can maintain without contradiction that something hostile to the hostilities that we direct toward life is nevertheless itself hostile to life, only if we reject a sharp dichotomy between making sense and not making sense—between intelligibility and faith. And this is exactly what Nietzsche does. The beliefs to which our faith drives us represent, according to him, precisely the sense that we make of life when trying not to make sense of life. In this spirit, he asks in section 346 of *The Gay Science* whether the man of knowledge's talk of overcoming morality altogether might not itself in some way be hostile to life.

> Have we not [in proposing that the value of morality be called into question] exposed ourselves to the suspicion of an opposition—an opposition between the world in which we were at home up to now with our reverences that perhaps made it possible for us to endure life, and another world that consists of us *[die wir selber sind]*—an inexorable, fundamental , and deepest suspicion about ourselves that is more and more gaining worse and worse control of us Europeans and that could easily confront coming generations with the terrifying Either/Or: "Either abolish your reverences or—yourselves!" The latter would be nihilism; but would not the former also be—nihilism?— This is our question mark. (*GS*, sec. 346, p. 287)

On this account, the hostilities that we direct toward life are, in fact, nothing other than the sense we make of life. This, indeed, is all that they can be. Our reverences are, after all, part of life. One cannot, therefore, pretend simply to abandon the former in the name of the latter.

Let us consider again Nietzsche's case against Socratism. The demand for reasons represents the principal form of reverence we have examined in this book. As we have seen, though the Socratic life of reason is rooted in the error of treating obedience as interpretation, it nevertheless serves as a means of survival for someone who is inclined to make that error. Thus, although Nietzsche believes that the demand for reasons represents philosophical nonsense, he considers it nonetheless to make excellent psychological sense. Consequently, to treat Socratism as a falsehood and nothing more is, in effect, to disown it in a way that gives voice to a wish to divorce oneself from the sense one used to make. And although Nietzsche considers it important to recognize that we can now make only psychological sense of the ostensibly philosophical sense we used to make, our desire to disown our errors itself expresses a fantasy of standing outside and apart from our own history.

Nietzsche insists that we cannot *but* make sense, even (indeed especially) when, in a philosophical context, we seem to make no sense. This, I think, is what he means in claiming at the end of the *Genealogy* that man would rather will nothingness than not will. As I have said, not willing is not a live option for human beings. Psychology, Nietzsche claims, is "morphology and *the doctrine of the development of the will to power*" (*BGE*, sec. 23, p. 31). But then to show that, contrary to what it pretends,[23] Socratism is after all a form of will to power is to show that it is a way of making sense. And to show that, and how, Socratism is a way of making sense is precisely the goal of Nietzsche's inquiry into the modern will to knowledge in general. Thus, the dichotomy that threatened to ruin our account of the piety of the modern will to knowledge is, in the end, merely apparent.

I have not meant to suggest that Nietzsche believes the man of knowledge should in any way *retain* his reverences. They are, after all, false. And one cannot just *decide* to believe something—certainly not something one already believes to be false. But Nietzsche is suggesting in section 346 that there is something life-denying in pretending simply to discard our former philosophical beliefs. Then what, if anything, is to be retained here? I think the answer must be, 'nothing at all.' Nevertheless, Nietzsche would have us recognize that our obedience to the imperative to be truthful is of a piece with the beliefs that obedience renders unbelievable. There is nothing more for the man of knowledge to *do* here than simply to tell the truth—to figure out what he believes. But a life-affirmative will to truth is not in a position to speak of any dichotomy between its former commitments and its present one other than that expressed by the difference between truth and falsehood.[24]

[23] Contrary to what it pretends, of course, because Socratism would have us believe that the life of reason transcends the conditions of ordinary life and rises above the instincts.

[24] As we should expect, this account implies that, even though the unconditional will to truth is itself hostile to life, it is nonetheless a way of making sense of life, indeed a way of making sense for someone who suffers from the fact of making sense. In other words, it is because we are inclined to resist the authority of the will to knowledge that our commitment to truth becomes unconditional. Our unconditionality, in short, is a form of melancholia, a hostility to the fact of having a past at all.

Section 346 therefore suggests that Nietzsche can indeed hold, without either contradiction or nostalgia, that the man of knowledge's commitment to truthfulness is a pious commitment. Where he encourages us to seek a properly psychological account of the needs that express themselves in the very problems the philosophical sense of which escapes the will to knowledge, the unconditional will to truth refuses to recognize that beings who make sense in the ways we do cannot fail to make sense in the ways we do. The piety of the unconditional will to truth, then, is a matter of its accepting the dichotomy from which we have tried to wrestle it here.[25]

What a Conditional Will to Truth Might Be

I have been trying in a very general way to articulate my understanding of how Nietzsche thinks we (men of knowledge) make sense of our lives in the present age. We have wanted to know how he thinks we should understand the death of God, and to make clear what he seems to think is life-denying about treating it as the mere unbelievability of the beliefs that express our reverences. The problem has been that to understand the death of God in the way the nihilist does seems to be the only intelligible response for someone committed at any price to truthfulness. For, as Nietzsche admits, the beliefs in question are, after all, false.

I have asked why Nietzsche considers the unconditional will to truth a kind of piety—as, in effect, a form of morality. In other words, I have asked what, in his view, makes our ostensibly life-affirming commitment to knowledge—the very commitment that ruins Christianity as dogma—a moral or life-denying commitment after all. I argued that it was not a philosophical conception of the nature of truth, but rather what Nietzsche considers to be the unconditional nature of our commitment to it that he thinks justifies the charge of piety. What makes the man of knowledge's will unconditional is his tendency to think that his present commitment to truthfulness represents a clean break with the past. Nietzsche, however, would have him acknowledge, on the one

---

[25] As I understand it, the more common interpretation of Nietzsche's talk of piety in this context insists that the will to truth has to learn, so to speak, to humble its pride, by recognizing that it is just one way among others of confronting the world. But I have argued that there is no room to speak intelligibly of humility here. Learning that our commitment to truthfulness is of a piece with the errors it uncovers is not learning that, like them, it is optional. Rather it is learning that, like them, it is fateful.

hand, that his will to truth grows out of the very Socratism that, on the other, it allows him to overcome.

According to Nietzsche, someone committed to truthfulness at any price will inevitably understand the growing unbelievability of Christianity as dogma as the progress of human reason. He will see himself, in other words, as coming to be able to do without such illusions and errors as his Socratic predecessors found necessary for life. But he will not be able to see anything of himself in his ancestors, and he will conceive of himself as having—although perhaps only eventually— nothing to do with his past. Such a person, on Nietzsche's account, desires to be wholly free of the past.

Nietzsche insists that, the nihilist's pretensions notwithstanding, the man of knowledge's life in the present age makes sense only as an achievement, as an overcoming of his past. But no sense can be made of the idea of achievement in this context if he insists that the past he overcomes is not in some sense his own. Nietzsche's claim appears, therefore, to leave us with the following question: in what sense is the past overcome by the man of knowledge his own? Both Nietzsche and the nihilist agree that that past is a constellation of consolations and reconciliations grounded wholly on errors. What, then, is the difference between their attitudes toward this fact? What is the difference between a self-conscious will to truth and an unself-conscious one? What, in other words, is a conditional will to truth?[26] I want to suggest that, although apparently natural, these questions are ill formed. In a sense, there is no single difference that serves to distinguish a conditional from an unconditional will to truth, no extra ingredient added to one's commitment to truthfulness that makes it self-conscious. Just as membership, in the sense explained in Chapter 1, in Greek culture is not something constituted by a special internal relation between the Greek individual and his or her community, so properly tragic obedience to the imperative to truthfulness is not so constituted. Rather, Nietzsche claims, resistance to the imperative must be overcome. Thus, although there is a failure on the part of the nihilist properly to understand the significance of the death of God, there is nothing that, in the nihilist's sense, constitutes success on the part of someone who, in Nietzsche's view, understands that event.[27]

---

[26] By a conditional commitment, of course, I do not mean a provisional one—one upon which we place conditions—but rather one that we let condition us.

[27] Here is another place where Nietzsche's thinking and Heidegger's cross paths. It is common to suppose that Heideggerian authenticity reflects a kind of insight into the nature of our situatedness that is denied inauthentic human beings. But, as I read him, Heidegger means to deny the picture of situatedness (or being-in-the-world) that underlies this conception of authentic human being. Authenticity is much

Because both the nihilist and Nietzsche agree that God is dead, the latter seems to have no way of specifying the putative object of the nihilist's resistance. But that Nietzsche's charge of resistance is therefore empty is a conclusion that the nihilist draws only because, like Socrates, he desires a philosophical insight where only a tragic one will do. There is nothing to do by way of manifesting one's obedience to the will to knowledge, beyond pursuing the sorts of historical and psychological investigations of our former reverences that occupy the man of knowledge in, for example, the *Genealogy*.

By contrast to the men of knowledge, the tragic Greeks were, according to Nietzsche, especially good at making sense of their place in the world. But the tragic Greeks made sense of their lives by resisting the temptation to treat their obedience to the authority of their culture as an interpretation of themselves and the world. They sought nothing behind or beyond their obedience in terms of which to justify it to themselves. Nietzsche likes to say that they were, in this way, superficial.[28] This means that, initially anyway, the problem life posed for them was not one of justification or grounding, for they did not take the Socratic description of their situation for granted. The tragic solution to their problem consisted, in effect, of a correct diagnosis of the suffering that Socrates and Euripides erroneously characterized as a need for reasons. The Socratic solution, on the other hand, accepts that characterization and responds to it accordingly. Everyone else, Nietzsche says, perished.

These considerations suggest that if, as Nietzsche maintains, God himself turns out to be our most enduring lie, then the attempt utterly to disown our moral past is itself a fundamentally moral endeavor. The man of knowledge cannot stand apart from the sense he makes. And the sense he makes is that of having overcome himself. This is why Nietzsche says that the attempt to reject our reverences is a form of nihilistic self-denial. The thought, therefore, that Nietzsche himself wants somehow to stand outside the morality whose value he seeks to uncover is part of this same nihilism.

Thus, when in section 380 he speaks of presupposing "a position outside morality, some point beyond good and evil, to which one has to rise, climb, or fly—and in the present case at least a point beyond *our* good and evil, a freedom from everything 'European,' by which I mean the sum of the imperious value judgments that have become part

---

more a matter of clearing up certain sorts of confusions than it is of producing novel philosophical insights.

[28] See sec. 4 of the second preface to *The Gay Science*.

of our flesh and blood" (*GS*, sec. 380, p. 342), we should take him seriously when he goes on to say that "the question is whether one really *can* get up there" (ibid., p. 343). Nietzsche, however, is not here lamenting the existence of limitations on our part. For, as he says, "that one *wants* to go precisely out there, up there, may be a minor madness, a peculiar and unreasonable 'you must'—for we seekers for knowledge also have our idiosyncrasies of 'unfree will'" (ibid., pp. 342–43). That is to say, the wish in this way to step outside morality is a sign of weakness in one's responsiveness to the constraint of the will to truth— a sign, as Nietzsche also puts it, of one's romanticism.

The proposed resolution of the difficulty to which our reading of section 344 pointed us reminds us not to identify making sense—what Nietzsche calls 'life'—simply with power. Being intelligible is *will* to power, and the will in question can be either strong or weak depending upon the kind of responsiveness in question.

> Every art, every philosophy may be viewed as a remedy and an aid in the service of growing and struggling life; they always presuppose suffering and sufferers. But there are two kinds of sufferers: first, those who suffer from the *over-fullness of life*—they want a Dionysian art and likewise a tragic view of life, a tragic insight—and then those who suffer from the *impoverishment of life* and seek rest, stillness, calm seas, redemption from themselves through art and knowledge, or intoxication, convulsions, anaesthesia, and madness. (*GS*, sec. 370, p. 328)

We will want, therefore, to know whether there is some way of overcoming the man of knowledge's resistance to understanding what he has become in the present age, and whether there is an unromantic way of expressing hopes for the future. This is what maturity—being a 'good European'—comes to for Nietzsche.

To represent the will to knowledge as an alternative to morality means, therefore, to think that, in the name of knowledge, we can simply disown our old faiths. It is in this sense, then, that Nietzsche believes the unconditional will to truth represents itself as an alternative to the ascetic ideal. From the standpoint of the will to knowledge, we conceive of ourselves as having simply outgrown the errors and illusions in terms of which we formerly made sense of our lives. To show that the unconditional will to truth is itself moral is, thus, to deny that, in this sense, the will to knowledge represents such an alternative to morality.

Morality represents a denial of life; this is what makes it objectionable to Nietzsche. But that which morality denies itself inclines toward such denial. In other words, the idea that the will to knowledge represents a complete break with the past is itself a rejection of the human, an expression of our same dissatisfaction with ourselves, of a desire to be less than we are. Man is not—in this sense anyway—a thing to be overcome.

Genealogy and Nihilism

Nietzsche's most dramatic announcement of the death of God echoes a famous story about Diogenes: "Have you not heard of that madman who lit a lantern in the bright morning hours, ran to the market place, and cried incessantly: 'I seek God! I seek God!'—As many of those who did not believe in God were standing around just then, he provoked much laughter. Has he got lost? asked one. Did he lose his way like a child? asked another. Or is he hiding? Is he afraid of us? Has he gone on a voyage? emigrated?—Thus they yelled and laughed" (*GS*, sec. 125, p. 181). What is the significance of the reaction of those in the market-place to the announcement that God is dead? And why have a *madman* make that announcement? These are the questions that will be occupying us, in one form or another, for the rest of this book.

I have been arguing, in effect, that the practice of genealogy counts for Nietzsche as obedience to the will to truth. Properly understood, such obedience is what he believes the man of knowledge's Socratic inheritance to be. The growth of the will to truth's self-consciousness is, in turn, a matter of clearing up confusions about the status of that obedience—and hence a matter of understanding the status of genealogical investigation in general. For Nietzsche, however, self-consciousness about our obedience is manifested not in anything we may believe about such obedience, but rather in overcoming our resistance to the authority of knowledge. Nietzsche's most blatant figure for this sort of resistance is the derision to which the madman in *The Gay Science*, section 125 is exposed. The people to whom he announces the death of God are, in effect, unwilling to let that event matter to them, to count it *as* an event. Overcoming such resistance would be a matter of a shift in their relationship to the madman, but it would not involve any further beliefs about what he actually says. Section 125 suggests that the people in the marketplace understand well enough what the madman says; they simply cannot see why they should care about it. As I will argue in the next chapter, it is a mistaken conception of what it would mean to care about what he says that hinders their comprehension here. By way of anticipation, let us explore this train of thought in a little more detail.

Nietzsche maintains that when refined into intellectual conscience, the moral imperative to truthfulness leads to the death of God.

> Looking at nature as if it were proof of the goodness and governance of a god; interpreting history in honor of some divine reason, as continual testimony of a moral world order and ultimate moral purposes; interpreting one's own experiences as pious people have long enough interpreted theirs, as if everything were providential, a hint, designed and ordained for the sake of the salvation of the soul—that is *all over* now, that has man's conscience *against* it, that is considered indecent and dishonest by every more refined conscience—mendaciousness, feminism, weakness, and cowardice. In this severity, if anywhere, we are *good* Europeans and heirs of Europe's longest and most courageous self-overcoming. (*GS*, sec. 357, p. 307)

Because it contributes to the growing unbelievability of Christianity as dogma, the practice of genealogy is itself one such refinement of intellectual conscience. The genealogist's self-consciousness about the will to truth is achieved by appreciating the price he pays for his pursuit of truth. It is so-called Christianity as morality—that is, the unconditionality of the will to truth—that limits his self-consciousness here. Nietzsche, however, thinks of such self-consciousness primarily in terms of overcoming resistance to the idea of letting the death of God matter, and not as a matter of further insight into the nature of knowledge or truth. As the preface to the *Genealogy* hints, then, self-consciousness in this context is not, strictly speaking, a matter of self-knowledge.

Genealogy is meant, in short, both to encourage and to express tragic insight into what we (men of knowledge) have become in the present age. Producing such insight, I have suggested, is the aim of genealogical inquiry generally. Genealogy is meant to help us appreciate in particular the fact of our commitment to the value of truth, and this commitment is precisely what motivates the practice of genealogy. To this extent, therefore, genealogy is always the genealogy of itself (and hence of the genealogist as well). Genealogical practice is meant, in other words, to help us understand the nature of our commitment to the very value that motivates our inquiry into that value. By appreciating the price we pay for that commitment, we are to understand that that commitment is in fact definitive of what we are. What makes such insight tragic, in Nietzsche's sense, is the fact that we understand our commitment to truth to be an achievement. And this, ultimately, is the significance of the fact that that commitment is shown by the genealogist to have a history.

As I have claimed, it is often thought that Nietzsche believed that the fact that our practices have a history was enough to show that in some significant sense they are contingent, that they—and, consequently, we ourselves—could have been other than they happen to be. On this kind of reading, Nietzsche is thought to have believed that, because they have grown stale, our old values require replacement and that, by seeing that what is most dear to us is the result of changes in the self-conceptions of different cultures, we would somehow be freed up for new values. On this reading, genealogy is thought to be a primarily negative or critical aspect of Nietzsche's larger revaluation of all values. This conception of genealogy, however, involves precisely the error Nietzsche elsewhere denounces as historicism.

While it may in a trivial sense be true that, had our values a substantially different history, they might well have been different from what they in fact turned out to be, such is not the insight Nietzsche believes genealogy to promise. To the question 'Couldn't something matter to us other than the will to knowledge?', Nietzsche means in effect to reply 'Us as opposed to whom?' The point of arguing that our commitment to truthfulness has a history is, for him, not to show that it is a merely contingent development, but rather to show that the hold that value has upon us is in some way fateful for who we are. In other words, we are to see that our will to knowledge represents a historical achievement—what Nietzsche conceives as an 'inheritance'.

The historical sense of which Nietzsche speaks in *On the Use and Disadvantage of History for Life* is, therefore, not to be confused with the historicist thesis that who we have become in modern times is the merely contingent result of wholly contingent historical factors. The suspicion that Nietzsche himself was prone to such historicism stems from a recognition of his rejection of the modernist tendency to look upon modern achievements as inherently superior to past doings. And though Nietzsche found various complacent versions of such historical chauvinism both childish and distasteful, it is wrong to conclude from this fact that he sought to encourage us to treat the will to truth as just one more way of doing things. We are not now superior in all respects to what we were. We are, however, supposed to be more honest.[29]

This last point is worth stressing, because Nietzsche is commonly taken to have been hostile to the Enlightenment, in the sense that he

---

[29] We men of knowledge, that is.

is thought to have argued that it signaled nothing more that the triumph of merely contingent historical configurations of will to power.[30] It is true that Nietzsche had little love for modernist pretensions to superiority. But his goal in general was to show in what sense we could intelligibly claim our Socratic inheritance as an achievement, and to demonstrate our habitual unwillingness to do so. We are to see ourselves as standing—perhaps shakily—at the end of certain lines of development, but the mere fact that we have developed is not meant to fuel a historicist commitment to the idea of the contingency of our practices (and certainly not of the practice of genealogy), not even in response to modernist affectations of preeminence.

The model for the kind of insight that genealogy promises remains the tragedies of Sophocles and Aeschylus: they showed the Greek audience what it meant to be Greek by displaying the authority of their culture in such a way that the threat of contingency was disarmed. Genealogy, on the other hand, is meant to show us who we are by disarming whatever our own version of the threat of contingency turns out to be. Genealogy is meant to show that the will to knowledge matters to us—that, as I put it, it constrains us—by showing us that having become men of knowledge represents something in which we have, as it were, mixed our labor. Because recognizing the modern will to knowledge as an achievement is deeply opposed to treating it as a mere historical accident, the nihilist's apparent complacency about the death of God is what Nietzsche believes the threat of contingency comes to in the present age.

The reaction of the people in the marketplace to the madman's announcement of the death of God is, therefore, meant to figure the nihilist's reaction to Nietzsche's claim that we in the present age are the inheritors of the Socratic will to knowledge. Some illusions may indeed die hard, the nihilist maintains, but they remain illusions all the same. I have been suggesting, however, that from the madman's standpoint, the people in the marketplace fail to hear the announcement of the death of God in the right way. And for him, this amounts to failing to hear it altogether. The event of the death of God is 'still on its way', he says, and has 'not yet reached the ears of men'. Yet, as I have said, there is no suggestion in section 125 that the people of the marketplace fail to understand what the madman says. They know what he knows. The truth of the claim that God is dead is not in dispute.

[30] This is how, for example, Jürgen Habermas reads Nietzsche in *Philosophical Discourses of Modernity* (Cambridge: M.I.T. Press, 1987). Charles Taylor is prone to such a reading as well. See his "Foucault on Freedom and Truth," in *Philosophy and the Human Sciences* (Cambridge: Cambridge University Press, 1985), pp. 152–84.

Nevertheless, it is fair to say that if the people of the marketplace underreact to the news of the death of God, then, in a sense, the madman *over*reacts to it. Tragic insight into the will to knowledge consists in closing this gap. The gap is closed—nihilism is overcome—as the people in the marketplace learn to let the death of God matter to them. Nietzsche conceives of such a transformation as a change in their hearing, and indeed as a change in their (and, hence, in our) relationship to *him*. This is why, according to Nietzsche, culture may now be said to be a matter of a certain kind of reading. To make this point out in any detail requires that we look more carefully at the reaction of those in the marketplace, and at the way in which Nietzsche thinks they refuse to let the death of God matter to them. We will also need to understand better what Nietzsche believes stands in the way of their hearing the news that they have overcome themselves: namely, their morality. This is what we will do in the next chapter. Once we understand their refusal a little better, we can turn our attention to the figure of the madman.

At the outset, however, it should be clear how I am suggesting we fit these two parts of Nietzsche's story together. On the one hand, he maintains that the practice of genealogy is obedience to the will to truth. The investigation into the origins of our values—into the means whereby we have struggled not to make sense—is our Socratic inheritance. On the other hand, however, Nietzsche needs some way to respond to the man of knowledge's resistance to this form of authority. Someone such as the nihilist who is committed at any price to the truth maintains that there can be no important consequences of the pursuit of truth—that the death of God is simply a matter of our having outgrown the illusions we formerly found necessary or at least expedient. Regret over the loss of these illusions, the nihilist maintains, is either madness or nostalgia. Indifference, he insists, is the only intelligible response.

CHAPTER 5

THE INDIVIDUAL AND THE HERD

Nietzsche's Critique of Morality

> How is it possible to keep to one's own way? Constantly, some
> clamor or other calls us aside; rarely does our eye behold any-
> thing that does not require us to drop our own preoccupation
> instantly to help. . . . Indeed, those who now preach the moral-
> ity of pity even take the view that precisely this and only this
> is moral—to lose one's own way in order to come to the assist-
> ance of a neighbor.
>
> *The Gay Science*, sec. 338, p. 270

My aim in this chapter is to understand the role the notion of individuality plays in Nietzsche's attack on morality. Though his writing is,
as I have claimed, guided by his desire to understand the relations
between individual and community, I have not yet done justice to the
centrality of the former notion to his thought as a whole. Nietzsche
maintains that morality is hostile to the very idea of individuality. And
it is in this context, I believe, that his ostensibly positive conception of
the individual is most clearly presented.

The individual, in Nietzsche's view, should not be construed as someone who stands outside his community and speaks a different language. To speak is to be intelligible, to make sense; and intelligibility,
as I have used the term, expresses one's membership in community.
This reading thus recommends a reassessment of what is often thought
to be the antagonism between the individual and the community. In
this chapter I begin such a reassessment.[1]

[1] By 'antagonism' I mean the thought that the demands of life in the community
are somehow inimical to those of the life of the individual. As Alexander Nehamas

As we have seen, a principal goal of *The Birth of Tragedy* is to show how a Socratic demand for the justification of the employment of moral concepts rests upon a misunderstanding of—and resistance to—membership in the community of speakers who use those concepts. In this context, being an individual is nothing more, but also nothing less, than being a member of the culture at hand. Because there is here no herd to which to oppose the individual, the latter notion plays a much less pronounced role in Nietzsche's conception of the tragic age of Greece than it does in his later work.[2] Nevertheless, *The Birth of Tragedy's* account of culture provides an important clue to understanding Nietzsche's conception of what it means to be an individual in the present age: we are not to achieve a standpoint outside the present age, but rather to overcome resistance to the perspective that is ours: that of the will to knowledge.

I have in the last three chapters tried to assess the positive role that Nietzsche assigns to Socratism in the wake of the collapse of Greek tragedy. On his account, what begins as a way of making sense of a life

has reminded us, Nietzsche's attack on dogmatism is an attack on the idea that any one way of looking at the world is the right way for everyone. An emphasis on the question of dogmatism therefore suggests that Nietzsche's criticism of morality's concern with universalization might hold a clue for understanding his conception of individuality. A Kantian insistence, for example, that one must be able to justify to all comers claims to the fairness of one's actions appears, from Nietzsche's point of view, distinctly herdlike; the individual appears, accordingly, to be warned away from it. But this reading tends to imagine two *different* moralities here: one for the herd, and one for the individual. In his *Friedrich Nietzsche and the Politics of the Soul: A Study of Heroic Individualism* (Princeton: Princeton University Press, 1990), Leslie Paul Thiele proposes this sort of reading. "The individual," Thiele writes, "is a law unto himself, unpredictable and unmanageable. Society, then, cannot be composed of individuals. It requires members" (p. 38). He goes on: "Nietzsche's individualist valuations are the antitheses of those stemming from any generalizable moral system" (p. 39). As I try to show, however, Nietzsche believes that the herd's self-conception actually represents a *failure* of intelligibility and is therefore not a genuine alternative to individuality.

[2] As elsewhere, so in the case of the idea of individuality, there is more going on in *The Birth of Tragedy* than meets the eye clouded by Schopenhauerian formulas. Though Nietzsche does not there actually call him one, Socrates is, of course, the prototype of the modern individual. Indeed, his role is quite like the one Nietzsche assigns to himself; to make clear the incoherence of the ways those around him speak. As becomes clear in "The Problem of Socrates," Nietzsche holds that Socrates had *rightly* recognized the Athenians' unwillingness to take responsibility for what they said. Although this insight is distorted by the specifically Socratic conception of responsibility (i.e., that to speak responsibly is to make judgments in the light of carefully articulated definitions of one's moral concepts), Nietzsche nevertheless agrees with Socrates that he stands out from the Athenians precisely by knowing that he does not know. We may, therefore, say that Socrates plays the individual to the Athenian herd.

184 NIETZSCHE'S GENEALOGY

that has become unintelligible develops over time into the form of the will to knowledge responsible for the death of God. I have more recently asked what Nietzsche believes constitutes a proper understanding of this development. In what, that is, does he hold our Socratic inheritance to consist?

Asking this last question, I said, is Nietzsche's way of inquiring into the value of the will to truth. In his view, the man of knowledge's understanding of the death of God is expressed by the character of his commitment to truth. As Nietzsche sees it, then, the task of the individual is, in this context, to overcome the piety of that commitment. My aim in this chapter is to show how the morality of pity prevents him from doing so.

Though the tragic age of Greece is Nietzsche's favorite example of culture, I do not believe he expects that particular civilization to serve as a model of the sort of community that he thinks we in the present age might achieve.[3] He denies that the particular features of Greek culture have clearly modern equivalents. An individual's sense of himself as a modern European is very different from what Nietzsche supposes to be the tragic audience's sense of itself as Greek. But, then, how *does* Nietzsche conceive what we might think of as membership in the present age? In what does he think modernity consists?[4] (This, I have claimed, is the question being posed when he asks about the value of truth, and it is by answering it that the will to truth becomes self-conscious.)

As we noted in the last chapter, Nietzsche thinks of the present age in specifically historical terms. This alone is enough to distinguish modernity from the tragic age of Greece. He writes, "When I contemplate the present age with the eyes of some remote age, I can find nothing more remarkable in present-day humanity than its distinctive virtue and disease which goes by the name of 'the historical sense'. This is the beginning of something altogether new and strange in history" (*GS*, sec. 337, pp. 267–68). By contrast, Greek culture during the tragic period lacked the sort of historical self-consciousness with which Nietzsche here credits (at least some of) modern Europe. Unlike the

[3] This claim is, of course, open to debate. For an interesting discussion of this topic, as well as of the issue of German nostalgia for ancient Greece, see Philippe Lacoue-Labarthe, *L'imitation des modernes* (Paris: Galilée, 1986).

[4] Of course, there need be no one thing in which it consists in general. But I think Nietzsche believes that the modern man of knowledge understand himself as such only on the condition that he recognizes what is unique about his position in the present age. He must, as I have put it, recognize himself as an achievement. And it is, as we shall see, a form of morality that, in a very particular fashion, stands in the way of such recognition.

Greeks, in other words, modern Europeans have—or anyway should have—a sense of themselves as standing at the end of a particular historical development. More specifically, the men of knowledge think of their honesty as compelling them to reject the errors and illusions of the past. To ask about the value of the will to truth, therefore, is to ask how the historical sense of the men of knowledge in particular should be understood, and in this way to inquire into the nature of their modernity.

Nietzsche's exploration of the relation between community and individual in the present age, then, is more complicated than his criticism of Socratism might lead one to expect. The latter tells us, in effect, that to be an individual is to be intelligible. And to be intelligible, we saw, means, for Nietzsche, to be a member of one's linguistic community. It is precisely to such community, however, that he believes we in the present age cannot lay claim. We fail, as I have put the point, to speak—fail, in other words, to let ourselves be intelligible to one another. This, I think, is why Nietzsche says we are a herd. Our situation in the present age is, therefore, structurally different from that of the tragic Greeks: on the one hand, there is for us no standing culture of which an individual might now construe himself as a member; and, on the other hand, for us membership in culture is to be construed in specifically historical terms.[5]

'Morality in Europe today is herd animal morality'. A remark like this suggests that, in Nietzsche's view, individuality in the present age will be possible only if one does not use the language of one's community. This suggestion in turn gives rise to a distorted understanding of Nietzsche's untimeliness. Being untimely is often misconceived as a matter of having a conceptually independent standpoint on one's historical situation. In the case of the will to knowledge, in particular, such independence is sometimes understood to be a matter of recognizing the contingency of the modern commitment to truth and as an openness to some other way of life. On the reading I am recommending here, however, this interpretation is symptomatic of resistance to the imperative to truthfulness—indicative of the weakness of our will to knowledge.[6]

[5] Our situation in the present age is, in this first respect at least, like that of the decadent Greeks who find the Socratic demand for reasons intelligible, and who need Socratism as a way of making sense of life.
[6] Again, the mistake here is not that of thinking that one can or cannot step outside one's historical situation, but rather that of thinking of one's historical situation as something on the outside *or* the inside of which it makes sense to suppose one might try to stand in the first place. Nietzsche's point is that, as we presently live our lives, we are not properly historical at all.

Consequently, the Nietzschean image of looking down on one's age must be handled with care, for it easily misleads us into thinking that, in his view, the individual stands outside his or her historical situation.[7] In Nietzsche's view, however, we in the present age clearly do not constitute a culture in the sense that interests him. Thus, there is nothing, in that sense, on the outside of which the individual might try to take up conceptual residence. Now Nietzsche suggests that it is our inability properly to acknowledge our historical character—our unwillingness to see the death of God as an event—that constitutes us as a herd. But it is precisely this suggestion that implies that there is no historical situation from which the individual might strive to distance him or herself. The herd, therefore, does not have a particular view of the world; it aims, rather, to cloud our vision of what having such a view would entail. The distinction Nietzsche draws between the individual and the herd is the distinction between a life in which what we have become matters to us and a life in which it does not.

As I have said, it is, in Nietzsche's view, morality—specifically, the morality of pity—that stands in the way of acknowledging this distinction. In a community ruled by the morality of pity, he says, the most an individual can be is an exception to a general rule of unintelligibility.[8] The exception, however, does not speak a different language than the herd's, but rather the one that, by and large, the herd fails to speak. From Nietzsche's point of view, then, the reason the would-be individual can be said not to speak the language of the herd is simply that the herd does not *speak* at all. Where the individual would do so, they merely mouth their words.

The difference Nietzsche intends between the individual and the herd is thus the difference between speech and what we might call 'mere talk'. The effect of the morality of pity, Nietzsche suggests, is to obscure this distinction—to make it appear as though speech were something *more* than talk, rather than allowing us to see that the latter is really something less than the former. To say that we live under the sway of the morality of pity is, I will argue, to say that we remain private, cut off from each other. Pity, we might say, makes us inscrutable to one another by perturbing our vision of what scrutability might be for us. Paradoxically enough, then, it is precisely where the morality of pity aims to bring us closer together (by putting us in touch with each other's suffering) that it actually has the result of driving us apart. As

---

[7] See, for example, *Beyond Good and Evil*, sec. 286, and *Daybreak*, sec. 369.

[8] See *Beyond Good and Evil*, sec. 26. I will return to this important section at the end of this chapter.

we will see, however, the effect of the morality of pity is that the man of knowledge remains less than he is, and that he continues to live, as Nietzsche puts it, "at the expense of the future" (GM, preface, sec. 6, p. 20).[9]

I have suggested that, for Nietzsche, overcoming the unconditionality of the will to truth would be a matter of appreciating the price one pays for that commitment. Such unconditionality is, in his view, a failure of intelligibility—as failure to recognize that commitment *as* a commitment. Thus, when the man of knowledge pretends that the death of God does not matter, Nietzsche holds he is not speaking meaningfully. Such unintelligibility is what is most herdlike about him and represents his own distinctive form of nihilism. It is ultimately the herd 'in' the man of knowledge that resists seeing the sense in which the modern commitment to truthfulness represents an achievement. The herd's failure to recognize the death of God as an event is clearly not the only fault Nietzsche finds with it, but this particular shortcoming is central to what he thinks of as our inability to become what we are in general.[10]

Where I have discussed the question of the relationship between individual and community in terms of the ideas of speaking and mere talk, the *Genealogy* speaks of 'reading' and of 'having the right to make promises'. To say of someone that he has the right to make promises means, for Nietzsche, that he speaks intelligibly—that he takes responsibility for what he says. The morality of pity, on the other hand, conspires to deny us the right to make promises, thus threatening to make us unintelligible. Odd though it sounds, however, Nietzsche believes that it does so by preventing us from reading his own works in the right way.

[9] Here, as elsewhere, the temptation I am urging us to resist is that of taking Nietzsche's talk about the future to refer to some point in time when we would have new values in the sense of a radically different conceptual scheme. Our lives in the future, as Nietzsche imagines them, would indeed be different from what he takes them now to be, indeed, different in content, but only in the sense that we would then truly be living them as opposed to the current situation of as it were merely going through the motions of doing so. This, to repeat, is not a difference captured by talking of a shift in one's interpretation of the world.

[10] Of course, on Nietzsche's view, it is more than just the morality of pity that tends to make us herdlike. And the men of knowledge are not the only ones Nietzsche accuses of failing to be individuals. There are, in other words, plenty of moral and religious practices in which we engage, on the one hand, and intellectual habits that condition us, on the other, that are not associated with pity but that Nietzsche does believe level down our lives in ways that he relates to herd morality. But insofar as we are trying to understand the possibility of the man of knowledge becoming an individual, we have to be able to make sense of the idea of his overcoming what is herdlike in *his* life. Pity, Nietzsche says, that is the last enemy of the man of knowledge, and the distinctively modern moral danger.

This last claim directs us to an aspect of Nietzsche's thinking that is among the most difficult to assess, but whose centrality should not be ignored. In general, Nietzsche's claims on behalf of his work can seem simply incredible, if not downright offensive. Even if we can get an intellectual handle on the idea of culture as linguistic community and even if we are not unsympathetic to the claim that, as we stand, we fail to amount to a culture in this sense of the word, it is terribly difficult to know how to respond to the suggestion that Nietzsche himself might somehow be responsible for correcting this situation. For how, we may well wonder, could becoming what *we* are depend upon reading the works of this author in particular? Our ability to see in what sense one might meaningfully speak of dependence in this context turns on our understanding of the kind of reading Nietzsche believes is in question here. He does not suppose that, at this level, his works offer *information* to the men of knowledge. He aims, however, to alter their relationship to what he takes them already to know. In a Platonic vein, we might say that he wants to remind them of something that they know but have forgotten. The *Genealogy* aims, in other words, at the creation of a special kind of memory. And it is precisely the morality of pity that Nietzsche holds responsible for our amnesia as readers. For it is the morality of pity, I mean to argue, that makes us think that reading can be a matter only of gleaning information.

These are, as I have said, extremely difficult claims to evaluate, and it is worth trying to articulate them in yet another way before we endeavor to do so. Nietzsche says that where we lack a certain form of memory we lack the right to make promises, and he suggests that lacking that right signals our inability to take responsibility for what we say. The goal of the *Genealogy* is to provide the kind of memory he thinks we lack, and thus to give us the right to make promises. This is the work he gives his work to do. The morality of pity and the attitude toward reading that it implies, however, thwart our ability properly to respond to genealogical writing, and *thereby*, in Nietzsche's view, encourage us to avoid taking responsibility for what we say.

There are, therefore, two features of Nietzsche's critique of morality on which I want to concentrate in this chapter. On the one hand, he insists that morality—specifically, the morality of pity—is hostile to the very possibility of individuality. As I read him, this means that our morality makes us unintelligible to one another. On the other hand, he claims that morality permits us to live at the expense of the future.[11]

[11] See, in particular, *On the Genealogy of Morals*, preface, sec. 6, p. 20.

These claims, I suggest, represent two sides of the same point Nietzsche is trying to make about life in the present age. For, in his view, to be an individual is to have the right to make promises, and someone who has that right is someone who can 'stand security' for his future. The morality of pity, however, threatens the speaker's ability to do so and is in this way inimical to the very possibility of individuality.

We need, then, to understand what it means to treat having the right to make promises as the mark of individuality. I will address this question in the next section. We also need to understand in what sense he believes that our morality denies us that right. I would like to discuss this issue briefly in the remainder of this introductory section, and I will return to it in the third section. In the fourth section, I will try to make explicit what light Nietzsche's discussion of promising, morality, and reading sheds on the question of self-consciousness about the will to truth. And finally, I will, in the concluding section, suggest how these issues play themselves out in the text of the *Genealogy* itself. For the moment, however, let us explore briefly the claim that morality is hostile to individuality.

To make sense of Nietzsche's attack on morality, we need to make sense of the following sort of remark: "For this is how things are: the diminution and leveling of European man constitutes *our* greatest danger, for the sight of him makes us weary" (*GM* I, sec. 12, p. 44). It will help, I think, to begin by contrasting Nietzsche's disgust with what, for these purposes, we might as well call 'the meaninglessness of modern life' with that of some of his near contemporaries. Thus, in a strikingly Nietzschean moment of *On Liberty*, Mill writes:

society has now fairly got the better of individuality; and the danger which threatens human nature is not the excess, but the deficiency, of personal impulses and preferences. . . . In our times . . . everyone lives under the eye of a hostile and dreaded censorship. Not only in what concerns others, but in what concerns only themselves, the individual or the family do not ask themselves, what do I prefer? or . . . what would allow the best and the highest in me to have fair play and enable it to grow and thrive? They ask themselves, what is suitable to my position? what is usually done by persons of my station and pecuniary circumstances? or (worse still) what is usually done by persons of a station and circumstances superior to mine? I do not mean that they choose what is customary in preference to what suits their own inclination. It does not occur to them to have any inclination except for what is customary . . . [U]ntil by dint of not following their own nature they have no nature to follow.[12]

Emerson similarly decried what he saw as our growing conformism, and described each of us as ashamed of ourselves. Self-reliance is, for Emerson, conformity's 'aversion'; and he set himself the goal of, as Stanley Cavell puts it, making us ashamed of our shame. From yet another direction, Kierkegaard excoriated the present age for having become so dispassionate and reflective as to leave us unable any longer to make sense of so much as the idea of human commitment. In his view, we live lives whose "qualitative distinctions [between what is worthwhile and what is not] are weakened by a gnawing reflection."[13] In the present age, he believed, no particular way of life—that is, no particular position that one might occupy in the social order of things—has any more claim on us than any other. Consequently, he thought, we simply pass from one entertainment to the next with no direct experience of the emptiness of our so-called interests. In response to this situation, Kierkegaard set himself the task of trying to make clear just what a life of concrete commitment might be for us.[14]

Like Mill, Emerson, and Kierkegaard, Nietzsche was infinitely galled by the mediocrity of modern life. But he tended in general to blame our morality rather than our reflectiveness for the difficulties that beset anyone who would, in the present age, be an individual. We will not go far wrong, for our purposes here, if we think of a person's morality as the basic outlook she has on the character of her relationship to her community. The specific form of morality that Nietzsche condemns— the so-called morality of pity—expresses something like the demand for conformity. This idea suggests that the outlook he condemns represents the voice of the community in the individual.[15] Nietzsche means, then, to attack those attitudes toward oneself and toward others that

[12] John Stuart Mill, *On Liberty* (Indianapolis: Hackett, 1978), p. 58. This passage is cited in a similar connection by Stanley Cavell in *Conditions Handsome and Unhandsome* (Chicago: University of Chicago Press, 1990). Cavell makes clear the Nietzschean overtones in Mill's thinking and has done the most to trace the influence of Emerson on Nietzsche's work generally.

[13] Søren Kierkegaard, *The Present Age*, trans. Alexander Dru (New York: Harper and Row, 1962) p. 43.

[14] This approach to Kierkegaard is due to Jane Rubin. See her doctoral dissertation, "Too Much of Nothing: Modern Culture, the Self, and Salvation in Kierkegaard's Thought" (University of California, Berkeley, 1984).

[15] Which is why Nietzsche so often appears to treat morality as the outlook that the community has on the individual rather than, as I have suggested here, the other way around.

encourage the individual to confuse her needs with those of the people around her.

To put the point in quasi-Kantian terms, we can say that, for Nietzsche, no action done out of fear of the opinion of others has moral worth. Indeed, his chief complaint about us is that our actions are everywhere governed by a sense of guilt. We have, he says, bad consciences and, consequently, lack the right to make promises. Thus, his complaint about our morality is not that keeping promises, say, levels us down and makes us mediocre, but rather that our mediocrity prevents us from making real promises in the first place.[16]

That it is specifically *individuality* that Nietzsche believes is ruled out by modern morality is made clear in the following sort of remark: "There is today perhaps no more firmly credited prejudice than this: that one knows what really constitutes the moral. Today it seems *to do everyone good* when they hear that society is on the way to adapting the individual to general requirements, and that *the happiness and at the same time the sacrifice of the individual* lies in feeling himself to be a useful member and instrument of the whole. . . . What is wanted—whether this is admitted or not—is nothing less than a fundamental remoulding, indeed weakening and abolition of the *individual*" (*D*, sec. 132, p. 83). Though, as we will see, Nietzsche sometimes treats the antipathy of society to the individual as an aspect of anything he considers to be the morality of custom or mores, the specific form of hostility that the morality of pity directs toward the individual is something he believes to be distinctly modern. In the present age, in other words, society's hostility to the individual is not simply a matter of condemning as evil whatever does not define itself in terms of the reigning customs and traditions. This is merely the sort of hostility that society directs toward anything it finds unintelligible or, as Nietzsche puts it, incalculable. By contrast, the morality of pity's hostility to the individual is the hostility that an unintelligible herd aims at the very possibility of making sense. This, I suggest, is how we should understand Nietzsche's claim that herd animal morality "resists with all its power" the possibility of "other types [of morality], above all higher moralities" (*BGE*, sec. 202, pp. 115–16).[17]

---

[16] In other words, Nietzsche does not consider us capable, as we stand, of being moral in a meaningful sense in the first place. We are, as Vicki Hearne has put the point to me in conversation, *bad* at being good.

[17] It is in this context, I think, that we should locate Nietzsche's objection to morality's concern with universality. I take his point to be not that universality per se is harmful, but that our image of universality is distorted and that, consequently, what we are capable of making of universality is bad for us. Once again, this amounts to

In section 287 of *Beyond Good and Evil,* Nietzsche draws the distinction between the herd and the individual in this way: "What is noble? What does the world 'noble' still mean to us *today?* What betrays, what allows one to recognize the noble human being, under this heavy, overcast sky of the beginning rule of the plebs that makes everything opaque and leaden? It is not actions that prove him—actions are always open to many interpretations, always unfathomable—nor is it 'works'. . . . [I]t is the *faith* that is decisive here, that determines the order of rank. . . . *The noble soul has reverence for itself*" (*BGE,* sec. 287, pp. 227–28; my emphasis). Because Nietzsche elsewhere says that an order of rank and a pathos of distance also separate his mythical masters from their slaves,[18] it is reasonable to conjecture that he considers what in *Beyond Good and Evil* he calls "the difference in value between man and man" to be something that at least *began* as a distinction between different social classes.[19] But it is doubtful that he believes that the notions of order of rank and pathos of distance have content in that context any longer.[20] If we are to see what sort of content these notions might have in the present age, we need to know more both about the distinction between the individual and the herd and about how Nietzsche thinks of morality's hostility toward the former. His insistence on the leveled character of modern life suggests that we cannot now make good sense of that distinction in terms of social hierarchies. It must be drawn differently.

For help, then, I turn to the second essay of the *Genealogy:* it is here that Nietzsche characterizes the individual as someone who has the right to make promises. According to the *Genealogy,* morality's hostility toward the individual derives from its opposition to that right. In the next section, I address the first question posed above: what does it mean to treat having the right to make promises as the mark of individuality? My suggestion has been that it is only if we come to terms with this

---

the claim that we are not capable of being moral—that our morality is moral in name alone.

[18] See the first essay of the *Genealogy,* as well as sec. 260 of *Beyond Good and Evil.*

[19] See *Beyond Good and Evil,* sec. 257.

[20] Consider, for example, the following passage from *The Will to Power:* "What does 'underprivileged' mean? Above all, physiologically—no longer politically. The unhealthiest kind of man in Europe (in all classes) furnishes the soil for this nihilism: they will experience the belief in the eternal recurrence as a curse. . . . It is the value of such a crisis that it purifies, that it pushes together related elements to perish of each other, that it assigns common tastes to men who have opposite ways of thinking—and it also brings to light the weaker and less secure among them and thus promotes an order of rank according to strength, from the point of view of health: those who command are recognized as those who command, those who obey as those who obey. *Of course, outside every existing social order*" (*WP,* sec. 55, p. 38; my emphasis).

claim that we can understand the further claim that morality is hostile to the individual.

An Animal with the Right to Make Promises

In saying that having the right to make promises is the 'real problem regarding man', Nietzsche suggests that we may think of human speech as a form of promising.[21] As we shall see, part of the point of this suggestion is to remind us that speech is something exchanged between speakers: one cannot give one's word where there is no one to take it.[22] We will return to this idea in the fourth section of this chapter. Here, however, I want to stress a different, though related, aspect of Nietzsche's vision of speech as promising: the idea of responsibility. One has the right to give one's word only where one can take responsibility for what one says. Responsibility in this sense, Nietzsche says, is the ability to stand security for the future.[23] He insists, however, that it is only the "sovereign individual" who *may* in this sense—who has the right to—give his word. That is to say, it is only the individual who speaks with full intelligibility, because it is only he who takes responsibility for what he says. Only he has the right to make promises.

[21] The *Genealogy* asks: "To breed an animal with the right to make promises—is not this the paradoxical task that nature has set itself in the case of man? is it not the real problem regarding man?" (*GM*, II, sec. 1, p. 57). Nietzsche's German reads: "Ein Thier heranzuechten, das *versprechen darf*—ist das nicht gerade jene paradoxe Aufgabe selbst, welche sich die Natur in Hinsicht auf den Menschen gestellt hat? ist das nicht das eigentliche Problem vom Menschen?" In what follows, I will, on stylistic grounds, generally refer to the speaker—and, hence, to the individual—as 'he'. Nietzsche is certainly not committed to the view that only men can be individuals in this sense. Indeed, he speaks in this context of the *person—der Mensch*. But insofar as Kaufmann's translations of the passages I will discuss from the second essay of the *Genealogy* and elsewhere use the masculine pronoun in this connection, I will do so too. The suggestion that, for Nietzsche, speaking is a form of promising is, as far as I can see, hardly an interpretation of the opening sentences of the second essay of the *Genealogy*, but rather something he more or less explicitly says. The rest of the essay is responsible for fleshing out his claim. The connection itself between speaking and promising or giving one's word is itself not especially surprising. Two recent discussions of this idea spring to mind: Stanley Cavell touches upon this part of Nietzsche's thought in *Conditions Handsome and Unhandsome* (see especially p. 115); and in *Memoires for Paul de Man* (New York: Columbia University Press, 1986), Jacques Derrida explores the resonances between *sprechen* and *versprechen* in connection with both de Man and Heidegger.

[22] It is in this context that the *Genealogy's* concerns with the concept of exchange —specifically between creditors and debtors—should be understood.

[23] The German is striking: "für sich *als Zukunft* gut sagen zu können" (GM II, sec. 1, p. 58).

The claim of the second essay, however, is that, by and large, we in the present age speak irresponsibly. As we stand, we do not count as individuals in this sense. Our promises are hollow, for we give our word without the right to do so. As we will see, for Nietzsche, this is as much as to say that we—at least as we live right now—are less than fully human.

On the face of it, the *Genealogy's* discussion of promising, punishment, and bad conscience looks like a naturalistic account of certain features of ourselves that we like to think distinguish us from mere beasts.[24] The point of such an account appears to be, among other things, to debunk the idea that human beings are *essentially* different from the beasts. Thus, by offering a psychological, rather than, say, a theological account of the notions of guilt, the soul, sin, redemption, and so on, Nietzsche would be trying to undermine the traditional vision of a sharp distinction between human beings and the other animals. He argues, for example, that the fact that we feel both responsible for what we do and yet ultimately powerless to do other than we do— that we feel, as it were, victims of ourselves—is a feature of our lives that has a complicated psychological and sociological history. Such feelings represent, in particular, an animal response to the pressures of a social environment and therefore are not the voice of an innate conscience in us.[25] On this reading, then, the peculiar intricacies of human aggression show not that we are *more* than animals, just different.[26]

On the other hand, however, Nietzsche is also concerned in this essay to make clear the sort of creatures he thinks we *are*. Ultimately, I think, his concern with how we live our lives now trumps the interest he might have had in specifically naturalist anthropological hypotheses about the underlying continuity of human beings with the other animals. The latter concerns must, in other words, be assessed in the light of the former. In his estimation, we are after all *very* different from the other beasts. In particular, we are social animals, a point Nietzsche

[24] To say that God is dead is, among other things, to say that the development of reason has reached a point where we produce accounts of religion in terms of fear. See Stanley Cavell, *The Claim of Reason* (Oxford: Oxford University Press, 1979), p. 419. Nietzsche offers just such an account in the second essay of the *Genealogy*. See sec. 19 especially. But I mean nothing more technical than this by my use of the term 'naturalistic'. Given his particular understanding of culture, I do not think that Nietzsche has a Humean naturalism in mind when, in *The Gay Science*, sec. 109, he asks, "When may we begin to 'naturalize' humanity in terms of a pure, newly discovered, newly redeemed nature?"

[25] Attacking this last idea is surely part of the point of showing "what *bestiality of thought* erupts as soon as [man] is prevented just a little from being a *beast in deed!*" (*GM* II, sec. 22, p. 93).

[26] Again, without suggesting that the particular account Nietzsche offers represents no contribution to our psychological understanding of ourselves, I have meant to

expresses by explaining how human beings come to reason. For "reason, seriousness, mastery over the affects, the whole somber thing called reflection, all these prerogatives and showpieces of man" (*GM* II, sec. 3, p. 62) are achieved by means of the institution of punishment, and punishment, Nietzsche holds, is a distinctly social practice. Thus, after listing some of what he considers to be the "fearful means" the Germans have used to "master their basic mob-instinct and its brutal coarseness" (ibid.), Nietzsche writes, "with the aid of such images and procedures one finally remembers five or six 'I will not's', in regard to which one had given one's promise so as to participate in the advantages of society—and it was indeed with the aid of this kind of memory that one at last came 'to reason'!" (ibid.). Thus, although what sets us apart from the other animals—namely, our reason—is in fact merely a feature of our own animality that first emerges in response to the pressures of communal life, Nietzsche wants to emphasize that our reason does nevertheless—or anyway ought to—*distinguish* us from our four-footed cousins.

Aside from being in this sense social animals, we are also set apart from the other beasts by both the kind and the degree of pleasure that we take in certain forms of cruelty. Not only do we delight in inflicting pain upon each other, but, in the right circumstances, we take even greater pleasure in inflicting it upon ourselves. According to Nietzsche, when conjoined with a primitive sense of indebtedness to God, our inability as members of society immediately to express our instincts of aggression leads to a distinctively human form of self-denial: namely, the experience of sinfulness. On this account, our bad conscience reinterprets the very fact of our animality as irredeemable guilt before God, and on this basis Christianity then advances the idea that only the suffering of God himself can redeem us. Finally, coming to believe that our animality is radically opposed to our spiritual natures leads to what Nietzsche calls the "moralization of the concepts of guilt and duty" (*GM* II, sec. 21, p. 91). No other animal seems to Nietzsche to be so at odds with its own nature.

Nietzsche's talk of breeding an animal with the right to make promises is, thus, his way of raising the question of what is involved in the passage out of mere animality and into humanity.[27] In the *Genealogy*,

stress the fact that he takes for granted his readers' willingness to entertain such hypotheses as he offers as relevant to the matters at hand. This willingness is itself a new development, our responsiveness to which Nietzsche aims to challenge. It is in this sense that I am suggesting he has nothing new to tell his rightful readers.

[27] I take it that Nietzsche believes that man is the 'promising animal' in both senses that expression suggests. Our ability to speak, in other words, is (or ought to be) what distinguishes us from the other beasts. But here, as in the case of the will,

however, he means not only to explain what kind of animal we are but also to indicate the sort of animal that, by and large, we *fail* to be. As I have said, he denies that, as we stand, we actually have the right to make promises. He believes that we lack that particular mark of humanity. Where we give our word without the right to do so, we are less than completely intelligible, and therefore less than fully human animals.

According to the *Genealogy*, then, our humanity depends upon taking responsibility for what we say. This, as we will see, is part of the point of treating promising as a relationship between debtor and creditor. But Nietzsche suggests that our currently moralized versions of that relationship demonstrate that we are presently incapable of standing security for ourselves in the way that someone must who truly has the right to make promises.

Now the idea that we in the present age fail to make sense—are not fully intelligible—is, of course, not a new idea in this book. I have tried to assess Nietzsche's attack on Socratism in these terms. And I have all along been asking, in particular, whether the nihilist can be understood to be taking responsibility for saying that God is dead. But because there seem to be two different notions of making sense at work in my reading—only one of which is at stake here—I should say something about this apparent dichotomy before we examine Nietzsche's discussion of responsibility more closely.

Where we seem to be able to make sense of the idea that there is something like a standing culture, the claim that an individual is someone who speaks intelligibly functions as little more than a reminder that individuality is not a matter of speaking a language different from the language of the culture at hand. As I have said, the more intuitive notion of an individual—as someone who does not confuse her needs with the needs of those around her—has no obvious application in this context. For where he can imagine a standing culture, Nietzsche has little use for the distinction between the individual and the herd.[28] On

---

Nietzsche's aim is not to provide a properly philosophical account of the difference between man and the other animals. From a philosophical point of view, his naturalistic point is, I suppose, that we are indeed animals. There is no divine spark within us. What keeps us from being *human* animals, however, is our inability adequately to respond to the fact of our recognition of our own animality. We need to keep in mind, however, the peculiarly psychological status of this last claim. The point is that, as long as our consciences are bad and our actions governed by a sense of guilt, we are, in effect, no better than the beasts. We only become human in the relevant sense to the degree that our "proud awareness of the extraordinary privilege of *responsibility*, the consciousness of this rare freedom," has become our "dominating instinct" (*GM* II, sec. 2, p. 60).

[28] And although, as we will see shortly, he stresses the hostility of custom and tradition—what Kaufmann translates as 'mores'—to the incalculable individual, where the culture functions properly, *such* an individual can only be an anomaly.

the other hand, where—as Nietzsche takes the case to be in the present age—there is no standing culture, the idea of an individual as someone who speaks intelligibly takes on a more positive cast. For in these circumstances to be an individual is clearly *not* to speak the language of one's fellows: where there is no standing culture, speakers have become spectators, neither responsible for what they say nor responsive to what they hear.

Consider, once again, Nietzsche's conception of the situation in Greece at the time of Socrates: the Athenians have become decadent, and their instincts are in disarray. In such circumstances, they are prepared to treat how the world appears to them as merely a fact about them. Because the Socratic life of reason allows them to make sense of their situation, they are in what Nietzsche considers to be the regrettable position of taking the demand for reasons seriously. As we have seen, however, where making sense is unproblematic, the notion of individuality has no positive content because there is no herd. In the case of the tragic Greeks, therefore, offering reasons is at best only one practice among many; someone who wanted to do so all the time would simply have failed to understand the role such a practice plays in ordinary life.

It is, therefore, Nietzsche's criticism of Socratism that appears to recommend distinguishing two different forms of intelligibility.[29] Understood on its own terms, Socratism is, in Nietzsche's view, a species of philosophical nonsense. This is because, according to him, the attempt to adopt a spectator's stance with respect to one's culture at large is, strictly speaking, impossible. Being unintelligible in *this* sense is, therefore, simply not an option for human beings. But precisely because he believes that Socratism makes no sense on its own terms, Nietzsche must struggle to develop an intelligible interpretation of it.[30] On his reading, the sense Socratism makes is to be found in the idea of the demand for reasons as a cure.[31] Nevertheless, although Socratic unintelligibility is impossible on its own terms, from Nietzsche's point of view, nothing is more common than our distinctively modern forms of unin-

[29] To put the point in Heideggerian terms, we might say that one of them would be 'ontological' and the other 'ontic'. As I suggest, however, once we properly appreciate the ostensibly ontological point, we will see that the only sort of responsibility of which we can meaningfully speak is ontic responsibility. That is all responsiveness comes to.

[30] He must struggle, in other words, to understand which form of will to power it is. This, Nietzsche says, is the proper task of the psychologist. Psychology is "morphology and *the doctrine of the development of the will to power*" (*BGE*, sec. 23, p. 31).

[31] As I have argued, Nietzsche sums up this line of thought in the *Genealogy* by saying that 'man would rather will *nothingness* than *not* will'.

telligibility: in particular, our failure to make sense of ourselves as 'men of knowledge'.[32] It may on these grounds seem tempting to try to distinguish two different sorts of 'sense' one can be said to make: the one we cannot help but make and the one Nietzsche thinks we fail to make.

It is not at all obvious, however, what sort of distinction may really be drawn here. There is, after all, only the sense we make—and no *other* sort of sense that we do not. Socratism expresses a human wish to speak outside the ordinary (human) conditions of intelligibility. But there is, as Nietzsche sees it, nothing outside these conditions, and therefore no content to Socratic talk of being confined to them. As the confusions on which the Socratic demand for reasons rests are cleared away, we should, in Nietzsche's view, begin to lose our sense that the notion of intelligibility might have any determinate philosophical content. I think, therefore, that in the end Nietzsche simply had no interest in the nature of what I just called 'standing culture'. His psychological concerns are always—can only be—particular.

Like the ascetic ideal generally, Socratism makes no sense on its own terms because it fails—at least in those terms—truly to oppose itself to anything. There is, in short, only one kind of thing that taking responsibility for what one says can be: obedience to the ordinary conditions of intelligible speech. And there is, of course, no one thing that constitutes such obedience. What counts as responsibility to meaning varies from context to context, of course, just as it can be avoided in a variety of ways. But there is no sense in speaking of a bottom level of intelligibility from which Nietzsche believes we cannot deviate.[33]

We should not, then, lose sight of the fact that, even in *The Birth of Tragedy*, Nietzsche was interested above all in what he took to be the

---

[32] See *The Gay Science*, sec. 347, p. 287. Because Nietzsche sometimes insists that we mostly still need Christianity, it is quite natural to think that he believes that, compared with the Christian herd, *atheism* represents a form of individuality. But he is quite explicit that mere atheism does not suffice to distinguish the individual from the herd in the present age. The values that lead to atheism are, after all, Christian (herd) values. Assuming that such people as Nietzsche considers modern Christians to be do in fact believe in God, they are not guilty of the same sort of self-blindness as is the man of knowledge whose will to truth is unconditional. From Nietzsche's point of view, they deceive themselves, because God does not exist. But when he discusses our modern failure to make sense of ourselves, Nietzsche has the 'last men' in mind, those in the marketplace of sec. 125 of *The Gay Science* who do *not* believe in God.

[33] Humanity, in other words, is nothing magical. It is therefore important to appreciate the fact that even in *The Birth of Tragedy*, Nietzsche is concerned primarily with the present age's failure to amount to a culture. His account of Socratism is best read in the context of that particular problem, and not as a general theory of intelligibility (whatever that might be).

man of knowledge's failure to make sense of his situation in the present age. There appear to the nihilist to be two different ways in which the news of the death of God may be greeted: as either pertinent or indifferent. Nietzsche insists, however, that indifference in this context is a symptom of resistance, and a sign of the man of knowledge's unwillingness to take responsibility for his commitment to truthfulness. As we saw, Nietzsche puts this point by saying that his will to truth is unconditional, pious. Our present considerations, however, suggest that Nietzsche understand the nihilist's indifference to the death of God to be a form of unintelligibility, and not, as the nihilist pretends, merely an alternative way of understanding the commitment to truthfulness.[34] It is, therefore, highly misleading to suggest that there are two different ways to understand what it means to be conditioned by the will to knowledge, two different ways of responding to the announcement of the death of God. It is, indeed, nihilism to think so. For the nihilist's posture of indifference is an attempt to master the will to truth and is, as such, a form of disobedience. With these points in mind, then, let us turn our attention back to the second essay.

My claim was that talking about having the right to make promises was Nietzsche's way of expressing a certain conception of the idea of taking responsibility for what one says, and thus of marking a distinction between speaking and merely talking. To say that someone makes promises without the right to do so is to say that he fails to be fully intelligible, that he is not fully human. In the case of the will to knowledge, in particular, to say that someone has the right to make promises is to distinguish him from someone whose will to truth is unconditional. Nietzsche insists, however, that the conditionality of one's will to truth depends upon the acquisition of a certain form of memory. This implies that, for Nietzsche, our humanity depends upon memory. Let me explain briefly, by way of introduction to our discussion of the second essay.

According to the genealogist, memory is the path to what is best in us. Two points about this idea are worth noting at the outset. First, and fairly obviously, the *Genealogy* itself is a book written with the aim of overcoming some form of forgetfulness in its readers. That is to say, Nietzsche presents genealogical investigation as a form of recollection: the genealogist aims, roughly, to recover memory where he believes it is presently lost. Second, Nietzsche believes that the means the genealogist employs to this end are themselves terrible in the sense that they

---

[34] For Nietzsche, to say that one can, if one likes, treat the death of God as an event is just as nihilistic as the claim that it makes no sense at all to do so.

call upon the reader to acknowledge difficult or painful truths. We might say that, on his view, the road to the present is, in this sense, paved with suffering.[35] But more important, he supposes that recalling this last fact will itself be painful, something his readers will be inclined to resist. I am suggesting, in short, that the *Genealogy*'s claim "'if something is to stay in the memory it must be burned in: only that which never ceases to *hurt* stays in the memory'—this is a main clause of the oldest (unhappily also the most enduring) psychology on earth" (*GM* II, sec. 3, p. 61) applies to the *Genealogy* itself.[36] These considerations imply that, in Nietzsche's view, it is the *Genealogy*—the memory it produces—that is in some way responsible for what I have called our humanity, at least as men of knowledge. Without it, we remain in our animal or prehistorical state.

Our forgetfulness, on the other hand, opposes itself to the acquisition of the kind of memory Nietzsche believes is necessary for the right to

[35] For example, Nietzsche considers it painful to acknowledge that punishment can serve to pay off a debt simply because it is painful to acknowledge that inflicting pain on someone is pleasurable. He says that "the depths of such subterranean things [as the origins of 'the moral conceptual world'] are difficult to fathom, *besides being painful*" (GM II, sec. 6, p. 65, my emphasis). He says, moreover, that "to see others suffer does one good, to make others suffer even more: this is a hard saying" (ibid.). When trying to assess the tone of such remarks, it is worth remembering that Nietzsche is above all concerned to point out the pleasure we take in self-torment. Unlike our barbaric past, this feature of our present may well not be something that we willingly acknowledge. The hard truths to which we have confined ourselves in this book are those having to do with overcoming our faith in the errors that give rise to the Socratic will to knowledge. Of course Nietzsche believes that there are other such truths. The point to bear in mind for the sequel, however, is that the morality of pity's hostility to suffering makes it difficult for us to understand what is involved in 'coming to reason' in *two* senses. On the one hand, Nietzsche believes that we are likely to find it difficult to understand how mere *obedience* can produce understanding. For we are not able properly to assess the sort of suffering involved. (See *Beyond Good and Evil*, sec. 188.) On the other hand, he also believes it likely that we will find objectionable—because incomprehensible—the special kind of suffering he understands to be involved in reading the *Genealogy* itself. In both cases, the morality of pity stands in the way of the acquisition of memory.

[36] I am claiming, in other words, that that of which the *Genealogy* seeks to remind us is not primarily that, for example, our reason is of a piece with our animality. For this is not what we men of knowledge are in danger of forgetting. When I say that the *Genealogy* does not seek to convey information to the man of knowledge—that Nietzsche does not aim to tell him something he does not already know—I do not mean to suggest that Nietzsche believes that, left to his own devices, any man of knowledge will come up with his particular account of, for example, bad conscience. This much is clearly not true. But the *point* of the sort of account Nietzsche offers is that such an account can be offered at all. That is to say, this is the kind of explanation we men of knowledge can now understand. Genealogy asks us to reflect upon what *that* fact says about us.

make promises. Such forgetfulness therefore stands in the way of our humanity. And though Nietzsche maintains that without forgetfulness "there could be no happiness, no cheerfulness, no hope, no pride, no *present*" (ibid., p. 58), this "active and in the strictest sense positive faculty of repression" (*GM* II, sec. 1, p. 57) governs only our prehuman—he says prehistorical—or merely animal state. The form of memory at which the genealogist aims represents the suspension of this state. For memory "involves no mere passive inability to rid oneself of an impression, no mere indigestion through a once-pledged word with which one cannot 'have done', but an active *desire* not to rid oneself, a desire for the continuance of something desired once, a real *memory of the will:* so that between the original 'I will', 'I shall do this' and the actual discharge of the will, its *act*, a world of strange new things, circumstances, even acts of will may be interposed without breaking this long chain of will" (ibid.).[37] According to the *Genealogy*, then, a 'real memory of the will' is what humanity requires.

Nietzsche says that the acquisition of this form of memory presupposes many things. Most important, "man himself must first of all have become *calculable, regular, necessary,* even in his own image of himself, if he is to be able to stand security *for his own future*" (ibid.). 'Calculability' and 'regularity' are explained in the *Genealogy* in the following terms: "The tremendous labor of that which I have called 'morality of mores' . . . —the labor performed by man upon himself during the greater part of the existence of the human race, his entire *prehistorical* labor, finds in this its meaning, its great justification, notwithstanding the severity, tyranny, stupidity, and idiocy involved in it: with the aid of the morality of mores and the social straitjacket, man was actually *made* calculable" (*GM* II, sec. 2, p. 59). Saying that someone is calculable, regular, and necessary is Nietzsche's way of saying that we can make sense of what that person does. Only if we bear in mind the idea of human speech as a form of promising can we appreciate his point in

[37] It is perhaps easier to appreciate what Nietzsche has in mind in talking here about a long chain of will if one has in mind marriage rather than, say, promising to meet someone for drinks as one's example of giving one's word. In any case, if my suggestion that Nietzsche means genealogy itself to overcome our forgetfulness is accurate, then it is primarily the genealogist's own promise to tell the truth that is in question here. The point of the *Genealogy's* discussion of forgetfulness and memory is not to remind us that promising is impossible where one cannot recall what one has promised. The forgetfulness Nietzsche discusses at the beginning of the second essay is *our* forgetfulness; it is we in the present age whose memories are short. The form of humanity achieved by the abrogation of *our* animal or prehistorical forgetfulness is the kind of memory Nietzsche associates with *our* being able to stand security for what we say.

insisting in these terms on the idea of promising as a specifically social activity. For he is not saying merely that promising involves both a promisor and a promisee. This much, of course, is true. But Nietzsche's point lies elsewhere. Minimally, his claim is instead that nothing counts as a promise where nothing counts as anything at all: where no two events are remembered as alike, where no similarities are perceived, nothing counts as breaking a promise, and so nothing counts as making one. If we keep in mind the idea of speaking as a form of promising, then the point of saying that man must be made calculable if promising is to be possible is that no one speaks—no judgments are made—where there are no similarities between the judgments we make. It is in this deeper sense that promising may be said to be a social activity. A concept, that is to say, cannot be employed just once.

As we saw, however, the topic of the second essay is, more specifically, the question of the passage of *Nietzsche's readers* from merely forgetful animality into recollecting humanity (from prehistory into history). Nietzsche's question about them is whether they can stand security for their future or whether they live at its expense. In the passage we are now considering, he says that, in general, such a transformation is effected in part by the force of tradition: the morality of custom is responsible for turning the animals that they were into intelligible animals—ones who are "to a certain degree necessary, uniform, like among like, regular, and consequently calculable" (ibid.). Tradition and calculability, however, are only part of what makes human beings human; something further is required. The social straitjacket of custom, in other words, is only a *pre*condition of actually having the right to make promises.

Nietzsche writes:

> If we place ourselves at the end of this tremendous process, where the tree at last brings forth fruit, where society and the morality of custom at last reveal *what* they have simply been the means to: then we discover that the ripest fruit is the *sovereign individual*, like only to himself, liberated again from the morality of custom, autonomous and supramoral (for "autonomous" and "moral" are mutually exclusive), in short, the man who has his own independent, protracted will and the *right to make promises*—and in him a proud consciousness, quivering in every muscle, of *what* has at length been achieved and become flesh in him, a consciousness of his own power and freedom, a sensation of mankind come to completion. (Ibid.)

The sovereign individual has, in short, a sense of the order of rank, and, consequently, a sense of what separates him from the herd.[38] Thus, Nietzsche asks: "This emancipated individual, with the actual *right* to make promises, this master of a *free* will, this sovereign man—how should he not be aware of his superiority over all those who lack the right to make promises and stand as their own guarantors, of how much trust, how much fear, how much reverence he arouses—he '*deserves*' all three—and of how this mastery over himself also necessarily gives him mastery over circumstances, over nature, and over all more short-willed and unreliable creatures?" (ibid., pp. 59–60). This, then, is how Nietzsche draws the distinction between the individual and the herd in the second essay of the *Genealogy*.[39] The implication for the idea of speaking as promising is that responsibility, as well as the social strait-jacket of custom, is required for true humanity. We might say that, from Nietzsche's point of view, not only must speech be a possibility, it must be an *actuality*. For the latter, having the *right* to make promises is required.[40]

[38] The notions of 'order of rank' and 'pathos of distance' are among the most perplexing in Nietzsche's work. In the first essay of the *Genealogy*, he suggests that any healthy individual or social class will have a sense of both. They will, in other words, view themselves both as fundamentally different from the others and as superior to them in value. This sort of view understandably gives rise to charges of elitism, as well as to worries that Nietzsche held that the few should somehow be permitted to live at the expense of the many. Readers reasonably enough find the idea that any one human life might be worth more than any other both incredible and offensive. We are, after all, all equal in worth. Indeed, Nietzsche himself seems committed to what looks, from his point of view, like the disheartening conclusion that we have at least *become* equal in this sense. As he puts it, the slave rebellion in spirit has been successful. Part of the difficulty here is that we have no obvious way of making sense of the troublesome ideas in question except in terms of an ostensibly social hierarchy. But I think it is reasonably clear that, in the present age, Nietzsche considers the distinction between those who have the right to make promises and those who do not have it to embody his crucial distinction. In a quasi-Kantian fashion, he favors the former and asks, 'What do the *rest* matter?'. From Nietzsche's point of view, the latter lack what Kant called 'moral worth'. Because my interpretation leaves Nietzsche's position as elitist as we might either fear or wish, what I am suggesting may, in the end, be no less offensive than the usual reading. But at least it points us in the right direction, and, unlike the usual reading, it forces us to try to say something intelligent about precisely what we find offensive here.

[39] I think we can make immediate intuitive sense of the idea that someone who has the right to promise him- or herself to someone or to something 'come what may' will draw a distinction of something like rank between him or herself and those who do not have the right to do so—especially if they go ahead and promise anyway. 'Promising', in short, is another word for commitment. The fact that it may be difficult to avoid a tone of sanctimoniousness here is not entirely Nietzsche's fault.

[40] For an interesting discussion—not at all unrelated to the matters at hand—of the nature of the conceptual relationship between notions of regularity and custom, see T. S. Champlin, "Solitary Rule-Following," *Philosophy* 67 (1992): 285–306. I am indebted to Ed Minar for bringing this article to my attention.

How, then, does Nietzsche conceive of that right? First, we should notice that the distinction he draws between the individual and the herd is not that between being able and not being able to make promises, but rather between having and lacking the *right* to do so.[41] The latter distinction is the one we need to understand. To begin, however, it will help to look first at Nietzsche's account of promising itself. As I have said, he argues that our modern moral concepts of guilt, duty, and so on are moralized versions of more primitive forms of human relationship. Taking his cue from the fact that the German word *Schuld* means 'debt' as well as 'guilt', he traces the origins of our "moral conceptual world of 'guilt', 'conscience', 'duty', 'sacredness of duty'" (*GM* II, sec. 6, p. 65) back to what he describes as prehistoric relationships established between creditors and debtors. Promises, he says, were first made in the context of such relationships. "To inspire trust in his promise to repay, to provide a guarantee of the seriousness and sanctity of his promise, to impress repayment as a duty, an obligation upon his conscience, the debtor made a contract with the creditor and pledged that if he should fail to repay he would substitute something else that he 'possessed', something he had control over" (*GM* II, sec. 5, p. 64). Nietzsche says that it was in this context "that promises were made; it was here that a memory had to be made for those who promised" (ibid.). In such circumstances, however, the willingness to keep one's promises is grounded only in expedience, in a desire to avoid punishment, and not yet either in a moral sense or in a properly Nietzschean understanding of responsibility. The latter phenomena are built upon these more rudimentary relationships. This is why Nietzsche says that "the actual *effect* of punishment must beyond question be sought above all in a heightening of prudence, in an extending of the memory, . . . in a kind of improvement in self-criticism" (*GM* II, sec. 15, p. 83), and not in the awakening of the malefactor's guilty conscience. The latter, he insists, represents a much later development, and responsibility a later development still. Punishment, at this early stage, merely impresses upon the promisor the undesirable consequences of not keeping his word.

Initially, then, promising was a contractual relationship. Such contracts, Nietzsche says, formed "the oldest and most primitive personal relationship[s]" (*GM* II, sec. 8, p. 70). "[I]t was here one person first

[41] My emphasis on the word 'right' may mislead, for it is not a question here of *political* rights in any straightforward sense. Indeed, Nietzsche does not even use the word *Recht* in this context. He speaks, rather, of 'ein Thier . . . das versprechen *darf*'. But Kaufmann's translation provides a convenient way of marking the distinction Nietzsche has in mind.

encountered another person, that one person first *measured himself* against another. . . . Setting prices, determining values, contriving equivalences, exchanging—these preoccupied the earliest thinking of man to so great an extent that in a certain sense they constitute thinking as such" (ibid.). Part of the point of saying that the ability to establish equivalences is the mark of primitive humanity and the origin of "the feeling of superiority in relation to other animals" (ibid.) is to say that human beings are animals for whom something can stand for or symbolize something else.[42] The ability in this sense to measure and to settle on the value of something is necessary, Nietzsche maintains, to any form of social relationship.[43] The significance of this last claim becomes clearer in the context of section 9 of the second essay. Nietzsche there makes his interest in the relationship between individual and community quite explicit. As we will see presently, he understands that relationship, too, as one of promising.

Because the primitive contractual relationship of promising binds debtors to creditors generally, Nietzsche explains, it also ties the community to its members.[44] With respect to his community, the individual member of a social body is, in effect, a debtor. "One lives in a community, one enjoys the advantages of a communality (oh what advantages! we sometimes underrate them today), one dwells protected, cared for, in peace and trustfulness, without fear of certain injuries and hostile acts to which the man *outside,* the 'man without peace', is exposed—a German will understand the original connotations of *Elend*—since one has bound and pledged oneself to the community precisely with a view

[42] Some will find it tempting to read this as a claim about the origins of writing as opposed to those of speech. But I think that Nietzsche is primarily concerned here to develop the idea that the morality of mores makes human beings calculable, regular, and necessary. In this connection, sec. 9 of *Daybreak* repays the second look that the *Genealogy* suggests we give it. The *Genealogy's* talk of establishing equivalences tends, I think, to support my claim that regularity and necessity in the context of custom and tradition are aspects of intelligibility.

[43] A more complete reading of this section than I have proposed here would need to come to terms with Nietzsche's use of the notion of justice. We would need in particular to know what, for him, justice, reckoning, and thinking all have to do with one another. As I have suggested, these sections of the *Genealogy*—sec. 9 explicitly— help to articulate further Nietzsche's conception of the relationship of individual and community, and his remarks about justice there must be understood in that context. The 'great generalization' that "everything has its price; *all* things can be paid for" signals for Nietzsche our entrance into *language.* This is why he says that determining values, contriving equivalences, and so on, constitute—Nietzsche's use of the present tense here is not insignificant—*thinking* as such.

[44] In *GM* II, sec. 17, Nietzsche expresses his distaste for social contract theory. In sec. 9, however, he is concerned with the particular relationship between the community and its members that constitutes a culture in his sense of the word.

to injuries and hostile acts. What will happen *if this pledge is broken?* The community, the disappointed creditor, will get what repayment it can, one may depend on that" (*GM* II, sec. 9, p. 71).[45] In obeying the laws of the community, the individual member is keeping what Nietzsche considers to be a promise—a 'pledge'—in order to enjoy the advantages of society. Punishment for breaking that promise consists in being deprived of the benefits the defaulter has hitherto enjoyed and, therefore, in being reminded of their worth. "[T]he law breaker," Nietzsche says, "is above all a 'breaker', a breaker of his contract and his word with the whole in respect to all the benefits and comforts of communal life of which he has hitherto had a share" (ibid.).

One may be misled here into thinking that Nietzsche is making a relatively familiar point about the so-called state of nature. But his talk of laws and of the advantages of a communality is meant instead to flesh out his claim that the capacity for meaningful speech is the mark of our humanity. In particular, the idea of *exile* as a form of punishment is meant to drive home the fact that speaking intelligibly—that is, allowing oneself to be understood—is something for which the community holds the individual responsible, and for miscarriages of which it will exact 'what repayment it can'. It is, in other words, precisely the individual's failures to make sense that are punished by banishment.[46]

In this section of the *Genealogy*, I suggest, Nietzsche is refining his earlier discussion of the morality of mores, specifically that of section 9 of *Daybreak*.[47] The point there was that custom and tradition are responsible for making us calculable, regular, and necessary—in a word, intelligible. That what one does makes sense is, in Nietzsche's view, the result of a demand for a certain kind of conformity.[48] Section 8 of the second essay of the *Genealogy* suggested that such intelligibility is to be

[45] The suggestion here is that a certain sort of exclusion from the community is the worst form of punishment. Nietzsche's last remark in this passage is, however, double-edged. For he is saying, on the one hand, that someone who makes no sense at all will be exiled from a community of language speakers and, on the other, that someone who actually succeeds in making sense will be exiled from a group of talkers who resist doing so. As should become clear, Nietzsche has no authority beyond that which his readers are willing to grant him for his claim to be in the latter situation.

[46] Indeed, in *The Birth of Tragedy* Nietzsche cites exile as the appropriate punishment for Socrates himself. See sec. 13, p. 89.

[47] Sec. 2 of the second essay refers us explicitly to secs. 9, 14, and 16 of *Daybreak*. See *GM* II, sec. 2, p. 59. *Daybreak*, sec. 14 brings out another feature of the hostility of custom and tradition to the individual, a feature that will become important later on in my discussion.

[48] There remains, of course, a different demand for conformity, one that insures that we remain *un*intelligible: namely, the morality of pity. But that kind of conformity is not yet at stake here.

understood as a matter of being able to count something as something—for example, being able to count a certain gesture as one of friendship, of warning, or, for that matter, of punishment.[49] Section 9, in turn, expands on this idea.

According to the *Genealogy*, then, the individual's relationship to the community may be understood on the model of promising. As I have interpreted this idea, Nietzsche's point here is that we may think of any given instance of letting something count as something as a kind of promise. A speaker promises, in effect, to be responsible to the meaning of her words—for example, to be open to certain sorts of challenge to her authority, to requests for clarification or explanation, to the facts, and so on. It is only in *this* sense that, on this account, we can be said to give our words meaning—only in this sense that their meaning depends upon us. Failures to make sense, on the other hand, are treated as a form of criminal wrongdoing—the punishment for which is said to be exile or banishment, specifically from the community of language users. This, I submit, is the thought behind the *Genealogy's* suggestion that human speech in general may be thought of as a kind of promising.

Such, in outline, is the *Genealogy's* view of promising.[50] I have urged

---

[49] Here, as in Chapter 3, I am indebted to Stanley Cavell's treatment of the idea of counting in connection with his interpretation of Wittgenstein's concept of criteria. It may be worth remarking that, at one point in *The Will to Power*, Nietzsche himself appears to use the verb *gelten* in something like this sense. He writes, "Kurz: das Wesen eines Dinges ist auch nur eine Meinung über das 'Ding'. Oder vielmehr: das 'es gilt' ist das eigentliche 'das ist', das einzige 'das ist'" (*Der Wille zur Macht*, 12. Aufl. [Stuttgart: Alfred Kröner Verlag, 1980], p. 381).

[50] Calling this a view or an account of promising is, of course, very misleading. Nietzsche's goal is not to provide an explanation of why, for example, our promises are binding on us. Indeed, his point is that, as we stand, they are not. In other words, unlike Kant, Nietzsche does not aim to articulate a philosophical analysis and justification of our employment of the idea of moral responsibility. Furthermore, unlike Hume, he does not even mean to propose a naturalistic account of the institution of promising. The sense in which promising may be said to be basic to anything we can count as human life is different for Hume or Kant, on the one hand, and for Nietzsche, on the other. Nietzsche's point is, if one likes to put it that way, 'normative' in character: he aims to remind his readers that speaking intelligibly is a matter of taking responsibility for what they say, and he considers the price of having forgotten this fact to be their very humanity. And though this claim sounds Kantian enough, there is nothing in which Nietzsche believes humanity *consists*. Because, however, the *Genealogy* does indeed provide a psychological account of that which Nietzsche believes we tend to confuse with responsibility—namely, what he calls guilt and bad conscience—it can appear tempting to suppose that there is room to provide a similar account of the notion of conscience. I think, however, that it is totally unclear what such an account might look like. There is, indeed, plenty to say about the ways in which speakers try to avoid taking responsibility for what they say—that is, about the ways in which their ill will against the historical conditions of intelligible speech manifests itself—but there is no one thing that taking responsibility amounts to, and

that Nietzsche's remarks be read in the wider context of his interest in the relationship between the individual and the community. That relationship, he holds, can be understood as one of promising. Whoever neglects his responsibilities as a speaker may be thought of as a debtor who breaks his promise to the community and is turned out by the latter as someone who fails to make sense. On this view, the individual member of a community is merely a debtor who is by and large able to make good on his promises.[51] On the other hand, however, where the community itself fails to make sense—where talking the way the herd does is in fact a failure to speak—the notion of an individual can be understood in a more positive light. And it is in this context that the distinction Nietzsche draws between having and not having the right to make promises makes most sense.[52]

According to Nietzsche, the right to make promises, like the modern will to knowledge, is a late development: it has no role to play either in the primitive contractual relationships discussed in the opening sections of the second essay or in the life of someone whose talking is governed by bad conscience. Both sorts of person lack the relevant sort of genealogical memory. "To possess the right to stand security for oneself and to do so with pride, thus to possess also the *right to affirm oneself*—this, as has been said, is a ripe fruit, but also a *late* fruit: how long must this fruit have hung on the tree, unripe and sour! And for a much longer time nothing whatever was to be seen of any such fruit: no one could have promised its appearance, although everything in the tree was preparing for and growing toward it!" (*GM* II, sec. 3, p. 60). I think we can understand Nietzsche's point here in the terms suggested above: to give one's word is to incur an obligation to let oneself be understood—an obligation, in particular, to overcome one's unwillingness to do so, to renounce one's desire to remain opaque. To be a sovereign individual is, in effect, to have the right to incur this obligation.

---

therefore no one thing of which Nietzsche might be seeking an account. I am indebted to Irad Kimhi for pushing me on this point.

[51] Nietzsche says that because of a natural equivalence between a certain amount of pain and what the creditor will have to cede to a defaulting debtor, the debtor is able to understand the price he would pay for defaulting, and the creditor is willing to risk his doing so. A sense of prudence or expedience alone is enough to guarantee the keeping of promises. But once again we should not fail to notice that neither the notion of a guilty conscience nor that of responsibility plays any role in this account of the primitive forms of promising.

[52] The ability to exercise that right, however, depends upon there being someone with whom to do so. And as we will see, the goal of the morality of pity is to *isolate* the individual in such a way as to make him merely exceptional. This is the subject of the next section.

In this sense, then, the individual is someone who takes responsibility for his potential failures to make sense. Intelligibility, for him, is not just possible; it is actual. Such an individual has, as Nietzsche puts it, 'a proud consciousness . . . of what has at length been achieved and become flesh in him . . . a sensation of mankind come to completion'. What has been achieved in him is the capacity for speech, in the sense that concerns us here. His memory of *this* fact permits the individual to keep his promises solely on the grounds that he made them.

The idea here is, roughly, that someone who has the right to incur an obligation to let him- or herself be understood will not try to transfer that responsibility to anyone or anything else. The sovereign individual, Nietzsche says, has a proud consciousness of having no one but himself to whom to turn should he fail to let himself be understood. This is as much as to say that, in having the right to give his word, the individual acknowledges his *separateness* from his creditors. The *Genealogy* suggests that such separateness is a condition of true community.[53]

Let us return now to the idea that having the right to make promises establishes an order of rank between the person who has that right and whoever does not. In the *Genealogy*, Nietzsche suggests that the relevant contrast may be made clear in terms of the idea of freedom. The individual whose will is free, he says, looks down upon those whose wills are not.

> The "free" man, the possessor of a protracted and unbreakable will, also possesses his *measure of value:* locking out upon others from himself, he honors or despises; and just as he is bound to honor his peers, the strong and reliable (those with the right to make promises)—that is, all those who promise like sovereigns, reluctantly, rarely, slowly, who are chary of trusting, whose trust is a mark of *distinction,* who give their word as something that can be relied on because they know themselves strong enough to maintain it in the face of accidents, even "in the face of fate"—he is bound to reserve a kick for the feeble windbags who promise without the right to do so, and a rod for the liar who breaks his word even at the moment he utters it. (Ibid., p. 60)

What Nietzsche refers to here as the sovereign individual's freedom

[53] That is to say, linguistic community of the sort that is of interest to Nietzsche depends upon the assumption of this sort of responsibility. This is why he believes some form of the 'pathos of distance' and the 'order of rank' are necessary for anything we can count as culture, in his sense of the term. As we will see shortly, it is the morality of pity's hostility to such separateness that makes it inimical to the kind of responsibility Nietzsche considers essential to speech as opposed to mere talk.

of will may be understood in terms of our discussion of the modern commitment to truthfulness. As we saw, the man of knowledge's will may be said to be free only if he gives up his pretense to unconditionality—that is, only insofar as he manifests the proud consciousness of what has been achieved in him.

As we have seen, then, the individual's sense of his higher rank with respect to those who promise without the right to do so depends, in Nietzsche's view, upon his memory. In this context, however, memory is to be understood neither as a matter of simply recalling what has in fact been promised, nor as a primitive awareness of the price of not keeping one's promise. Rather, Nietzsche says that the sovereign individual is conscious of himself as an achievement, conscious that something has been accomplished—brought to completion—in him. Only *as such* does he have the right to make promises.[54] This idea suggests, in turn, that only someone who has the right sort of memory has a future.[55] Without such a memory, "anyone who manages to experience the history of humanity as a whole as *his own history* will feel in an enormously generalized way all the grief of an invalid who thinks of health, of an old man who thinks of the dreams of his youth, of a lover deprived of his beloved, of the martyr whose ideal is perishing, of the hero on the evening after a battle that has decided nothing but brought him wounds and the loss of his friend" (*GS*, sec. 337, p. 268). It should be clear, then, that Nietzsche considers the memory the *Genealogy* aims to produce in its readers to be necessary for *their* future as men of knowledge.

Indeed, Nietzsche says that to give one's word is "für sich *als Zukunft* gut sagen zu können." Kaufmann's translation has: "to be able to stand security for [one's] own future." But this attempt to render Nietzsche's German into less jarring English ignores the fuller sense of the text. For his striking turn of phrase here—to be accountable *'as* future' (and not merely *'for* one's future')—suggests that, in his view, to say that someone has the right to make promises is as much as to say that he *is* a future.[56] In the preface to the *Genealogy*, however, Nietzsche insists that our morality is to be blamed for the fact that we live 'at the expense

---

[54] The nihilist, however, misinterprets Nietzsche's talk of memory as mere nostalgia for the past—an unwillingness to face facts.

[55] It is, I think, in this insistence on the principle that a certain form of memory is necessary for having a future, as much as in any other part of his thinking, that Nietzsche shows himself to be Freud's precursor.

[56] See for example the end of sec. 16 where Nietzsche more or less says that man is, or anyway ought to be, a promise. Of course, the idea behind saying that someone is responsible for his future is that no one *else* is responsible for it. And this is surely part of Nietzsche's meaning.

of the future'. The implication is that morality is in some way hostile to the possibility of intelligible speech. Let us now consider in what sense Nietzsche believes this to be so.

Promising and the Morality of Pity

We have been following one strand of Nietzsche's criticism of modern morality: his claim that our current ways of life are hostile to the very possibility of individuality. On the interpretation offered here, an individual in the present age would be someone who has the right to say that God is dead—someone, that is, who can take responsibility for claiming to be committed to the truth. Not to have the right to do so is to live at the expense of the future. Nietzsche insists, however, that our morality stands in the way of our having the right to make promises and thus prevents us from, in his words, becoming what we are. He holds, more specifically, that it is our inclination to *pity* that diverts us from the demands of individuality. Pity and responsibility are, as Nietzsche thinks of them anyway, incompatible. This is the claim we now need to understand.

In maintaining that the morality of pity is opposed to the task of 'keeping to one's own way', Nietzsche is clearly sounding an Emersonian theme of self-reliance.[57] And while it remains difficult to assess the depth of his debt to Emerson, the very fact of it is not always respected in readings of his criticism of morality.[58] Nietzsche's attack on pity, in particular, is sometimes interpreted only within what are taken to be the broader bounds of his assault on altruistic virtues in general, as though pity were, in his view, merely one vice among many.[59] In his

[57] See especially sec. 338 of *The Gay Science*, part of which provides the epigraph to this chapter.

[58] Stanley Cavell's work is a notable exception to this rule.

[59] Richard Schacht reads Nietzsche in this way. See his *Nietzsche* (Boston: Routledge and Kegan Paul, 1983), especially pp. 359–62. Unlike Schacht, Tracy Strong underscores the centrality of Nietzsche's attack on pity to his conception of life in the present age. See his *Nietzsche and the Politics of Transfiguration* (Berkeley: University of California Press, 1975), especially p. 254. Pity on Strong's account is a psychological mechanism for maintaining the last man in existence, for avoiding what Nietzsche sees as the historical necessity of overcoming this form of life. The morality of pity, Strong argues, encourages an attitude toward others that is analogous to nationalism at a more properly political level: both are ways of keeping slave morality from disintegrating. This reading has the virtue of showing why Nietzsche considers the morality of pity to be a distinctly *modern* phenomenon. "Pity," Strong writes, "is . . . a form of the will to power engendering and characterizing nihilism: it preserves that which is characteristic of nihilism" (p. 254). For more recent discussion of Nietzsche's attack on pity, see Martha Nussbaum, "Pity and Mercy, Nietzsche's Stoicism," in *Nietzsche,*

earliest writings, for example, he appears to some commentators concerned to do little more than to deny that such virtues exist and, consequently, to endorse what he seems to think of as the inherent selfishness of the human species.[60] In that context, the point of his attack on pity would appear to be only that the individual ought not to attend to the sufferings of others where doing so will keep her from striving for the satisfaction of her own ends.[61]

Some of what Nietzsche says in his discussion of morality, especially in his earliest writings, appears to recommend this sort of reading. For he does indeed advocate an attitude he sometimes calls 'egoism' in the face of the conception of our relationship to others that he condemns. 'Altruism' and 'selflessness' are two names he gives to this conception. 'The morality of pity' is, of course, another. I want to suggest, however, that his attack on altruistic virtues and his praise of egoism should both be read in the context of his more general investigation of the relation-

---

Genealogy, Morality, Essays on Nietzsche's Genealogy of Morals, ed. Richard Schacht (Berkeley: University of California Press, 1994), pp. 139–67. Nussbaum appreciates the centrality of Nietzsche's rejection of the morality of pity, but underestimates the degree to which, as Nietzsche saw, that same morality tends to infect one's reading of his work in general.

[60] The outlines of such a reading can be found, for example, in Alexander Nehamas's *Nietzsche: Life as Literature* (Cambridge: Harvard University Press, 1985). See especially pp. 204–5. See also Maudemarie Clark's dissertation, "Nietzsche's Attack on Morality" (University of Wisconsin, Madison, 1976). Nehamas claims that we may discern at least three different stages in the development of Nietzsche's attack on morality. In his earliest writings, Nietzsche appears simply to deny that there is anything properly to be called morality, because there are no properly moral—i.e., nonegoistic—motives. This view is later rejected as unsatisfactory, and replaced with a view that acknowledges the importance of 'the morality of mores'. This last view is finally replaced with a more complex account that acknowledges the importance of the sort of psychological investigations that occupy Nietzsche in his latest writings. There is, for example, no room in the morality of mores account for a developed notion of moral responsibility or for our modern conception of guilt; these, therefore, must be described in different terms. Clark's dissertation offers a much more detailed reconstruction of what she takes to be Nietzsche's developing views of morality. From my point of view, the principal shortcoming of this sort of reconstruction is that it fails to show how those views fit into Nietzsche's concerns with what I have called 'the fact of intelligibility'. These concerns are most evident in the *Untimely Meditations*, and therefore antedate the apparent rejection of morality on the grounds of egoism.

[61] Richard Schacht recommends this sort of reading of Nietzsche's attack on pity and selflessness. Schacht stresses—as do I, though with a different emphasis— Nietzsche's claim that pity's recommendation that life should be viewed primarily under the aspect of suffering is inimical to the sort of self-enhancement his philosophy advocates. As Schacht puts it: "Suffering . . . is inseparable from the qualitative enhancement of life; and instead of taking the former to warrant repudiation of the latter, Nietzsche takes the latter to sanction the former, and to require a reversal of the basic intention of the morality of pity" (*Nietzsche*, p. 461).

ship between community and individual. For if, as I have maintained, Nietzsche is primarily concerned with our failure to let ourselves be intelligible, then his attack on altruism should be understood as a criticism of one particular way in which we fail to do so. On the reading I am recommending he is not claiming that pity is a simple psychological error on which the many somehow capitalize in order to defend themselves against the depredations of the few.[62] Let us see, then, what sense can be made of Nietzsche's hostility toward pity when viewed in the light of his interest in the fact of human intelligibility.

The morality of pity expresses, for Nietzsche, a particular attitude toward others, one he considers harmful both to the pitier and to the sufferer.[63] We need to understand how this attitude contributes to our unintelligibility, to what the *Genealogy* presents as our not having the right to make promises. How, in particular, is it incompatible with and hostile to the attitude that Nietzsche would have the individual adopt toward him- or herself and others? In what *way*, that is, does Nietzsche consider pity and responsibility to be incompatible?

Nietzsche speaks of our "deadly hatred of suffering generally" (*BGE*, sec. 202, p. 116); and he says that those who pity "want, if possible . . . *to abolish suffering*" (BGE, sec. 225, p. 153). Such remarks suggest that the morality of pity treats the fact of someone's suffering as objectionable in itself: anything or anyone that causes suffering is, by virtue of that very fact, to be condemned. As a first attempt at interpreting this claim, we may begin by considering—all too briefly, I am afraid—a few cases in which a kind of suffering might be thought to be an integral part of someone's effort to develop or to perfect some part of his or her nature. It is in this context that the pitier's desire to help might most obviously be thought to be in some way harmful to the sufferer. I think we can agree at the outset that an ethics whose *only* permitted motivation for action was a desire to avoid suffering would not have much to recommend it. There are many otherwise worthwhile aspects of human life that, if not essentially, then at least not incidentally involve suffering, and one would be understandably reluctant to give them up in the name of comfort alone. It will, to pick an obvious example, be difficult to hold onto the idea of honesty as a virtue if one is never allowed to cause suffering. Nietzsche's antipathy to the so-called morality of pity is not unrelated to this last suggestion, but we will have to see more

[62] It is indeed the case that the morality of pity is designed to protect the herd against the demands of individuality, but we shall see that it does so by distorting their understanding of the nature of communication.

[63] Of course, as we will see in the next section, Nietzsche considers *self*-pity to be a danger as well.

specifically how he understands the idea of suffering if we are to come to grips with the way in which he thinks pity is inimical to the very idea of responsibility.

Nietzsche sometimes suggests that the pitier's reflexive desire to leap to the aid of the sufferer tends to prevent the latter from confronting challenges necessary to his or her efforts at what we might call 'self-enhancement'.[64] "[A]ll such things that may be involved in distress are of no concern to our dear pitying friends; they wish to *help*" (GS, sec. 338, p. 269). Suppose, for example, that someone sets herself the task of developing certain of her athletic talents. Suffering will almost certainly be involved in accomplishing this goal, if only because the means to this particular end are likely to be painful: there will be injuries, exhaustion, deprivation, frustration, doubt, and so on. Moreover, there will be the sort of suffering that is involved in most attempts to transcend a certain level of accomplishment. Insofar as the morality of pity recommends that all suffering be avoided, it will recommend that it be avoided here. But then, should the person who sets herself the task of developing her talents fall prey to the morality of pity, her task will be made that much more difficult, especially if, as seems likely, she is already at odds with herself. The pitier will discourage her from further painful exertions, will insist that nothing could be worth what she is going through, and so on. An athlete might well want a trainer who understood the kind of suffering involved in developing these particular talents—a trainer, for example, who could listen. But a good trainer will, at the very least, keep whatever pity she may feel to herself. It is, I think, fairly clear what kind of obstacle to self-enhancement pity could produce in such a case. And it is also clear that, other things being equal, an overwhelming imperative to seek comfort represents something from which one would wish to protect the athlete. Furthermore, while it may seem less clear that anyone really is motivated in this way by the morality of pity to establish such obstacles, this might be because we are by and large ignorant of the sorts of suffering serious athletic training actually involves.[65]

[64] This is a dominant theme in, for example, *Thus Spoke Zarathustra*, part I, "On the Friend."

[65] Nietzsche would have us ask ourselves what we are really feeling when, for example, we feel offended that a young gymnast is pushing herself or that she is being pushed too hard by her trainer. Under what circumstances and in which contexts, that is, are we confident that we can distinguish discipline from cruelty? How much and what sort of thing does one have to know here? There may, of course, be room to raise a sort of pushpin vs. poetry objection to these kinds of consideration. But Nietzsche's reply, like Mill's, will be that that sort of objection is rooted in a thoroughly debased conception of human happiness.

Consider, alternately, the case of someone who decides fundamentally to change her intellectual outlook and surroundings. Suppose, for example, that she finds her current intellectual environment stifling, that she cannot see how to continue working with the tools she has inherited. She may well find it tremendously difficult to give up the comforts of what she finds familiar. Here the very fact of shedding the past may be painful. In this context, it is difficult to see how action motivated by pity—whether her own or that of someone else—could be anything other than counterproductive. Again, compassion of some sort might be in order in such circumstances, but pity's insistence that all suffering be avoided will likely have exactly the "depressive effect" (AC, sec. 7, p. 118) for which Nietzsche reproaches it. We can also imagine more or less psychoanalytic equivalents of this last sort of example: it is often tremendously difficult to renounce particular images of ourselves and our relationships to others, just because those images are so satisfying. Yet in many cases giving them up may be the only thing that permits us the possibility of a future. A pitying analyst will not, Nietzsche suggests, be doing his job properly.

In cases such as these, then, the emotion of pity can be used to restrain someone who is, as we might want to put it, too hard on herself, and to prevent her from attaining what she would otherwise recognize as a better, higher, state of herself. From this point of view, to say of someone that she is governed by the morality of pity is to say that she tends to want to avoid anything that would challenge her to overcome a certain stage of her self-development. In general, I think, the morality of pity encourages us, where possible, to prevent anyone—ourselves included—from confronting such challenges.[66]

The actual psychology of pity in such cases is, obviously, far more complex than these cursory remarks suggest. Among other things,

---

[66] One of the clearest examples of this aspect of the morality of pity can be found in certain aspects of various animal rights movements. As Vicki Hearne reminds us, a great deal of cruelty is inflicted, in the name of kindness, upon animals (as well as upon the people who own them) by some of those committed to animal rights. This form of kindness protests that all forms of discipline and breeding are cruel because they involve suffering. There is, however, plenty of room to suspect that a moral opposition to, for example, certain kinds of dog training has its roots in precisely the sort of confusion Nietzsche diagnoses as a failure to distinguish obedience from slavishness. Entering into intelligible relationships with domestic animals (not to mention bringing children—or adults, for that matter—into language) requires making them—and, hence, oneself—calculable, regular, and necessary. Real cruelty, Nietzsche would argue, begins with the disavowal on putatively moral grounds of the necessity for this sort of responsibility. See Vicki Hearne, *Adam's Task: Calling Animals by Name* (New York: Vintage, 1987) and *Bandit: Dossier of a Dangerous Dog* (New York: HarperCollins, 1991).

what I have said so far ignores what is for Nietzsche the more basic question of why anyone would find the forms of suffering involved in what I called self-enhancement offensive in the first place. It explains nothing to say that some people find suffering in any form whatsoever to be objectionable. We need to know why they would fail to draw a distinction between cruelty and discipline. From Nietzsche's point of view, then, the conviction that all suffering is inherently bad calls for some sort of explanation. Part of the desired account might be that, by and large, we tend to repress the pleasure we take in the sight of suffering. But it may also be the case that the sight of the suffering involved in self-enhancement reminds the spectator of his or her solitude faced with another human being.[67] We find hints of both sorts of explanation in Nietzsche's work, especially, as we will see, of the latter. These are, in any case, complicated psychological questions, and I mean here to discuss only one aspect of the issues involved: what Nietzsche suggests we may refer to as the epistemological confusions of pity.

The sort of example we have considered so far nevertheless illuminates one important feature of Nietzsche's complaint about the emotion of pity: the idea, namely, that it diverts us from the often painful struggle to articulate what is best in us, and that it is, to that extent, harmful. But it is not immediately clear what light these considerations shed on the *Genealogy's* claim that the morality of pity leads to the form of nihilism Nietzsche associates with our inability to take responsibility for what we say. In other words, pity's hostility to the rigors of the kind of self-enhancement considered so far is not obviously responsible for the sort of unintelligibility for which Nietzsche denounces the present age.

It helps here to remember that the *Genealogy* expresses the idea of self-enhancement by talking of breeding an animal with the right to make promises, and that the particular form of such self-enhancement that most occupies Nietzsche in this work is the perfection of the man of knowledge's will to truth. I want to suggest, therefore, that the morality of pity is hostile to *that* particular form of the perfection of human life. It is *this* sort of hostility that keeps us inarticulate and herdlike. But how?

---

[67] Imagine, for example, the sort of anxiety provoked by watching someone trying to learn something new. At some point, the pupil has to figure it out for herself. A pitying teacher, however, will feel that the pupil's hand must somehow be guided all the way to understanding. A responsible teacher, Nietzsche suggests, will know when to leave off. Most generally, I think, what the so-called morality of pity finds most offensive are these sorts of hierarchical relationships. That there may be certain sorts of hardship involved in such relationships is, Nietzsche suspects, largely a pretext for avoiding the solitude and rigors of responsibility.

Nietzsche's answer to this question is likely to seem both uncomfortably abstract, on the one hand, and impossibly direct, on the other. I want to suggest that, in his view, it is in the first instance his *own* suffering that our inclination to pity makes us unable to understand. Moreover, he appears to believe—odd though it sounds—that the inability to understand his suffering is what keeps the man of knowledge in his leveled state of mediocrity. In other words, Nietzsche suggests that he himself might somehow be responsible for strengthening the man of knowledge's commitment to truthfulness. To make sense of these unusual claims, we will need to underscore a related but different feature of pity than that thrown into relief by our previous discussion. To begin, we should recall that the person inclined to pity is, according to Nietzsche, unable to *let* someone suffer.[68] Letting someone suffer is Nietzsche's metaphor for a certain form of *reading*. For the idea of letting someone suffer implies a kind of passivity, a capacity for letting someone speak, a capacity for listening—all things Nietzsche associates with a certain conception of the nature of reading. And it is of *this* kind of passivity that Nietzsche complains we in the present age are least capable.[69] The idea of letting someone suffer suggests that the morality of pity makes us hard of hearing. This is why those he considers to be his rightful readers must be, in the words of *The Antichrist*, 'predestined for the labyrinth' (see *AC*, preface, p. 114). It is also why the madman of section 125 of *The Gay Science* complains that the news of the death of God has "not yet reached the ears of men" (*GS*, sec. 125, p. 182).[70] Pity, in short, makes us bad readers.

It is in these terms, I suggest, that we should understand Nietzsche's

[68] Nietzsche says that anarchists, for example, are at one with the democratic herd "in their almost feminine inability to remain spectators, to *let* someone suffer" (*BGE*, sec. 202, p. 116).

[69] This is how I propose to understand Nietzsche's repeated complaints that he lacks the sort of reader he needs, that he writes for 'the very few', and so forth. As I read them, such remarks—most conspicuous in the various prefaces Nietzsche adds to later editions of his works in 1886—are not at all extrinsic to the content of Nietzsche's work. They are instructions in reading. The question of learning how to read Nietzsche properly cannot be divorced from that of learning what he has to say.

[70] I find it difficult to know how much to try to make of the idea of reading as a form of passivity. It helps to remember that Nietzsche does not suggest that the madman *knows* more than his audience does. They know what he knows; they do not believe in God. But the madman complains that they do not react in the right way to what they know—they do not hear it properly. In this context, it is primarily the idea of hearing that suggests that, in Nietzsche's view, reading involves a form of passivity that we find it difficult to accept. Nietzsche's point, I want to say, is that we are not open to what we already know. Unfortunately, however, although corrective of certain misunderstandings, the idea of openness does not really shed much light on the relevant notion of passivity.

repeated complaints that he lacks readers of the sort he needs: as pitiers, we refuse to hear what he says in the right way. This claim needs,
however, to be handled with some care. He is not insisting merely that
there is a right and a wrong way to read his work. He is making the
far more striking and perplexing claim that by failing to read him in
the right way we remain unintelligible to ourselves.[71]

My interpretative suggestion, then, is that Nietzsche believes that it
is at our own peril that we are bad readers of his work. Moreover, he
believes that it is in *this* way that the morality of pity ensures that we
in the present age live at the expense of the future; it is in *this* way that
it leads to nihilism. The interpretative upshot, clearly, is that Nietzsche
means to assign a unique place to his writing in the present age.[72] This
is what he takes to be the significance of his untimeliness. So I do not
believe we can get much further with his attack on pity unless we try
to take this claim as seriously as possible.[73]

[71] Nietzsche does not usually go so far as to say that reading him is the *only* way
out of our inarticulateness, but he certainly believes that it is *one* way, and he offers
it as such. There is, of course, a weaker reading of this claim available: namely, that
our inability to read his work is merely *symptomatic* of our inarticulateness. Nietzsche
certainly believes that this much is true. But I think that his critique of the morality
of pity points in the direction of the stronger reading under consideration here. These
readings might, nevertheless, be reconciled if we could make sense of the suggestion
that it is a specific *kind* of nihilism with which the inability to read Nietzsche threatens
us: namely, that associated with not understanding the death of God. This reading
would leave room for the idea that there is a *broader* sense in which the morality of
pity threatens us with nihilism: namely, our generalized inability to let ourselves be
understood. If we reconcile the readings in this way, then our alleged inability to
read Nietzsche properly does indeed seem in some sense to be merely symptomatic
of a more general phenomenon.
[72] I do not think, therefore, that the more hyperbolic moments of even *Ecce Homo*
represent a fundamental change in Nietzsche's conception of the importance of his
own work. If there is a change in his understanding of the special role he plays in
modern culture, it is at the level of his understanding of his increasing isolation
from his audience. Tracy Strong makes a related suggestion in "Nietzsche's Political
Aesthetics," in *Nietzsche's New Seas*, ed. Michael Allen Gillespie and Tracy B. Strong
(Chicago: University of Chicago Press, 1988), pp. 153–74.
[73] There are two points here. First, I do not mean to say that there are no limits to
how seriously we can take Nietzsche's claims for his own writing. Admittedly, what
he says can seem quite incredible. Nietzsche is, however, his own best critic here: he
is quite aware that he can claim no authority but his own for such claims, and, as
he knows, that authority comes to nothing without our obedience. This is another
way of bringing out the point about promising with which this chapter began: that
speaking, or writing, is an exchange between two or more individuals. Nietzsche
needs readers. A voice in the wilderness is only half a voice. Second, it is important
to recognize that Nietzsche's attack on pity is intelligible independent of its application to his own case. 'Pity', remember, is his name for those attitudes that contribute
to what he thinks of as a particularly modern misunderstanding of the relationship
of individual and community. As it happens, however, the most sustained and imme-

Before we try to do so, however, let us once again consider in a formulaic way Nietzsche's point about the incompatibility of pity and responsibility. His basic idea is that the morality of pity would have us avoid the kind of suffering involved in taking responsibility for what we say. I think we can conceive of this as a quite general diagnosis—though perhaps not the only one—of the trouble with modernity: Nietzsche believes that we in the present age speak irresponsibly, and, from his point of view, that means that we do not *speak* at all. What, in his view, prevents us from doing so is, in part, our attitude toward the kind of suffering he associates with responsibility. His name for that attitude is 'the morality of pity'. Individuality, in other words, is a burden the herd would rather not bear. This is, as I said, a quite general point, but Nietzsche makes much more specific use of it in suggesting that the herd also endeavors to suppress anyone who would try—as he himself tries—to remind it of those burdens.

This reading suggests that, as I claimed in Chapter 4, the aim of Nietzsche's genealogical hypotheses is in large measure to bring home to us the fact of our unintelligibility—specifically, as men of knowledge. 'We are unknown to ourselves', he says, 'we men of knowledge—and with good reason. We have never sought ourselves—how could it happen that we should ever *find* ourselves'. In Nietzsche's view, the men of knowledge would not have the same need of such hypotheses if they were not threatened by the morality of pity.[74] Without this threat, he suggests, they would be free to recognize the sense in which what they have become represents an accomplishment. Thus, about even his earliest genealogical writings he insists:

> what was at stake was the *value* of morality. . . . What was especially at stake was the value of the "unegoistic," the instincts of pity, self-abnegation, self-sacrifice, which Schopenhauer had gilded, deified, and projected into a beyond for so long that . . . he *said No* to life and to himself. . . . It was precisely here that I saw the *great* danger to mankind, its sublimest enticement and seduction—but to what? to nothingness?—it was precisely here that I saw the beginning of the end, the dead stop, a retrospective weariness, the will turning *against*

diate (though still uncomfortably abstract) example of this misunderstanding articulated in Nietzsche's own work does indeed concern his own case: the men of knowledge, he believes, need his work to become what they are. This is, again, the work he gives his work to do.

[74] Once again, this is not to deny that various uses can be made of Nietzsche's hypotheses. They are interesting enough in their own right. But their *point*, so to speak, is not simply to convey information about the origins of our moral values.

life, the tender and sorrowful signs of the ultimate illness: I understood the ever spreading morality of pity that had seized even on
philosophers and made them ill, as the most sinister symptom of a
European culture that had itself become sinister, perhaps as its by-
pass to a new Buddhism? to a Buddhism for Europeans? to—*nihilism?*
(*GM*, preface, sec. 5, p. 19)

'Nihilism', in this context, is Nietzsche's name for the fact that we lack
the right to make promises—a fact that manifests itself, in particular,
in the modern man of knowledge's will to truth. The nihilist's relationship to the announcement of the death of God—his unwillingness to
see himself as an achievement—is, in Nietzsche's view, the most dangerous effect of the morality of pity. How, then, does the morality of pity
distort our understanding of our particular position in the present age?
By what mechanism does pity make us inarticulate?

As I suggested above, Nietzsche contends that the emotion of pity is
prey to a kind of epistemological confusion. More specifically, his attack
on the morality of pity turns on his rejection of the idea that compassion
lifts the pitier out of himself and places him in a more intimate relationship to the sufferer than he normally enjoys.[75] And, as we will see, it
is precisely the idea that the emotion of pity allows the pitier as it were
to *inhabit* the sufferer that, in Nietzsche's view, prevents the pitier from
listening to him in the right way. Strictly speaking, "one simply knows
nothing of the whole inner sequence and intricacies that are distress
for *me* or for *you*" (*GS*, sec. 338, p. 269). The intellectual attitude toward
someone who suffers recommended by the morality of pity—its vicari-
ousness—is, Nietzsche concludes, impossible. A failure to appreciate
this fact tends inevitably to cloud one's relationship to someone who
suffers. Consequently, even in those passages in which he insists on
the egoistical character of the emotion of pity, Nietzsche, I think, wants
above all to emphasize the sufferer's *solitude*—his or her unavailability
to the pitier.[76] An unwillingness to acknowledge the sufferer's separate-

[75] The intuition behind this claim is fueled by the fact that the German *Mitleid*
means quite literally 'with-suffering'. Thus according to the morality of pity's description of itself, to pity someone is to take on his suffering as one' own.

[76] See, for instance, *Daybreak*, sec. 133. In this relatively early text, Nietzsche argues
that a particular kind of concern with other people is simply impossible. When pity
moves one to act, he says, it is always one's *own* suffering that one is trying to
diminish. The character of such suffering, however, is quite difficult to assess adequately and includes, among other things, the suffering brought on by the sight of
"human vulnerability and fragility in general" (*D*, sec. 133, p. 84). There are, of
course, a *variety* of motives one might have for trying to relieve someone's suffering;
pity represents only a certain range of them.

ness betrays what he calls the "intellectual frivolity" (ibid.) of the morality of pity.

Nietzsche maintains that we in the present age do not know what solitude is.[77] Consequently, he does not believe we are in a position properly to comprehend the sufferer's peculiar isolation, his or her difference from—and, hence, community with—us. But he clearly does not believe that one can never know *that* another person is suffering: often enough, nothing could be more obvious than this. He insists, however, that pity never provides special *access* to the sufferer. "That pity . . . is the *same kind of thing* as the suffering at the sight of which it arises, or that it possesses an especially subtle, penetrating understanding of suffering, are propositions contradicted by *experience*, and he who glorifies pity precisely on account of these two qualities *lacks* adequate experience in this very realm of the moral" (*D*, sec. 133, pp. 84–85). One's sufferings are, Nietzsche says, "distinctively personal" (*GS*, sec. 338, p. 269), "incomprehensible and inaccessible to almost everyone" (ibid.). In its desire to identify with the sufferer, however, the emotion of pity is, we might say, insufficiently skeptical toward the sufferer.

Nietzsche also believes that the pitier's desire to help demeans the sufferer. The idea that, other things being equal, pity is in at least some circumstances a degrading and disrespectful attitude is common enough. But it is not obvious what Nietzsche intends by it. He writes, "The whole economy of my soul and the balance effected by 'distress', the way new springs and needs break open, the way in which old wounds are healing, the way whole periods of the past are shed—all such things that may be involved in distress are of no concern to our dear pitying friends; they wish to *help*, and have no thought of the personal necessity of distress, although terrors, deprivations, impoverishments, midnights, adventures, risks, and blunders are as necessary for me and for you as are their opposites" (ibid.). Rather than letting the sufferer suffer, then, the pitier insists on eliminating his suffering, on calming him. Pity refuses to let him speak. But why does Nietzsche say that this attitude diminishes the sufferer's 'worth and will'?

One of the ways in which he seems to believe that pity decreases the value of the sufferer is, in effect, by humiliating him or her. He says, for example, that "to savages the idea of being pitied evokes a moral shudder: it divests one of all virtue. To offer pity is as good as to offer

[77] Of the free spirit who can question morality Nietzsche says: "Solitude encircles and embraces him, ever more threatening, suffocating, heart-tightening, that terrible goddess and *mater saeva cupidinum*—but who today knows what solitude is?" (*HAH*, preface, sec. 3, p. 7).

contempt: one does not want to see a contemptible creature suffer, there is no enjoyment in that" (D, sec. 135, p. 86).[78] Though the idea that pity conceals contempt is an important aspect of Nietzsche's criticism of any form of life founded on that emotion, I want to focus on a different feature of his discussion: the mistaken idea that pity can allow the pitier, as I put it, to inhabit the sufferer, to know exactly what she knows, to view the world through her eyes. We want to know what is demeaning about *this* attitude.

As we have seen, the idea that the pitier refuses to let the sufferer suffer implies that it is the independence or separateness of the sufferer to which the morality of pity objects. According to Nietzsche, the pitier tries to pry into the other's suffering, to reduce the distance between them. It is, I suggest, this intrusiveness—what I called the 'vicarious-ness' of pity—that diminishes the sufferer's worth and will.

The thought that pity allows the pitier actually to experience the sufferer's suffering betrays the fantasy that suffering conveys knowledge to which only the sufferer has access. Without this fantasy, Nietzsche suggests, the alternative to pity would be simply to *listen* to the sufferer. Though the notion of compassion might—as long as it caused no confusion—be thought to provide a handy way of referring to the latter attitude, Nietzsche himself scandalously recommends contempt as the healthy alternative to pity. But this last notion, he insists, cannot be properly understood from the slavish point of view of the morality of pity.

In Nietzsche's view, I want now to argue, the effect of the fantasy that the sufferer knows something the pitier does not is essentially to *isolate* the former, and thus to make his suffering irrelevant to anyone else's concerns. This is how pity debases him. The pitier's belief that the sufferer is unique in a way that only a fellow sufferer can appreciate effectively credits the sufferer with something he does *not* have—private knowledge—and ignores what is true of him: namely, that he suffers. Pity is, so to speak, *curious* before the sufferer. The fantasy of private knowledge supposedly conveyed by suffering thus leaves the person of the sufferer completely out of the picture.[79]

[78] This view lies behind Nietzsche's suspicion that, far from being a sign of benevolence, pity represents, in many people, a form of hostility. See, for example, *Daybreak*, sec. 138.

[79] The idea that suffering provides a kind of insight that cannot be understood as knowledge should be familiar to us from our reading of *The Birth of Tragedy*. In effect, Nietzsche suffers tragically from the death of God. The parallel with *The Birth of Tragedy* implies, of course, that Nietzsche does *not* know anything about the death of God that those who do not suffer fail to know.

The pitier believes that he can *identify* with the sufferer. For example, "If we love, honour, admire someone, and then afterwards discover that he is *suffering*—a discovery that always fills us with the greatest astonishment, for we cannot think otherwise than that the happiness that flows across to us from him must proceed from a superabundant well of happiness *of his own*—our feeling of love, reverence and admiration changes in *an essential respect*: it grows *tenderer*; that is to say, the gulf between us and him seems to be bridged, an approximation to identity seems to occur" (*D*, sec. 138, p. 87). It is as though, when the sufferer says to the pitier, 'You don't know what I've been through', the latter replies, in effect, 'Oh, but I do', and assumes that knowing what he has been through is a matter of actually feeling what he feels—something Nietzsche here calls 'an approximation to identity'.

We might say, then, that the morality of pity *secludes* the sufferer, sequesters him, refusing to allow him to do anything other than report on his state, as though crowding the sufferer leaves him unfrequented. To say that we lack the right to make promises is, on this view, as much as to say that our talking remains private—as though human speech were a matter of articulating inner states, and not a matter of communication.[80] For instead of listening, the pitier responds on the basis of a fantasy of what the sufferer's experience must have taught him. In this way, Nietzsche says, pity "strips away from the suffering of others whatever is distinctly personal" (*GS*, sec. 338, p. 269). Though this remark appears to suggest that pity's error consists in trying to make public what is in fact wholly private, Nietzsche's claim is, I think, nearly the opposite. Pity confuses the personal with the private, and transforms the sufferer's suffering into something wholly subjective, thus depriving it of significance.

I need now to make more explicit the consequences of these reflections for the claim that the morality of pity is hostile to the idea of taking responsibility for what one says, and therefore incompatible with Nietzschean individuality. In standing security for what he says, the speaker acknowledges his separateness from those with whom he speaks, insofar as the responsibility for making himself understood falls to him alone. For, on Nietzsche's view, the burden of overcoming resistance to being understood is borne by the speaker. As we have seen, there are various ways of trying to shirk that burden, to place it elsewhere. 'Socratism' is the name Nietzsche gives to the typically philosophical way of trying to do so. The pitier, similarly, is someone who wants to avoid having to stand by anything he says and therefore treats

[80] This is another way of underscoring the incompatibility of pity and responsibility.

everyone as immediately accessible to him. Pity amounts, accordingly, to a refusal to acknowledge that speakers can ever be mysteries to one another (and, hence, in Nietzsche's sense, understood), a refusal to recognize that, in Vicki Hearne's words, "my knowledge of you, my interpretation of your words, is not brain surgery. [Rather] it is the articulation of the ways your words interlock mine, and it comes to an end somewhere outside of your skin."[81]

On Nietzsche's account, then, making a promise is a matter of granting the person to whom the promise is made the authority to exact repayment should one default on one's debt. In making a promise, in other words, one agrees to accept the consequences of not fulfilling the obligation one thereby incurs. Similarly, accepting a promise is a matter of agreeing to adopt a position of authority over the person who has made the promise. To do so is to grant the promisor authority for what he or she says. (This, in turn, entails its own forms of obedience.) Having the right to accept and to grant authority in this way is what it means to be a responsible interlocutor. But precisely for this reason, Nietzsche concludes that one neither gives one's word to nor accepts the word of someone whom one pities. The pitier, in other words, does not have the right to make promises. He cannot take responsibility for what he says, because to take responsibility in *this* sense is to acknowledge the separateness of those with whom one speaks.

Pity is incompatible both with the authority I assume as a promisor and with the authority I grant to the person to whom I make a promise, my creditor. It is also incompatible with the kind of authority I grant to someone who promises me something. In each case, it is a matter of acknowledging another person's autonomy, and hence his separateness from me. In each case, I must adopt a particular stance of responsiveness with respect to my creditor or to my debtor. For if my interlocutor is going to occupy the position of creditor or debtor, I must, in effect, 'let' him do so.

These relationships of obedience and authority are central to intelligibility. The claim of the opening sections of the second essay of the *Genealogy* is that intelligibility entails a heavier responsibility than we are, by and large, willing to bear. In the case of the will to knowledge, in particular, one who pities cannot take responsibility for—does not hear in the right way—the announcement that God is dead. To say that one suffers from the death of God is to understand oneself as an achievement, and, hence, as an individual. The nihilist maintains that any suffering that attends the recognition of the falsity of our previous

---

[81] Hearne, *Adam's Task*, p. 116.

attempts to make sense of life is only a sign that such illusions are difficult to give up, and he denies that this suffering teaches us anything important about life in the present age. But Nietzsche's attack on the morality of pity is meant to show that the nihilist is looking in the wrong place for the significance of the death of God. The claim that what the man of knowledge has become represents an achievement is not meant to convey information to him, and Nietzsche does not recommend nostalgia as a response to the recognition of the mendacity of his former means of consolation. Nietzsche's aim, rather, is to bring home to the nihilist the fact of his weakness of will, to show him in what way he is at odds with himself. This is what the morality of pity refuses to let the nihilist see, by distorting his understanding of what 'seeing' amounts to here.

My suggestion, then, has been that, in Nietzsche's view, the morality of pity prevents us from reading his work in the right way, and that it *thereby* prevents us from becoming what we are. We fail, as he sees it, to constitute ourselves as a culture—as members of this particular historical epoch, the so-called present age—to the degree that we remain unwilling to acknowledge the fact that what we have become represents an achievement, a 'deed'. Moreover, he maintains that this is so in the face of the nihilist's insistence that the news of the death of God does not matter. What I have tried to make clear is that Nietzsche means to bring home only the fact of our resistance here, and that doing so is not a matter of conveying further *information* about who he thinks we are. Allowing him to 'read us' in this sense is what culture amounts to on the picture we are considering. Nietzsche writes from the standpoint of suffering—both from the fact that God is dead and from the fact of our indifference to that development. The morality of pity, however, insists that if indeed he has something to say about what it means to be human in the present age, then it *must* take the form of information about what we have become. Otherwise, the nihilist urges, Nietzsche's suffering either from the death of God, on the one hand, or from our modern mediocrity, on the other, is only a fact about him, and cannot have any wider significance. The morality of pity, in other words, cannot see that self-consciousness is anything other than self-*knowledge*, and therefore condemns us to the unintelligibility Nietzsche believes is involved in trying to deny the significance of his sense of modernity as an event.

That Nietzsche's rejection of the morality of pity is aimed at nihilism in *this* sense is confirmed, I think, by the section immediately preceding the long discussion of pity in section 338 of *The Gay Science*, titled "The 'humaneness' of the future." "When I contemplate with the eyes of some remote age, I can find nothing more remarkable in present-day humanity than its distinctive virtue and disease which goes by the name of 'the historical sense'. . . . We of the present day are only beginning to form the chain of a very powerful future feeling, link for link—we hardly know what we are doing" (*GS*, sec. 337, pp. 267–68). Memory—what Nietzsche here calls the historical sense—would guarantee us the right to make promises, to stand security 'as future'. But, just as in the opening section of the second essay of the *Genealogy*, section 337 goes on to accuse us of forgetfulness: "It almost seems to us as if it were not a matter of a new feeling but rather a decrease in all old feelings; the historical sense is still so poor and cold, and many people are attacked by it as by a frost and made still poorer and colder." Properly understood, however, memory is forward-looking; it produces a feeling of happiness that Nietzsche here associates with "humanity" (ibid.).[82] It is this form of memory that is promised by the *Genealogy*, and denied by the morality of pity.

The Madman

Nietzsche's notions of the individual and the herd are inextricably interwoven.[83] An individual, on his view, is someone who makes sense; but the latter idea, he suggests, has content only in the context of a failure to make sense. According to Nietzsche, our lives in the present age are distinguished precisely by such failure. This is, in large measure, the point of his saying that 'morality in Europe today is herd animal morality'. More specifically, the fact of our failure to understand our commitment to truthfulness leaves room for the notion of an individual who does understand it. Thus, my interpretation of the notion of individuality appears to suggest that, for Nietzsche, as long as one is not guilty of the present age's unintelligibility, one can reasonably claim to be an individual.

But this account is not quite true to the text. For Nietzsche maintains that the morality of pity ensures that the would-be individual remains merely an *exception*, unread; the exception, I want to say, falls short of

[82] Kaufmann has "humaneness" for Nietzsche's *Menschlichkeit* here. But this translation threatens to sentimentalize further a thought whose expression in this aphorism already strays in that direction.

[83] I have discussed some of the material in this section in "Who is Heidegger's Nietzsche?" in *Heidegger: A Critical Reader*, ed. Hubert L. Dreyfus and Harrison Hall (Cambridge: Blackwell, 1992), pp. 231–46.

true individuality.[84] Intelligible speech requires interlocutors, and precisely this is what the morality of pity denies the exception. This is the other salient feature of the idea that speaking is a form of promising that I mentioned at the beginning of the second section of this chapter: namely, that one cannot give one's word where there is no one to take it. In the last section, I tried to explain what Nietzsche means by suggesting that becoming what we are depends on reading his work in the right way. I tried, that is, to make clear the idea that the ability to read Nietzsche—to let him suffer—is a crucial feature of what it means for us to make sense of our lives in the present age. What needs to be made clear in the present section, however, is the significance of his claim that *he* needs readers of a certain sort, that without them he (and not just the man of knowledge) is as it were voiceless. Nietzsche's untimeliness, I want to say, is not an inherent virtue.[85] To see this, it will help to have a last look at the madman of *The Gay Science*, section 125. This section articulates in a more or less straightforward way Nietzsche's conception of his dependence on his audience.[86]

Section 125 suggests that we identify the madman with Nietzsche, on the one hand, and the people in the marketplace with Nietzsche's readers—that is to say, with ourselves—on the other. The figure of the madman, in other words, is meant to remind us that the point of view of the marketplace is in fact our own. Madness is not a standpoint Nietzsche encourages us to adopt. But this implies that part of his point in having a madman announce the death of God is precisely to underscore how apparently reasonable his audience is. As I have stressed, they already know what the madman knows: namely, that God is dead. The fact that it is a madman who announces the death of

---

[84] The term 'exception' is from sec. 26 of *Beyond Good and Evil*.

[85] I disagree, then, with Thiele's remark that, for Nietzsche, "the modern hero is destined for an alienated existence" (*Friedrich Nietzsche and the Politics of the Soul*, p. 46). Thiele feels entitled to this claim because, as I have noted, he accepts the view that there is one morality for the herd and another for the individual. I have endeavored to show why this reading is unsatisfactory: Nietzsche does not present herd morality as a coherent alternative to individuality. However, as I now wish to show, Nietzsche also seems to believe that individuality—responsibility—requires more than mere resistance to the herd's resistance to it.

[86] Other places to look, of course, are the various prefaces Nietzsche wrote in the late 1880s. As I have said, these prefaces are all quite self-conscious instructions in reading. The most blatant of these, I think, is the preface to the *Genealogy*, especially the last section thereof. Another obvious place to look for such instructions is *Schopenhauer as Educator*. But because section 125 dramatizes the sort of difficulty Nietzsche believes attends the announcement of the death of God, I have chosen to discuss this passage as most relevant to the form of nihilism with which we have primarily been concerned in this book.

God thus suggests that the overcoming of 'Christianity as dogma' is not something that can *simply* be told; it is news that must be taken in the right way. Doing so would, in turn, signal the demise of 'Christianity as morality'.

Those in the marketplace are forerunners of the 'last men' whom Zarathustra initially tries to teach. From their point of view, it is clear that only a madman could 'seek God'.[87] In other words, only a madman could be concerned in this way about something with which, as far as they can see, they simply have no reason to concern themselves. But it is important to notice that Nietzsche does not suggest that it is only from the point of view of the marketplace that the madman appears deranged. In some sense, it seems, he is indeed mad.

As we should expect, therefore, section 125 does not recount a clash between two different and mutually uncomprehending world views. From Nietzsche's point of view, madness does not represent a viable view of things at all. On the one hand, Nietzsche clearly does not suggest that the marketplace's indifference to the madman's announcement is really an alternative to taking that news to heart. For, as we have seen, he considers such indifference to be a failure of intelligibility. On the other hand, however, the announcement of the death of God is not made from a standpoint that is intelligible independent of the marketplace. In short, those to whom the news of God's death is told are not uncomprehending. The problem, once again, is that what they know means nothing to them.[88] But Nietzsche does not propose the figure of the madman as a model of what he thinks it would be for that knowledge to mean something. Section 125 is offered, instead, as instruction in reading.

As Nietzsche describes them, those in the marketplace appear not to take seriously what the madman says. They laugh and shout at him, and are not visibly threatened by his madness. But what is the significance of their response if the point is not that the madman merely *appears* mad from their perspective? How shall we understand his madness? Here, again, I turn for help to a relatively early text of Nietzsche's.

In a section from *Daybreak* to which I have already referred, Nietzsche associates madness with what he there calls 'new ideas'. "When in spite of that fearful pressure of 'morality of custom' under which all the communities of mankind have lived, many millennia before the begin-

---

[87] Heidegger reads this aspect of section 125 in a similar way. See his "The Word of Nietzsche: 'God is Dead'," in *The Question Concerning Technology and Other Essays*, trans. William Lovitt (New York: Harper and Row, 1977).

[88] In *The Antichrist*, Nietzsche writes, "Everyone knows, and *everyone nonetheless remains unchanged*" (AC, sec. 38, p. 150).

nings of our calendar and also on the whole during the course of it up to the present day . . . new and deviate ideas, evaluations, drives again and again broke out, they did so accompanied by a dreadful attendant: almost everywhere it was madness which prepared the way for the new idea, which broke the spell of a venerated usage and superstition" (*D*, sec. 14, pp. 13–44). Nietzsche says here, quite explicitly, that madness paves the way for new ideas *in the present age*. I think we may safely read section 125 in the light of this passage. But his point is not that new ideas somehow *drive* one mad, nor, as we have seen, is it that the possessor of new ideas will *appear* to be mad from the standpoint of the community in which he lives. For Nietzsche denies the intelligibility of the notion of culture on which this particular understanding of madness rests. Rather, he is suggesting that madness functions as the precondition—instead of the consequence—of the announcement of anything that is in this sense 'new'. He continues, "all superior men who were irresistibly drawn to throw off the yoke of any kind of morality and to frame new laws had, *if they were not actually mad*, no alternative but to make themselves or pretend to be mad—and this applied to innovators in every domain and not only in the domain of priestly and political dogma" (*D*, sec. 14, p. 14). Those who are moral innovators in this sense must feign madness as a way of believing in themselves. Because their form of innovation does not—indeed, from Nietzsche's point of view, *cannot*—propose a radically new way of looking at things, they cannot have the kind of confidence in themselves that might be thought to come from fresh insight. What Nietzsche calls madness is, instead, a way of making a show of conviction where, in his view, circumstances do not permit genuine certainty. He writes:

> To listen to the sighs of these solitary and agitated minds: 'Ah, give me madness, you heavenly powers! Madness, that I may at last believe in myself! Give deliriums and convulsions, sudden lights and darkness, terrify me with frost and fire such as no mortal has ever felt, with deafening din and prowling figures, make me howl and whine and crawl like a beast: so that I may only come to believe in myself! I am consumed by doubt, I have killed the law, the law anguishes me as a corpse does a living man: if I am not more than the law I am the vilest of all men. The new spirit which is in me, whence is it if it is not from you? Prove to me that I am yours; madness alone can prove it'. (Ibid., p. 16)[89]

[89] As if to underscore the tenuousness of the standpoint that madness provides, Nietzsche writes that "only too often this fervour achieved its goal all too well: in that age in which Christianity proved most fruitful in saints and desert solitaries,

When sanity no longer speaks intelligibly, a certain form of madness is Nietzsche's only alternative. But the irony of this passage's talk of 'proof' emphasizes the fact that such an alternative does not represent an independently intelligible standpoint.

Nietzsche says that the genealogist stands on the threshold of the event of the demise of Christian morality. He sees himself as living on the trailing edge of a given way of life. It is from *this* standpoint that he is supposed to be able to criticize modern moral values. This is the standpoint of the exception: "We ourselves dwell in the little world of the exceptions and, so to speak, in the evil zone" (ibid., p. 13). Writing from the 'evil zone' denies the genealogist the possibility of appealing to an external standard for his charge that the men of knowledge are less than human. It is for this reason that the *Genealogy* is a polemic; it rests on nothing more than the authority conferred by suffering.

The idea that suffering provides knowledge is, as we have seen, a common theme in Nietzsche's writing. Though such insight should not be construed in pity's terms, he often speaks as though profound suffering did provide the sufferer with *some* kind of personal insight. Consider the following passage from *Beyond Good and Evil:*

> The spiritual haughtiness and nausea of every man who has suffered profoundly—it almost determines the order of rank how profoundly human beings can suffer—his shuddering certainty, which permeates and colors him through and through, that by virtue of his suffering he *knows more* than the cleverest and wisest could possibly know, and that he knows his way and has once been "at home" in many distant, terrifying worlds of which *"you* know nothing"—this spiritual and silent haughtiness of the sufferer, this pride of the elect of knowledge, of the "initiated," of the almost sacrificed, finds all kinds of disguises necessary to protect itself against contact with obtrusive and pitying hands and altogether against everything that is not its equal in suffering. Profound suffering makes noble; it separates. (*BGE,* sec. 270, p. 220)

The morality of pity fails to understand this sort of suffering because it takes literally the sufferer's claim to know something that the pitier does not know. But taking this claim literally is, as we shall see presently, a mistake to which the sufferer himself, just as much as the pitier,

---

and thought it was proving itself by this fruitfulness, there were in Jerusalem vast madhouses for abortive saints, for those who had surrendered to it their grain of salt" (*D,* sec. 14, p. 15).

is prone. We can best understand Nietzsche's conception of the dangers of self-pity by reflecting on another passage in which he questions the nature of his relationship to his readers.

In section 354 of *The Gay Science*, Nietzsche argues that, strictly speaking, communication [*Mitteilung*] conveys only what is common. It is easy to take this claim to suggest that the individual is always left out of common speech. And, as we shall see, there is a sense in which this is true.[90] But he also insists that that which is, in this sense, common is more basic than, is prior to, any putatively private 'contents of consciousness'. For *"consciousness,"* he writes, *"has developed only under the pressure of the need for communication"* (*GS*, sec. 354, p. 298).[91] And this need, he maintains, is born of the sense of being endangered, and hence of needing help and protection.[92] He concludes that one's awareness of oneself as having this or that experience or as engaging in one action or another is—like everything else of interest to him—only a late development in our natural history. "Consciousness does not really belong to man's individual existence but rather to his social or herd nature; that, as follows from this, it has developed subtlety only insofar as this is required by social or herd utility" (ibid., p. 299). The conclusion Nietzsche draws from these reflections about the nature of reading is this: "given the best will in the world to understand ourselves as individually as possible, 'to know ourselves', each of us will always succeed in becoming conscious only of what is not individual but 'average'" (ibid.). On the view of communication articulated in section 354, therefore, there can be no purely private knowledge. More important,

---

[90] See section 354: *"On the 'genius of the species'."* Thiele relies upon this important text to buttress his claim that "the individual is in a permanent state of isolation. Experiences are never truly shared, only their simulacra. . . . Consciousness is . . . the ultimately futile attempt to turn the individual's monopoly of experience into common, communicable knowledge" (*Friedrich Nietzsche and the Politics of the Soul*, pp. 35–36). To my mind, however, Thiele's reading turns the spirit of Nietzsche's thought in section 354 on its head. For Nietzsche argues that there is, in effect, no private experience; he is not trying to register limits on what is communicable. This is not to deny that communication bears a complex relationship to one's individual experience of the world. Nietzsche does say that "all our actions are altogether incomparably personal, unique, and infinitely individual," and that "as soon as we translate them into consciousness *they no longer seem to be*" (*GS*, sec. 354, p. 299). But we should not construe individuality here in terms of privacy and isolation. I suspect that Kaufmann was righter than he knew when he suggested resonances—though *not*, I think those of style—between Nietzsche's argument here and Wittgenstein's so-called private language argument. See Kaufmann's footnote to section 354 (*GS*, p. 297).

[91] Compare *Beyond Good and Evil*, sec. 268.

[92] Once again, I think Nietzsche has himself in mind in this passage as the animal who needs help and protection.

Nietzsche does not pretend that his experience of the death of God provides *him* with any: he merely suffers from that event. This insight lies at the origin of the figure of the madman. In other words, until the news of the death of God has been acknowledged by the people in the marketplace—by Nietzsche's readers—it must remain merely a fact about the madman, a fact, in other words, about Nietzsche's particular 'private' experience of the present age. And as such, it can have no greater significance than that.

I have been trying to make what sense I can of Nietzsche's suggestion that the full intelligibility of his criticism of the present age depends in some way upon that criticism actually being taken to heart, upon his being read in the right way. It is, as should be clear, difficult to know what to make of the sort of authority Nietzsche claims for his writing in general. As we have seen, he appears quite explicitly to confer upon himself the authority for his reader's intelligibility. That is to say, he appears to believe that our very individuality depends upon reading his work properly, because only in this way does he think we adequately express our commitment to truthfulness. Only in this way, in other words, does the will to truth 'gain self-consciousness'. In this last section, however, I have also tried to shed light on Nietzsche's conception of the nature of his authority. What has emerged, I think, is that he thinks of his authority as that of a speaker. On his view, however, such authority is nothing at all without his reader's obedience.

The nihilist's response to all of this is to think that it is at best only Nietzsche's personal tragedy to have experienced a painful incapacity to feel himself understood in the terms of his age. But, as we have seen, it is Nietzsche's claim that it is, on the contrary, *our* tragedy that he has no readers. Such a claim can, of course, seem to represent the very pinnacle of hubris—a fact to which Nietzsche himself draws our attention when he says that suffering produces in the sufferer "downright convulsions of arrogance" (*D*, sec. 114, p. 70). Moreover, the first effect of 'convalescence' is "that we fend off the dominance of this arrogance: we call ourselves vain and foolish to have felt it—as though we have experienced something out of the ordinary! We humiliate our almighty pride, which has enabled us to endure our pain, without gratitude, and vehemently desire an antidote to it: we want to become estranged from ourselves and depersonalized after pain has for too long and too forcibly made us *personal*" (ibid., p. 70–71).[93] Such, for Nietzsche, is the nature of obedience and authority.

[93] The German text for "as though we have experienced something out of the ordinary" is instructive here: "als ob wir etwas erlebt hätten, das einzig wäre!"

I would like to try to sum up these remarks by commenting briefly on a final passage from *Beyond Good and Evil*. Here, it seems to me, Nietzsche is trying to indicate yet another danger to which he fears that both he and those he considers his rightful readers may fall prey: cynicism. Cynicism is a danger that threatens those who are disappointed in life, especially, as we shall see shortly, those who are not sufficiently disappointed in that disappointment.[94] He writes:

> Every choice human being strives instinctively for a citadel and a secrecy where he is saved from the crowd, the many, the great majority—where he may forget "men who are the rule," being their exception—excepting only the one case in which he is pushed straight to such men by a still stronger instinct, as a seeker after knowledge [*Erkennender*] in the great and exceptional sense. Anyone who, in intercourse with men, does not occasionally glisten in all the colors of distress, green and gray with disgust, satiety, sympathy, gloominess, and loneliness, is certainly not a man of elevated tastes; supposing, however, that he does not take all this burden and disgust upon himself voluntarily, that he persistently avoids it, and remains, as I said, quietly and proudly hidden in his citadel, one thing is certain: he was not made, he was not predestined, for knowledge. If he were, he would one day have to say to himself: "The devil take my good taste! but the rule is more interesting than the exception—than myself, the exception!" And he would go *down*, and above all, he would go "inside." (*BGE*, sec. 26, p. 37)

Once again, the overarching danger to the so-called exception is that of pity: the Socratic temptation to think of himself as standing outside of and apart from 'men who are the rule', as radically separate from them—as though not being in tune with one's age were a matter of speaking a different language. The danger, that is, is that the exception may become a spectator of his age, rather than an individual. This is why Nietzsche counsels the exception who would be an individual to go 'inside'. The danger facing the person who is able to do so, however, is what Nietzsche calls 'nausea'. How, then, does Nietzsche think the exception should find his way about the herd?

The 'higher man' should, he says, let his disgust with 'the rule' be his guide. In section 26, the shape taken by such disgust is cynicism.

---

[94] Nietzsche here echoes a theme of Emerson's that Stanley Cavell expresses by saying Emerson's "therapy is to become ashamed of our shame" (see his "Being Odd, Getting Even," in *In Quest of the Ordinary: Lines of Skepticism and Romanticism* (Chicago: University of Chicago Press, 1988), p. 112.

Cynics are people who "recognize the animal, the commonplace and 'the rule' in themselves, and at the same time talk of themselves and their like before witnesses" (ibid., p. 38). The 'higher man' is the witness in question—a witness to possibilities of humanity gone awry. This, anyway, is how Nietzsche would like to think of himself. For when he talks about the exceptional person's disgust with the herd, I take him to be pointing to the cynicism with which he himself feels threatened.[95] In avoiding cynicism, in other words, the exception must overcome a form of *self*-loathing.

Nietzsche suggests, however, that cynical disappointment with the rule in oneself is more frequently encountered in the form of an 'intellectual conscience' that is not quite the genealogist's. In such cases, he says, "a scientific head is placed on an ape's body, a subtle exceptional understanding in a base soul, an occurrence by no means rare, especially among doctors and physiologists of morality" (ibid.). Lovers of knowledge—those capable of being Nietzsche's rightful readers—must, therefore, listen especially carefully to the voice of this particular form of cynicism. They should attend carefully "whenever anyone speaks without bitterness, quite innocently, of man as a belly with two requirements, and a head with one; whenever anyone sees, seeks, and wants to see only hunger, sexual lust, and vanity as the real and only motives of human actions" (ibid.). But hunger, sexual lust, and vanity are just the sorts of things Nietzsche himself commonly cites as motives to action. There may, certainly, be additional motives at work in a given person, but nothing comparatively different in kind or worth.

The true cynic pretends to react indifferently (or even gleefully) to the discovery that these are the only sorts of instinct that function as motives for human action. Such a reaction to the death of God, Nietzsche maintains, is of more interest to the higher man and the philosopher than is the indignation of the person who, in his disappointment with not being more than the animal he is, turns on himself and his ideals and bitterly denounces both. The indignant have a form of what the *Genealogy* calls 'bad conscience'. Cynics accordingly chide them for their expressions of disappointment. For they feel that the desire to be more than human is part of the problem humans face—something they should grow out of. It is in this sense that, as I sug-

---

[95] See *Ecce Homo*, 'Why I Am a Destiny': "*Nausea* at man is my danger" (*EH*, 'Why I Am a Destiny', sec. 6, p. 331). Compare sec. 12 of the first essay of the *Genealogy*: "Here precisely is what has become a fatality for Europe—together with the fear of man, our hopes for man, even the will to him. The sight of man now makes us weary—what is nihilism today if it is not *that?*—We are weary *of man*" (*GM* I, sec. 12, p. 44).

gested a moment ago, cynicism represents a refusal to be disappointed by one's own disappointment. Ultimately, however, cynicism is an expression of pity.

The Unity of Nietzsche's Genealogy

In closing, I would like to sketch briefly an interpretative framework for reading the *Genealogy*. As I read them, the three essays of that work turn around the central issue of the modern commitment to truthfulness. My aim here is only to illustrate the economy of my interpretative claim that Nietzsche's work is centrally concerned with two sorts of response—roughly, an active and a reactive one—to the announcement that God is dead, two understandings of the commitment to which that announcement gives voice.

The *Genealogy* as a whole is centrally concerned with the significance of human life in the present age.[96] More specifically, as we have seen, Nietzsche wishes in this work to understand the particular character of the value that we attach to truthfulness. In this sense, then, the *Genealogy* is concerned—as I have claimed Nietzsche's work in general is concerned—with the meaning of the death of God. For as we have seen, and as the third essay makes very clear, to say that God is dead is simply to say that one is committed to truthfulness. It is this commitment, Nietzsche says, that forbids us the lie involved in the belief in God. My interpretative suggestion, then, is simply that we can understand the relationship among the three essays that make up the *Genealogy* in terms of the contribution they each make to the question of the character of our modern commitment to truthfulness.

In the first essay, Nietzsche introduces the idea of two opposing kinds of valuation: that of the masters and that of the slaves. I think that by 'valuation' we can understand him to mean 'a way of making sense of life', for this is what he believes one's values allow one to do. He describes the two sets of values in question in terms of the twin oppositions of 'good and bad' and 'good and evil'. But I think that what most interests him in the first essay is the difference between the *kinds* of valuations these oppositions represent—between the kinds of *lives* they express. He marks this difference by distinguishing between masterly activity and slavish reactivity. The *Genealogy* as a whole, I suggest, is

[96] This point is made quite explicitly in the preface—especially in secs. 5–6. But the particular aspect of modern life in which Nietzsche is most concerned only becomes completely clear near the end of the third essay.

intended as an exploration of this particular distinction. It is in terms of this distinction that Nietzsche hopes to understand the character of our modern commitment to truthfulness.

As I read it, the second essay is meant to *deepen* our understanding of the distinction between activity and reactivity introduced in the first essay.[97] Nietzsche begins by drawing the crucial distinction between having and lacking the right to make promises. As we have seen, it is in this way that he introduces the distinction between responsibility (conscience) and guilt (bad conscience). Fairly clearly, this distinction is not meant to mark the difference between two different classes of human action—two different sets of things people might do—but rather to contrast two different ways in which people may be said to act: actively and reactively. That the sort of action in question in the *Genealogy* may be thought of as human speech is suggested by the claim that promising is man's true problem.

Now, as I have claimed, what Nietzsche thinks we in the present age—the men of knowledge to whom the *Genealogy* is addressed—are most inclined to say is that we are committed to the truth, that truthfulness is our highest value. As the third essay makes clear, Nietzsche means to ask whether we in fact have the right to say that. This, I have said, is the *Genealogy's* way of asking about the meaning of the death of God. Nietzsche is very explicitly concerned in this essay to understand the character of our modern commitment to truthfulness. His investigation of the ascetic ideal leads him to ask whether our modern (scientific) intellectual conscience represents an alternative to the life-denying values of the past. As he explains in section 23, intellectual

---

[97] An alternative interpretation of the relation between the first two essays might be to maintain that insofar as the so-called slave rebellion of the spirit has been successful we cannot hope to make sense of the distinction between activity and reactivity—as well as of the central notions of order of rank and pathos of distance—in terms of the sort of ostensibly *social* hierarchy that the first essay's quasi-mythological reconstruction of the past allows us to envisage. The distinction between having and not having the right to make promises, then, appears to be, as it were, politically neutral, not to register a sense of two social classes. There may well be room to articulate such an interpretation, but even in the first essay, Nietzsche clearly associates the masters' activity with possibility of authentic human speech. He writes, "It was out of this pathos of distance that [the masters] first seized the right to create values and to coin names for values. . . . (The lordly right of giving names extends so far that one should allow oneself to conceive the origin of language itself as an expression of power on the part of the rulers: they say 'this *is* this and this', they seal every thing and event with a sound and, as it were, take possession of it)" (GM I, sec. 2, p. 26). Thus, I prefer to think that the second essay builds upon and deepens the analysis of valuation presented in the first essay, rather than attempting simply to apply that analysis to the very different social situation of the present age.

conscience might well *seem* to present such an alternative just insofar as it insists that we should confine ourselves to making hypotheses about *this* world, rather than turning our backs on it in favor of the philosophical, religious, or moral illusions of the past. But Nietzsche clearly rejects this idea. Indeed, as he argues in section 344 of *The Gay Science*, our intellectual conscience—our commitment to truth at any price—reveals itself as the highest and noblest expression of the ascetic ideal precisely in its insistence that it represents a distinct alternative to that ideal. This insistence reflects what Nietzsche considers to be the moral or pious wish to avoid the fact of our own history, the desire to see the will to truth as something other than our historical inheritance.

It is the third essay itself that directs our attention to section 344. In this long aphorism, Nietzsche argues that it is the *unconditionality* of our commitment to truth that makes it a moral commitment. As we saw, this claim suggests that we may distinguish a pious version of that commitment from a nonmoral one. This latter distinction, in turn, is cast in the third essay of the *Genealogy* in terms of the difference between a moral and a nonmoral will to truth. As section 344 makes very clear, whoever suggests that the unconditional commitment to truth (what the *Genealogy* calls intellectual conscience at any price) is an alternative to the ascetic ideal has failed to recognize the morality of his commitment to truth.

Nietzsche calls on us to recognize the historical character of our commitment to truth—to recognize, in other words, that who we are in the present age is something we have *become*. But he thinks that we—the men of knowledge—strive to deny the historical character of our commitment to truth precisely by denying the significance of our triumph over the illusions and errors of the past. This denial is what the unconditionality of our commitment to truth comes to: here is where our piety lies. In the terms introduced in the second essay, we may say that the unconditionality of our commitment to truth is our way of avoiding taking responsibility for that commitment.

But to call on us to acknowledge the historical character of our commitment to truth is not to demand that we recognize its contingency. On the contrary, Nietzsche seeks to overcome our resistance to its authority. The will to knowledge is fateful for us, and, he says, his 'formula for greatness in a human being is *amor fati*'. It is the idea of 'love of fate' that Nietzsche is trying to express when, at the end of the *Genealogy*, he talks about the growing self-consciousness of the will to truth.

It is in this way, then, that the *Genealogy* seeks to remind us of our hatred of history, of our desire to live without a memory. Only the creation of such a memory will keep us from living at the expense of the future. The point to bear in mind, however, is that taking responsibility for one's commitment to truth (for the conditionality of that commitment) is nothing more—but nothing less—than telling the truth. This is what obedience to the authority of the value of truthfulness amounts to here. For *all* we are called upon to do is to recognize the falsity of what the *Genealogy* calls Christianity as dogma, and to overcome our aversion to recognizing that dogma as having been our own.

The questions Nietzsche forces us to ask about the character of our commitment to truthfulness are, I have argued, absolutely central to his conception of life in the present age. That commitment is the only thing that, according to him, could serve to unite us in the present age. This is the only sort of community that we have. To stress this last point is not to say that such a community is merely better than none. For, on Nietzsche's account, there simply is no standpoint from which someone committed to truth could enter such a claim.

INDEX

Instinct
  in Greek culture, 48–49, 52n
  intelligibility and, 66, 145–46
  life-preserving errors and, 100
  sense making and, 66
Intellectual conscience. *See* Commitment to truthfulness:
  unconditional
Intelligibility. *See also* Commitment to
  truthfulness; Resistance; Speech
  constraints of, 132–33, 136, 144–45,
  147
  failure of, in present age, 196–99
  herd morality and, 20–22, 187
  instinct and, 66
  life-denial and, 38
  madness and, 229–30
  membership in community and, 182,
  185
  morality of pity and, 213, 224–26
  Nietzsche's use of term, 23–24
  notions of, 9–10, 196–99
  obedience and, 41–42
  of philosophical preconceptions, 87
  as practical, 21–22
  Socratism and, 13–15, 68, 197–99
  thing-in-itself and, 120
  tragedy and, 50n, 60, 62n, 63–65
  will to power and, 176
Interpretation, concept of. *See also* Perspectivism, doctrine of
  alienation from the world and, 89n,
  93–94
  knower's contribution to experience
  and, 113–19, 124
  perspectivism and, 108–9
  relation between knower and the
  known and, 113–19, 124–26
  responsibility vs. responsiveness
  and, 113
  Socratism and, 63–64, 82
  thing-in-itself and, 107, 112–19,
  125–26
  will to knowledge and, 159n
  will to power and, 127–39

Justice, notion of, 205n

Kant, Immanuel, 32–33, 84, 91n, 110,
  207n
Kierkegaard, Søren, 89n, 190
Knowledge, nature of
  Nietzsche's concern with, 3–4,
  105–7, 122–23
  theoretical optimist and, 82–83

Lacoue-Labarthe, Philippe, 184n
Leiter, Brian, 4n
Lessing, Gotthold Ephraim, 80–81
Life
  aesthetic justification and, 55–57,
  65–68
  Nietzsche's use of term, 92n, 103
  Socratic justification and, 62, 66–67
Life-affirmation, 33, 37–38, 170–72
Life-denial, *xiin*
  ascetic ideal and, *xviii–xix*
  historic character of will to truth
  and, 153–55, 157
  morality and, 33, 153n, 168n, 176–77
  as resistance to making sense, 37–38,
  119–21
  unconditional will to truth and,
  168–73
Linguistic community
  culture as, 28–29, 37–38, 185, 188
  notion of, 37n
  resistance to, 29
  responsibility and, 209n

Madman, the, 177, 180–81, 217–18,
  226–35
Masters vs. slaves. *See* Activity and
  reactivity
Maturity, 176
Meaningfulness
  resistance of men of knowledge to,
  17–18
  tragic Greeks as suffering from,
  62–63, 82, 138
Memory, 188, 199–201, 208, 210, 226.
  See also History; Practice of
  genealogy
Men of knowledge. *See also* Commitment to truthfulness; Modernity;
  Philosophy; Science
  belief and, 168–73
  as culture, 38–39
  error and, 88–89
  as expression, 5n
  history and, 184–85
  nihilism among, 153, 157, 174–75
  perfection of, and morality of pity,
  217–20, 224–26
  pious vs. self-conscious, 79–80
  resistance to meaningfulness and,
  17–18
  self-consciousness and, 177–78
  self-understanding and, 5, 7–8,
  67–68, 152, 184
  universe as chaos and, 96

On the Genealogy of Morals (cont.)
  production of culture and, 30n
  promising and, *xiin*, 192–211
  questioning the will to truth and,
    78n, 159
  reason and, 97n
  relation between first two essays in,
    235–37
  scientific claims to detachment and,
    166
  unconditionality of will to truth and,
    237
  will to power and, 127–28
Optimism vs. pessimism, 81–85
Overman, doctrine of the, 130

Perfection, 133. *See also* Memory; Self-
  consciousness
Perspectivism, doctrine of, 108, 122.
  See also Interpretation, concept of
Nietzsche's thinking and, 15–16, 109,
  115–16, 146–48
Pessimism of strength, 81–82
Phenomenalism, 91n, 168n
Phillips, Adam, 116n
Philosophy. *See also* Commitment to
  truthfulness; Men of knowledge
  hatred of history and, 131, 149
  intelligibility of preconceptions in, 87
  limitations of rationality and, 97
  problem of interpretation and,
    115–19
  resistance to intelligibility and, 147
  self-deception in, 88n
  Socratic detachment and, 29–30, 39,
    43, 51–52, 59, 65
  weakness of will and, 138
Piety, in men of knowledge, 79–80,
  124, 152–55, 157–58, 167, 172–73.
  See also Commitment to truthfulness: unconditional
Pippin, Robert, 130n
Pity. *See also* Morality of pity
  cynicism and, 235
  as incompatible with responsibility,
    213–17, 219, 223n, 224–26
  Nietzsche's attack on, 186, 211–13
  suffering and, 213–23, 231
Platonism
  Christianity and, 6–7, 89n
  death of God and, 11
  detachment and, *xix*
  errors of, 89n, 104
  responsibility for speech and, 63
  Socratism and, 19
Power. *See also* Will to power

as constraint, 123, 130, 133, 139
knowledge as, 43, 161
life and, 176
Nietzsche's usage of term, 123, 127
Practice of genealogy, 70n, 74. *See also*
  History; Memory
  humanity and, 199–200, 208
  nihilism and, 177–81
  Socratic demand for reasons and, 19
Pragmatism, 91n
Promising. *See also* Activity and reactivity; Speech
  as commitment, 203
  morality of pity and, 187, 211–26
  nihilism and, 220
  as real problem of man, 193
  responsibility for speech and, 21–22,
    187, 193–211
Psychology
  aesthetic justification and, 65–68
  Nietzsche's concept of will and,
    139–51
  self-consciousness of will to truth
    and, 159–60
  Socratic demand for reasons and, 46,
    171–72
  thing-in-itself and, 107, 112, 119–20
Punishment, 204–6

Rationality. *See* Cognition, limits of;
  Commitment to truthfulness; Reasons, Socratic demand for
Readers. *See also* Men of knowledge
  interpretation and, 129–30
  Nietzsche's conception of own, 5–6,
    24, 152–53, 195n, 217–19
  Nietzsche's conception of reading
    and, 8, 187–88, 200n, 227–35
  pity and, 217–19
  transformation of, 202–3
Reasons, Socratic demand for. *See also*
  Socratism
  The Birth of Tragedy critique of,
    13–15, 40–52
  collapse of culture and, 40
  as life-preserving error, 88
  membership in a culture and, 36–37
  practice of philosophy and, 39, 46
  as psychological, 46
Resistance
  action and, 144
  to authority of knowledge, and self-
    consciousness, 177
  belief in thing-in-itself and, 20,
    119–21